Massachusetts at a Glance

Massachusetts at a Glance

A USER'S GUIDE TO THE BAY STATE

Jack Tager

University of Massachusetts Press
AMHERST & BOSTON

Printed in the United States of America

LC 2003022002
ISBN 1-55849-439-1 (cloth); 440-5 (paper)

Designed by Jack Harrison
Set in Adobe Garamond and Avant Garde by Graphic Composition, Inc.
Printed and bound by The Maple-Vail Book Manufacturing Group

Library of Congress Cataloging-in-Publication Data
Tager, Jack.
Massachusetts at a glance : a user's guide to the Bay State / Jack Tager.
p. cm.
ISBN 1-55849-439-1 (cloth : alk. paper) — 1-55849-440-5 (pbk. : alk. paper)
1. Massachusetts—Miscellanea. 2. Massachusetts—History—Miscellanea.
I. Title
F64.T34 2004
974.4—dc22
2003022002

British Library Cataloguing in Publication data are available.

Contents

Introduction

Designed for general readers, this book offers an alphabetically arranged compendium of information about people, places, and events—past and present—in the Commonwealth of Massachusetts. Its aim is to provide a handy one-volume reference guide to a state that has played a central role in American history since the Pilgrims landed at Plymouth Rock in 1620. Site of the first Thanksgiving as well as the Salem witchcraft trials during the seventeenth century, the Massachusetts Bay Colony became a principal seedbed of revolutionary sentiment during the eighteenth. Behind the rallying cry "no taxation without representation," John Hancock, John Adams, Paul Revere, and others championed the notion of government by consent as well as the natural right of the people to revolt when such consent is denied.

After the Revolution, as the young republic moved into the nineteenth century, Massachusetts emerged as the center of the American industrial revolution. While businessmen like Francis Cabot Lowell built the textile mills and factory towns that began the shift from a rural to an urban nation, political leaders such as John Quincy Adams and Daniel Webster, reformers such as William Lloyd Garrison and Wendell Phillips, and writers such as Ralph Waldo Emerson, Nathaniel Hawthorne, and Louisa May Alcott helped shape the country's culture and politics.

During the twentieth century the Bay State again led the way as the United States underwent a prolonged and sometimes agonizing transformation from a manufacturing to a high tech and service economy. Companies such as Digital Equipment and Raytheon heralded the advent of the new information age, drawing on the cutting-edge research of MIT, Harvard, and other notable institutions of higher learning within the state. In politics, the Kennedy clan became important national figures, though they were not the only Massachusetts men and women to exert a larger influence on American life. Black leader W. E. B. Du Bois, jurist Louis Brandeis, rocket scientist Robert H. Goddard, poet Robert Frost, artist Norman Rockwell, and baseball slugger Ted Williams are just a few of the state's residents who gained prominence during the century.

To attempt to provide a comprehensive overview of this rich and complex history would be a monumental undertaking, requiring multiple volumes and a large staff of contributing scholars and experts. My purpose here is more modest. A professional historian with a long-standing interest in the history of Massachusetts, I set out to fill a gap in the existing literature by gathering under one cover a broad range of information about the Bay State and its people. As the work of a single individual, this book is necessarily incomplete and unavoidably idiosyncratic. I have made choices to include and to exclude material based primarily on my own sense of what is important. Some readers no doubt will question my selections and priorities and find omissions they consider egregious. But whatever the book's faults may be, it encompasses three decades of scholarly reading and research on Massachusetts and reflects in some small measure an effort to fulfill Diderot's belief that "the labors of the past ages may be useful to the ages to come."

The book is organized to allow readers to find answers to questions in a speedy and reliable manner. It begins with a compilation of basic facts about Massachusetts, including size in square miles, population data drawn from the latest census, state motto and seal, even the state bird. This is followed by the major section of the book, an alphabetical list of people, places, events, and other subjects inspired by Thomas O'Connor's *Boston A to Z* and Leonard and Dale Pitt's *Los Angeles A to Z.*

After using the A to Z list to satisfy their curiosity about specific subjects, readers can move on to a chronological list of events. This year-by-year narrative of key developments in Massachusetts is the most extensive available in print and can be read as a mini-history in its own right. Next comes a statistical appendix of the state's 351 towns and cities, with information ranging from their dates of settlement and incorporation to population figures by selected decades from 1790 to 2000. Also included is a list of the state's museums, historic sites, and state parks as well as its many colleges and universities, with addresses, telephone numbers, and websites for readers who might wish to contact these institutions directly. Finally, I have compiled an extensive listing of suggested readings for those who would like to explore further any of the topics covered in the book.

In carrying out this project, I incurred an enormous debt to a wide range of scholars and writers whose published work on Massachusetts furnished many of the facts and insights contained in this volume. Although it would be impossible to acknowledge them individually, most of their names and writings can be found in the bibliographical appendix of suggested readings. My own scholarly contributions to the history of the Bay State were also an important source of information and direction. These include *Massachusetts: A Concise History,* co-written with Richard D. Brown, *The Historical Atlas of Massachusetts,* co-edited with Richard W. Wilkie, and my recent monograph, *Boston Riots: Three Centuries of Social Violence.*

For those who live in the Commonwealth of Massachusetts as well as for those who come to visit, whatever their age or background, I hope this book proves useful and instructive.

Basic Massachusetts Facts

Massachusetts is one of the original thirteen states.

Name: Derived from the Massachusett tribe, who lived in the region south of Boston.

Nickname: Bay State

Motto and seal: *Ense Petit Placidam Sub Libertate Quietem* ("By the Sword We Seek Peace, But Peace Only under Liberty"). Adopted in 1780 and made official in 1885.

State features
- Citizenry: Bay Staters
- Bird: Chickadee
- Tree: American elm
- Flower: Mayflower
- Dog: Boston terrier
- Horse: Morgan
- Fish: Cod
- Insect: Ladybug
- Game bird: Wild turkey
- Shell: New England Neptune
- Beverage: Cranberry juice
- Song: "All Hail to Massachusetts" (composer, Arthur J. Marsh)
- Dessert: Boston cream pie

Government: Commonwealth, based on the Constitution of 1780. In 1637 John Winthrop used the term "Common weal" meaning "the consent of a certaine companie of people to cohabit together under one government for their mutual safety and welfare."

Capitol: State House in Boston

Governor: Chief administrative officer; elected for four-year term

Governor's Council: Advisory to the governor and approves appointments; elected for two-year terms

General Court: State legislature composed of two houses
Senate: 40 members; elected for two-year terms
House: 160 members; elected for two-year terms

Courts: Trial, Appeals, Supreme Judicial; all justices appointed

Constitutional officers: Elected for four-year terms
Attorney General: Chief legal officer
Secretary of the Commonwealth: Record keeper
Treasurer: Caretaker of all state funds
Auditor: Officer in charge of auditing all state accounts and expenditures

Counties: 14: Barnstable, Berkshire, Bristol, Dukes, Essex, Franklin, Hampden, Hampshire, Middlesex, Nantucket, Norfolk, Plymouth, Suffolk, and Worcester. Counties have no real governmental powers.

Municipalities: Governed either by mayors/councils or by selectmen/town meetings. Largest cities: Boston (589,141), Worcester (172,648), Springfield (152,082), Lowell (103,000), Cambridge (101,355), New Bedford (93,768).

Population: 6,349,097; thirteenth in nation

Size: 8,257 total square miles (7,838 land square miles); forty-fifth in the nation

Distance: East to west: 190 miles; north to south: 110 miles; 1,980 miles of shoreline

Largest body of water: Quabbin Reservoir (39 square miles)

Largest river: Connecticut, flowing north to south, with its tributaries—the Deerfield, Westfield, Chicopee, and Millers—makes up the major drainage area of the state.

Highest elevation: Mount Greylock (3,491 feet), near North Adams

Massachusetts A to Z

AN ALPHABETIC LIST OF PEOPLE, PLACES, EVENTS, AND MISCELLANY

African Meeting House, Smith Court, Boston, c. mid 1880s. Courtesy of Historic New England/SPNEA.

A

Abolitionists

Participants in the antislavery movement in the North, abolitionists fought to end slavery as a legal institution in the United States. In contrast to gradualists, who expected slavery as an economic institution to wither away, abolitionists were radicals who believed that, as a moral evil, it should be ended immediately. To achieve their goal, they advocated amending or even discarding the Constitution.

Massachusetts abolitionists were divided along the same lines as their counterparts in other states. For example, **John Quincy Adams** preferred to work within the political system, **William Lloyd Garrison** wanted slavery immediately declared immoral and illegal, and **Thomas Wentworth Higginson** contemplated the use of violence to overthrow the institution.

Southerners' political clout in Congress forced the Union into a series of "Compromises" (1820 and 1850) that would promote the establishment of slavery in the new territories, thereby eventually increasing the number of slave states. Southerners' growing obduracy also strengthened the position of Northern abolitionists. Massachusetts became the center of the antislavery movement in 1831 when William Lloyd Garrison began publishing the *Liberator* in Boston. This abolitionist newspaper called for an immediate end to slavery, but by peaceful means. Garrison, who also helped found the American Anti-Slavery Society in 1833 in Philadelphia, became the focal point of the movement. People from all over the Northeast joined the cause, but the most numerous and articulate leaders came from Massachusetts—among them **Wendell Phillips, Charles Sumner,** Theodore Parker,

Thomas Wentworth Higginson, **John Greenleaf Whittier, James Russell Lowell, Ralph Waldo Emerson,** and Lydia Maria Child, as well as **Frederick Douglass** and William Wells Brown, former slaves now residing in the Bay State.

Their constant, eloquent outcry against slavery finally awakened broad sympathy for abolitionism in Massachusetts and the rest of the free states. At the same time, the South was arousing resentment through attempts to enforce the 1850 Fugitive Slave Act. Meanwhile, the intense propaganda of Harriet Beecher Stowe's antislavery novel *Uncle Tom's Cabin* (1852) was making converts at home and abroad. In 1859 a secret group of abolitionists, most of them from Massachusetts, financed John Brown's abortive raid on the U.S. Armory at Harpers Ferry, Virginia.

Finally, the vehement objections of the abolitionists persuaded Northerners to oppose the spread of slavery in the territories, resulting in the election of Abraham Lincoln as president in 1860. His victory sparked the secession of the Southern states in 1861 and the beginning of the Civil War. Four years later, events proved radicals such as Thomas Wentworth Higginson right: it had taken unimaginable violence to put an end to slavery in the United States. (See also **Fugitive Slaves**)

Abigail Adams

Abigail Adams was the wife of **John Adams,** second president of the United States, but more important, she was also his intellectual collaborator and dearest friend. John Adams confided in her and sought her advice in developing his ideas, although he disagreed with her more advanced views on women's rights. Born in Weymouth on November 11, 1744, Abigail Smith was the daughter of a Congregational minister. Following custom, she received no formal education, but she engaged in a rigorous course of self-education. She married John Adams in 1764 and became his confidante, though because of his many years as a peripatetic diplomat for his young nation, the couple spent long periods apart. In addition to raising their family, she managed the family farm and controlled the family interests in Quincy. While apart, they dutifully wrote to each other. Abigail was not shy in apprising John of her views. In 1774, as John Adams was working on the Declaration of Independence with Thomas Jefferson and others, his wife admonished him, "I desire you remember the ladies."

After ten years apart she joined her husband in Europe in 1784, remaining with him during his diplomatic travels. When John Adams became president, Abigail Adams became the first woman to reside in the half-built White House in Washington, D.C. With his loss of the presidency in 1800, John and Abigail Adams returned to Quincy, where she helped her son **John Quincy Adams** in his political career. Abigail Adams died in Quincy on October 28, 1818. In 1840 her grandson Charles Francis Adams published many of her letters, revealing a mind of intelligence, maturity, and sophistication. Abigail Adams, like **Anne Hutchinson,** is now recognized as a precursor of modern feminism.

John Adams

The second president of the United States, John Adams was a famed Revolutionary leader and spokesman for the cause of independence. In addition to being a skillful diplomat, he was the chief author of the **Massachusetts Constitution** of 1780, which became the model for the U.S. Constitution. Born in Braintree (now Quincy) on October 9, 1735, to a family of farmers, Adams graduated from Harvard in 1755 and then practiced law in Boston. Of superior intelligence, Adams was also arrogant and difficult to get along with. Outside the elite circles of Boston, he struggled to gain prominence. Adams enlisted in the patriot cause by writing Braintree's 1765 objection to the passage of the **Stamp Act.** Citing its unconstitutionality under Magna Carta, Adams argued that the Stamp Act violated the right of the English freeman not to be taxed without his consent. The notion of rule by consent of the governed became the heart of American Revolutionary ideology. Forty other towns adopted these "Braintree Instructions." In 1773 he was jubilant over the **Boston Tea Party,** writing "the die is cast," confident that now independence would come.

After taking up residence in Boston, in 1768 he defended **John Hancock** after customs officials confiscated Hancock's sloop *Liberty* for smuggling. Although Hancock was guilty, Adams built his case on the argument that the Acts of Trade that prohibited smuggling had no legal standing in the colonies since they had been passed by Parliament without colonial representation. Because of the previous unrest caused by the Stamp Act riots, the Crown authorities dropped all charges, fearing that the popular Hancock would become a martyr, inflaming an already tense situation. Adams gained fame as a lawyer in 1770 when he and **Josiah Quincy,** at the behest of his cousin **Sam Adams,** successfully defended the soldiers accused in the

Abigail Adams, detail of an engraving from a painting by Gilbert Stuart. Library of Congress, Prints and Photographs Division.

John Adams, second United States president, helped write the Massachusetts Constitution, which was used as a model for the Federal Constitution. From George Bancroft, *History of the United States, vol. 4, 1866.*

Boston Massacre. That same year Bostonians elected Adams as representative to the General Court. By 1774 he was a well-known patriot, representing Massachusetts as a delegate to the first Continental Congress. After the battles of **Lexington and Concord,** Adams was again elected a delegate to the second Continental Congress, where he nominated George Washington as commander in chief of the Continental Army. He served on the committee that drafted the Declaration of Independence, penned by Jefferson.

Throughout the war, Adams served on committees and wrote many articles in support of American independence. In 1778 he sailed to France, where he successfully negotiated a treaty of alliance. During his years of diplomacy he was able to return to Massachusetts for a short time in 1779, when he wrote a constitution for the new state. His success as a diplomat resulted in his appointment as minister to England in 1785. He returned to the United States in 1788 to become the country's first vice president, under Washington. Elected again in 1792 as vice president, he became an important member of the newly formed Federalist Party, which was in opposition to the Democratic Republicans of Thomas Jefferson. In 1796 Adams vied for the presidency against Jefferson and won with 71 electoral votes to Jefferson's 68. Jefferson became vice president.

Adams's administration was fraught with conflict over relations with the new French republic, leading to the Quasi-War of 1797–1800. During this period Congress passed the Alien and Sedition Acts, aimed at suppressing dissent against the government's anti-French policies. Adams's support of these laws earned him condemnation from the Jeffersonians. Because of this controversy Adams lost his reelection bid in 1800 to the now formidable Jefferson. He retired to Quincy, where he lived quietly, continuing to write articles and letters on the issues of the day. He began a long-term correspondence with his former enemy Jefferson which comprises some of the finest essays ever written on government and politics. Adams died July 4, 1826 (Independence Day), the very same day his old rival Jefferson died, during the presidency of his son John Quincy Adams. His contributions as a Revolutionary, a diplomat, a president, and a statesman mark him as one of the greatest leaders of American history.

John Quincy Adams

A disappointing presidency but a long and glorious career as a congressman: such was John Quincy Adams's contribution to the nation and his state. Sixth president of the United States (1825–1828), Adams, like his father, **John Adams,** served only one term. The leading political figure of his time in Massachusetts, John Quincy Adams symbolized the shifting party structure of the period from the 1820s through the 1840s. He was many things—certainly an intellectual and a devoted public servant—but he was also a curmudgeon, a man who was difficult to get along with. From his birth in Braintree in 1767, his life was an endless struggle to measure up to the high standards set by his famous father and ambitious mother, **Abigail Adams.** In 1781, at the precocious age of fourteen, he started his public career by becoming secretary to the U.S. minister to Russia, later working in the same capacity for his father, who was minister to Britain. He attended Harvard, graduating in 1787. In 1794 he became minister to the Netherlands, then minister to Prussia in 1797. Family connections helped Adams's election to the Massachusetts Senate in 1802. The next year the Federalist Massachusetts legislature elected him to the U.S. Senate.

Demonstrating the rash streak of independence that epitomized his character, he began taking positions that the Federalist leaders back home found intolerable. He infuriated his party by voting for Jefferson's purchase of Louisiana. The conflict reached a crisis when he voted for Jefferson's Embargo Act of 1807, an economic calamity for Massachusetts. When the Massachusetts Federalists asked him to recant, he refused and resigned from the party, joining Jefferson's Republican Party. President James Monroe, a Republican, appointed Adams secretary of state in 1817.

His goal was to take back the presidency for the Adams family, but to achieve that he had to destroy the Massachusetts Federalists. He organized a new party, the National Republicans, and under this banner he ran for the presidency in 1824. Democrat Andrew Jackson won the most electoral votes, with Adams placing second. Jackson, however, did not receive the necessary majority required by the Constitution, so the choice was thrown into the House of Representatives for a decision. There Henry Clay worked an accommodation with Adams, and the House elected the second-place contender as president of the United States. Once again Massachusetts led the nation.

Forgetting that compromise had won the day, the hardheaded Adams initiated a nationalist federal program that was not well received by Clay and his Jeffersonian Republicans. Adams called for many changes, among them the creation of a national system of canals, turnpikes, and railroads, the establishment of a national university and a naval academy, federal support for exploration of the western territories, and the adoption of a uniform system of weights and measures. Parts of this farsighted and progressive program were not enacted until years later under various administrations. Lacking the will to compromise, Adams and his party lost in his bid for reelection in 1828, and Adams returned home in disgrace. But ever a fighter, he ran for and won office to Congress in 1830. Subsequently he had an influential congressional career, usually standing alone attacking the Southern "slavemasters" and their policies.

One of his most famous victories was against the "gag" rule by which Southerners prevented any attacks against slavery on the floor of the House. Fighting alone for many years, by the use of deft parliamentary maneuvers he succeeded in getting the House to abolish the gag rule. He was also an advocate before the Supreme Court for the liberty of the *Amistad* slave ship captives. Contentious to the end, "Old Man Eloquent," as he was called, collapsed on the floor of the House and died two days later on February 23,

1848. John Quincy Adams of Massachusetts is remembered today as a brilliant, principled advocate, a skilled diplomat, and a farsighted policymaker who was instrumental in changing party politics in the Bay State and the nation. His advocacy of abolition and equal rights was instrumental in promoting equality for all Americans.

Sam Adams

Samuel Adams was the foremost Revolutionary leader of Massachusetts, surpassing even his close associates **John Adams** and **John Hancock.** He was one of the signers of the Declaration of Independence and served as governor of Massachusetts. Born in Boston on September 27, 1722, Sam Adams was the son of a brewer and real estate investor. He graduated from Harvard in 1740, then received a master's degree in 1743. He started out in business but was mainly interested in politics. Adams became one of Boston's tax collectors in 1756, and in 1765 Boston town meeting elected him to the General Court, where he found his issue, joining with those who argued that Britain had no right to tax the colonies without their permission. Elected clerk of the assembly, he remained a representative until 1774. All the while he was a prime mover in the events leading up to the Revolution.

Adams instigated mobs to violence on several occasions, ranging from the **Stamp Act** resistance to the **Boston Tea Party.** He wrote voluminous broadsides and letters attacking British tyranny and the arbitrary nature of Crown rule. He was at Lexington when warnings arrived of the British approach. He became a delegate to the Continental Congress, where he swayed the other delegates to support Massachusetts in opposing Britain's Quartering Act and the **Coercive Acts.** He also persuaded them to endorse the **Suffolk Resolves,** calling for colonists to arm themselves and resist the British. After signing the Declaration, Adams served in the second Continental Congress throughout the Revolutionary War. He was instrumental in raising support for the passage of the new **Massachusetts Constitution** of 1780, written by his cousin John Adams.

In 1782 he became a member of the state Senate and was elected its president. He then served as lieutenant governor from 1789 to 1793, and became governor when the incumbent, John Hancock, died in office, remaining until he retired in 1797. He died in Boston on October 2, 1803, and is buried in the Granary Burying Ground on Tremont Street. His major contribution was as a Revolutionary propagandist who brought home to the people the principles of rule by consent of the governed, the virtues of republican government, and the natural right to resist tyranny. On the basis of these beliefs he supported the ratification of the U.S. Constitution and worked diligently to win its approval from a divided Massachusetts. He lives in the memory of the nation as one of its most influential founders.

African Meeting House

Located on Smith Court on **Beacon Hill** in Boston, the African Meeting House is one of the oldest black churches in the nation, founded in 1806 by Boston's black Baptists, who built themselves a meeting house after white churches forced them to sit in the balcony and refused to allow them to vote on church issues. The church became an important center for antislavery agitation during the antebellum period. On January 6, 1832, abolitionist **William Lloyd Garrison** founded the New England Anti-Slavery Society in the church building. It became a central venue for speakers on the other important issues of the day, such as women's rights, penal reform, and school integration. At the end of the nineteenth century, blacks began to migrate to other Boston neighborhoods and the church disbanded. Finally, the building was sold to immigrant Jews who turned it into a synagogue. In 1972 the Museum of Afro American History bought the building and restored the nineteenth-century design. It is now one of the stops on Boston's Black Heritage Trail. (See also **Abolitionists**)

Louisa May Alcott

Louisa May Alcott is remembered for writing the best-known American novel of female adolescence, *Little Women.* Born in Germantown, Pennsylvania, on November 29, 1832, the daughter of educator, Transcendentalist, and utopian reformer Bronson Alcott, she spent most of her life in Concord and Boston. Though living in genteel poverty for much of the time, the Alcotts maintained a household rich in culture and literature, supporting Louisa's dream of becoming a writer and her sister May in her painting pursuits. **Henry David Thoreau, Ralph Waldo Emerson,** and **Margaret Fuller,** among other authors and reformers, were frequent guests at the Alcott home in Concord, called **Orchard House.**

Louisa May Alcott. Library of Congress, Prints and Photographs Division.

With the outbreak of the Civil War, Louisa May Alcott volunteered as a nurse at a Washington, D.C., hospital, where she contracted typhoid fever. Although she recovered, her treatment consisted of liberal doses of mercury, which contributed to her ill health throughout the rest of her life. She returned home and began a writing career to help support the family, publishing her first romantic novel, *Moods,* in 1864 to mixed reviews. Her second novel was a young women's book, *Little Women,* published in two parts in 1868 and 1869. She wrote the novel in six weeks by hand, an effort made possible by the fact that she was ambidextrous. It was a smashing success, selling over 82,000 copies—a best-seller by the standards of the time. Much of the book was autobiographical, based on the Alcott family's daily life at home in Concord. The appeal of the novel then, as now, derived from Louisa May Alcott's superb insight into the lives and hopes of young women.

Alcott went on to write more books in this vein, including *Little Men* in 1871 and *Jo's Boys* in 1886, publishing over 270 titles in the course of her career. Her health continued to deteriorate, and the mercury poisoning caused periods of depression and emotional isolation. An advocate for women's rights, she never married. She died in Boston on March 6, 1888, two days after the death of her father. Her classic story of the March sisters remains a perennial favorite. Through it she has influenced generations of young women. (See also **Transcendentalism**)

John and Priscilla Alden (See **Myles Standish**)

Algonquins

The first settlers and long-term inhabitants of Massachusetts were descended from ancestors who originated in Asia or Asia Minor, arriving on the North American continent from ten thousand to forty thousand years ago, crossing over a land or ice bridge that emerged when the great glaciers began to retreat and sea levels fell off. When the land bridge disappeared under the waves, the tribes became isolated. The cool climate proved inhospitable to microbes and disease-bearing pests, and for many years these Paleo-Indians, untouched by other cultural contacts, remained free from the vast epidemics and countless disease strains that flourished in Europe and Asia. Evidence from the Bull Brook archaeological site near Ipswich shows that by the Early Archaic period, 8000–6000 B.C., these hunter-gatherers had reached the Atlantic coast. It was not until about A.D. 1000 that the agricultural revolution spread from Mexico and Central America to New England.

These settlers established a diverse and differentiated cultural system that existed in harmony with the natural environment, getting their food from a horticulture based on maize, beans, and squash combined with hunting and gathering of land and sea animals and plants. The major tribes or confederations—Mahican, Nipmuck, Niantic, Pequot-Mohegan, Massachusett, Wampanoag, and Narragansett—all engaged in similar social, political, and religious practices. All spoke a form of the Algonquian language, a distinct linguistic difference setting them apart from their northern and southern neighbors. With a well-defined village-based political structure of tribes acting in concert under local hereditary leaders (sachems), with clear-cut social roles based on the family, and with a complex set of ethical and religious values, the Algonquins developed a rich civilization well suited to their isolated environment.

Various estimates put their population at 90,000 to 144,000 on the eve of English colonization. First contacts with English fishermen, explorers, and traders exposed the Natives to a host of European diseases, such as plague, smallpox, chicken pox, and measles, to which they had no natural immunity. The epidemic of 1616–17 resulted in mortality rates as high as 80 to 90 percent, virtually decimating the coastal villages. Other epidemics followed in the 1620s, and a smallpox epidemic in 1633 killed up to 95 percent of Native villagers. The high rates of mortality had a devastating effect on a subsistence cycle based on planting and hunting. Disease destroyed the network of kin relationships and seriously undermined indigenous religious beliefs. As the surviving Natives engaged in European trades or became dependent on settlers' largesse, their society lost its agricultural infrastructure. Increasing English settlement and two disastrous wars soon pried the land away from the small number of Algonquins remaining. They became almost invisible as a group, farming marginal land, but maintaining their kinship ties. (See also **King Philip's War**)

Anti-Catholicism

Although the rhetoric of American popular culture trumpets a nation of religious liberty, anti-Catholicism has a long history in the United States, and particularly in the Commonwealth of Massachusetts. Boston's notorious history as a center of anti-Catholic bigotry may derive from its founding as a model of Puritan religious perfectionism, a "City on a Hill," and its unique retention of a homogeneous population of Protestant Yankees—New Englanders of British stock, from the social elite to small farmers and marginal laborers—until the migration of the Famine Irish after 1846. The **Puritans** conditioned citizenship on church membership, thus excluding all those of other faiths. Colonial statutes denied Catholics the right to worship or hold office. A 1647 law banished all Roman Catholic priests from entering the **Massachusetts Bay Colony,** with death the penalty for violations until 1700.

Throughout the eighteenth century, anti-Catholic celebrations, known as **Pope Days,** were held every year on November 5 in Boston. Despite French support of the patriots' cause during the American Revolution, Catholics could not worship publicly until 1780, and not until 1788 did Boston get its first Catholic church. The arrival of Irish Catholic immigrants in ever-greater numbers in the 1820s and 1830s inspired further intolerance. In 1834 Yankee mobs in Charlestown burned a Catholic convent to the ground. Three years later an anti-Catholic riot broke out on Broad Street in Boston, ravaging an entire Irish neighborhood. Ireland's Great Famine of 1846 triggered a staggering migration of Irish Catholics to the United States, with many coming to Yankee Protestant Boston, arriving penniless, lacking skills, and facing brutal intolerance. It took years for them to mount the ladder of social mobility.

The backlash against the Irish took many forms. In 1854 a political party, the **Know-Nothings,** came into being just to oust and subordinate the Irish. The party was short lived, but it put a face on the intolerance of Massachusetts, and Boston in particular. In 1863 the Irish of Boston's North End exploded into violence against the new draft law, which they believed was aimed directly at them. It was not until the early twentieth century that the Irish were able to succeed in politics in Boston, with popular leaders such as **John Fitzgerald** and **James Michael Curley.** Statewide it was not until after the Second World War that Irish Democrats came to control the state legislature. In 1960 the election of **John F. Kennedy** to the presidency marked the ultimate triumph of the Irish Catholics and their full acceptance by American society. (See also **Broad Street Riot** and **Ursuline Convent Riot**)

Mary Antin

Mary Antin is known for her autobiographical writings depicting how a Jewish immigrant girl came to America and made a place for herself in a new land. Born in Polotzk, Russia, on June 13, 1881, Mary Antin was the daughter of a scholar and shopkeeper, Israel Antin, who emigrated to the United States in 1891 because of religious persecution of the Jews. Three years later he sent for his wife and three daughters to join him in Boston. That year, 1894, thirteen-year-old Mary began first grade at public school. By the middle of the year she had learned English well enough to skip to the fifth grade. Her teachers took a special interest in her, making home visits and taking her on outings. She advanced rapidly, writing poems and exercises that delighted the school. On her graduation in 1897, Antin published a poem on George Washington that made her a local celebrity. Her fame earned Mary a place at the prestigious Boston Girls' Latin School. Her father, meanwhile, failed time and again in business, and the family moved from one slum to another. Though poor, she met important members of Boston society, who were taken with this immigrant girl's patriotism and her growing stature as a writer.

In 1899 she published her first book, *From Plotzk to Boston,* a series of letters originally written in Yiddish in 1894 to her grandfather, describing her emigration to the United States. The translated version brought her the attention of Boston's Yankee community, who were growing fearful at that time of the increasing immigration from overseas. In Mary Antin they saw the value of a public school education in promoting assimilation. She graduated from Boston Girls' Latin in 1901 and went to work in a settlement house. Soon after, she broke with her Jewish Orthodox background and married Amadeus Grabau, a geologist and son of a Lutheran minister. They moved to New York, where he took a teaching position at Columbia College. There Mary took courses at various schools, had a child in 1907, and then began to write in earnest describing her adjustment to American life.

The *Atlantic Monthly* published these articles in 1911, which were then combined into a book that appeared in 1912, *The Promised Land.* It brought her nationwide fame and sold well over the years. In it she rhapsodized about the assimilation experience, and her patriotic fervor touched many Americans. She went on the lecture circuit, and in 1914 published *They Who Knock at Our Gates,* a plea for the continuation of unrestricted immigration and tolerance for immigrants. The First World War led to a divorce, as her husband favored the German side and she the American allies. This personal loss, plus feelings of insecurity relating to her anomalous position of being caught between two worlds, brought on a nervous breakdown in 1918. In 1923 she entered a religious convalescent commune in western Massachusetts, where she lived for many years as an acolyte of a sort of pantheistic Christianity. She continued to speak out for tolerance toward immigrants and for a greater humanity until her death on May 15, 1949.

Nathan Appleton

Nathan Appleton, a rich Boston merchant, banker, politician, and early investor in the textile industry, epitomized the businessmen of Boston whose acumen and vision provided the impetus for the industrial revolution. Born in Boston on October 6, 1779, into a merchant family, he began work as a trader in 1794 and was one of the few merchants to prosper during the War of 1812. Appleton was an original investor in **Francis Cabot Lowell**'s textile factory in Waltham, and his firm sold the products of the mill. He was also one of the founding members of the **Boston Associates**—the group of merchants and bankers who invested in and developed the New England textile system. With other Boston Associates he participated in the creation of new mill towns, such as Lowell, Lawrence, and Manchester, New Hampshire. Elected to Congress in 1830, he was a staunch advocate of a high protective tariff.

Like other "Lords of the Loom," who formed a mutual relationship with the cotton-growing South, Appleton opposed abolitionism as a violation of the Constitution. By 1860, however, like so many other Bostonians, he was opposed to the extension of slavery into the territories. Throughout his lifetime he turned his attention to philanthropy as an obligation of his class, supporting a wide variety of cultural institutions such as the Boston Athenaeum and the Massachusetts Historical Society. He died on July 14, 1861, and was buried in Mount Auburn Cemetery in Cambridge.

Arbella

The ship *Arbella* was one of eleven vessels that set sail in the spring of 1630, carrying seven hundred passengers to New England to establish the **Massachusetts Bay Colony.** The leaders of the expedition were English religious dissenters known as **Puritans.** Those on board who would become the future colony's leading citizens included lawyer **John Winthrop,** high stewards Simon Bradstreet and Thomas Dudley, gentlemen Sir Richard Saltonstall, landowner Isaac Johnson and his wife, Lady Arbella Fiennes, and her friend the poet **Anne Bradstreet.** Many others were on board, including artisans and yeoman farmers. Also filling the ship's hold were farm animals of all sorts and provisions for the expedition. The *Arbella* and the other ships arrived at Salem harbor in June of that year.

Crispus Attucks

Very little is known about Crispus Attucks (ca. 1723–March 5, 1770), except that he was an African American and one of the first people killed by British troops in the **Boston Massacre** of March 5, 1770. He may have been a sailor and was perhaps part Indian. There is some evidence that at one point he had been a slave and ran away from his Boston owner in 1750. In his defense of the British soldiers accused of the massacre, **John Adams** referred to Attucks at the trial as one of the leaders of the mob who instigated the harassment of the troops by grabbing a soldier's bayonet.

Whatever the truth, Adams got the soldiers acquitted, including the soldier specifically accused of shooting Attucks. As an early hero of the American Revolution, Attucks exemplifies the diversity of the independence movement.

Main gates to Boston Common.

B

Back Bay

The Back Bay section of Boston reached its glory as the prime residential neighborhood for the city's well-to-do in the late nineteenth century. Originally mudflats and marshland, this area of 450 acres close to downtown and **Beacon Hill** attracted the attention of speculators in the early 1850s. Planned and executed after the grand design of Baron Hausmann's Second Empire boulevards of Paris, the Back Bay grew up alongside the green mall running the length of Commonwealth Avenue from the Public Garden on Arlington Street to Massachusetts Avenue. The plan called for splendid tree-lined streets with British names cutting across the great avenue, with its French-inspired brownstones with servant's quarters, roomy enough for families to live in the grand style. The Needham hills provided the gravel landfill to soak up the marshes and watery flats, and steam railroads transported the forty-five dirt carts with their gravel to the site, round the clock, beginning in 1859.

Over 1,500 Victorian row houses and educational institutions filled the once vacant area to become the new home to Boston's rich and mighty, including **Isabella Stewart Gardner.** Grand churches built in the Gothic and Romanesque styles soon followed. Other institutions arrived, such as the Museum of Natural History and the Massachusetts Institute of Technology in the 1860s, and the Harvard Medical School in 1883. With the construction of the neoclassical Boston Public Library on **Copley Square** in 1895, the Back Bay became the social and cultural center of the city. In addition to the rich, these splendid five-story Back Bay homes housed the city's Irish newcomers, who were the servants, toiling away in the basement kitchens and sleeping in cramped quarters under the roof.

The twentieth century took its toll on the Back Bay as rising social mobility eliminated domestic service, and as educational institutions increasingly turned their sights on Back Bay properties. Real estate speculators bought up the townhouses and divided them into apartments. Commercial life came to the area with chic retail shops and restaurants on Newbury Street, and hotels, office buildings, stores, and a convention center built on Boylston Street on the Back Bay's southern border. New apartment buildings have replaced some of the old brownstones, but more than enough remains to give the visitor a taste of a bygone era's grand architecture.

Sarah Bagley

Sarah Bagley is one of the ordinary people who appear only briefly in the historical record and then disappear. There is no listing of her birth or death, but we do know that in the 1830s she became one of the first female labor leaders in the nation's history. She seems to have worked in the mills for a while, in 1836 at the Hamilton Cotton Mills in Lowell. She was present during the mill women's strike in October of that year. Responding to the rapid decline of working conditions in the mills, Bagley organized a women's labor organization, the Lowell Female Labor Reform Association, in 1845. Starting with a few dozen members, it soon numbered five hundred and had become an important rallying force for the ten-hour workday movement, which had been a demand of the mill workers for some years.

Bagley wrote exposés, led petition drives, and did all in her power to publicize the plight of factory women, generally with no immediate success. In 1845 she charged that the company publication, the *Lowell Offering,* was captive to the interest of the owners. She and a few other young women published their own views in local newspapers and in labor journals for male workers. Bagley denounced the mill owners for cutting wages that were already too low, for increasing workloads, and for imposing long hours that left little time for social or intellectual pursuits. A pioneer labor organizer, she initiated the long, hard drive for worker equity that was not to come to fruition until well into the twentieth century. By 1847 she had left the mills to become a telegrapher, and, like many other workers, vanished from history.

Emily Greene Balch

The Nobel Peace Prize winner for 1946, Emily Balch was a pioneer women's activist who led a long life of social service, scholarship and teaching, and involvement in the worldwide peace movement. Born on January 8, 1867, she was raised in an upper-middle-class family of Boston Unitarians. Her father was a successful lawyer. Remarkably for the times, he wanted his daughter to become a lawyer, so he sent her to Bryn Mawr, where she graduated with the college's first class in 1889. At college she became keenly aware of the growing problems arising out of industrialization and urbanization. In 1892, with fellow college women such as Vida Scudder, she founded a settlement, Denison House, after the style of Jane Addams's Hull House in Chicago. At Denison House, located in a slum district of Boston's South Cove, she met **Mary Kenney O'Sullivan,** a labor activist, who shared her concern for the plight of working women in the factories. She continued her studies and her reform activities, joining a group of women who were leaders in the social reform movements of the day, such as Elizabeth Glendower Evans, Mary Kehew, and Mary Simkovitch, in addition to Scudder.

From 1896 to 1915 she worked first half-time, then full-time, as a professor of economics at Wellesley College. In 1902 she helped found the Boston Women's Trade Union League, an offshoot of Mary Kenney O'Sullivan's National Women's Trade Union League, organizations that sought to get women workers organized into unions. After a close study of Marx, in 1906 Balch announced that she was a socialist. With Scudder she organized a socialist conference that year in Boston. She also became interested in the plight of immigrants, particularly those from eastern Europe. After travel there and study, she published a book in 1910, *Our Slavic Fellow Citizens,* in order to counter the growing nativist alarm in the country over immigrants. She urged toleration, acceptance, and help so the newcomers could become assimilated.

The outbreak of the First World War brought her into an active role in the peace movement. With America's entry into the war in 1917, Balch and other socialists and pacifists, such as Jane Addams, came under attack for their views, which were denounced as unpatriotic. The trustees of Wellesley College refused to renew her contract in 1918. After the war she continued in her efforts to promote world peace. She helped organize the Women's International League for Peace and Freedom in Geneva in 1919, where she served as secretary and Jane Addams as president. Balch stayed in Geneva and devoted most of her remaining life to this organization, continuing to travel, write, and lecture on peace. In the 1930s she joined in the struggle against fascism. The outbreak of World War II forced her into a complete turnaround, since she believed that it was better to go to war than to allow fascism to triumph. For her many contributions, at age seventy-nine she was awarded the Nobel Peace Prize. She died in Cambridge on January 9, 1961.

Clara Barton

Clara Barton, founder of the American Red Cross, began her career of helping others during the Civil War. Born in North Oxford, Massachusetts, on December 25, 1821, she did not come to prominence until her fortieth year, while she was working as a clerk in the United States Patent Office in Washington, D.C. When rioting secessionists in Baltimore attacked a Massachusetts regiment, the Sixth, traveling to Washington, in what became a pitched battle, Barton and several others rushed to the train station to help the arriving troops. She took it upon herself to organize medical care and provisioning for the wounded soldiers. Recognizing the inadequate performance of the Quartermaster Corps, Barton subsequently devised a system for Massachusetts communities to send parcels of food and medical supplies to front-line troops. At her own expense she stored these provisions in three warehouses. Convincing the authorities of her good intentions, she was given wagons and passes to go to the front lines to help care for the wounded. Barton was present at several Civil War battles, acting as nurse and caregiver to those in need. Later, General Benjamin Butler of Massachusetts named her superintendent of nurses for the Union Army. After the war, she traveled worldwide, caring for victims in dangerous places devastated by war, flood, and other disasters. In 1881 she founded the American Red Cross and served for twenty-three years as the leader of the organization, known for its central purpose of helping casualties of warfare and natural disaster. Barton died on April 12, 1912, after fifty years of devoted service to others.

Basketball Hall of Fame

The Basketball Hall of fame is located in Springfield, where a young YMCA instructor, Dr. James Naismith, invented the game in 1891 at the School for Christian Workers, now Springfield College. The sport quickly developed and achieved international success when introduced at the 1936 Olympics in Berlin. The first home of the Hall of Fame was Springfield College, which opened a building in 1968 for induction of players and to house basketball artifacts. An expanded Hall of Fame opened off I-91 in 1985, loaded with basketball memorabilia and paraphernalia celebrating the major highlights and players of the game. In 2002 a newly renovated Hall of Fame opened to the public on the same site.

Beacon Hill

Beacon Hill was the neighborhood of choice for Boston's upper classes in the early nineteenth century. With merchant fortunes on the rise, there was a need for a new residential area to accommodate all this new wealth. Aside from the crowded North End and wharf area, the only place left was on the land occupied by the three hills, or Trimountain, of the Boston peninsula. These hills, Beacon, Pemberton, and Mount Vernon, soon became the source of earth to fill up the waterways and estuaries around Boston to make room for more settlement. Although two of the hills were completely shorn, remnants of Beacon Hill remain in the neighborhood that bears its name. In 1799 a gravity railroad using carts to take the fill downhill leveled Beacon Hill's crown, making way for construction to begin. In 1800 Federalist merchant **Harrison Gray Otis** hired architect **Charles Bulfinch** to design and build a house at 85 Mt. Vernon Street, which still stands as a monument to the taste and prosperity of Boston's elite two hundred years ago.

Further shaping of the hill in 1824 allowed for the construction of opulent row houses. Some sixty feet of hilltop was used to fill fifty acres of nearby Mill Pond for further building. With the use of steam railroads, the area became more fully developed in the 1830s. Its desirable location drew the well-to-do merchants and elite of Boston, who hired architects to design attractive Federal-style mansions. Today, portions of Beacon Hill near the **State House** and facing **Boston Common** remain an area of exclusive town houses, some with private cobblestoned nooks and parks, such as Louisburg Square. Residences on the side of the hill facing the Charles

River consist largely of middle-class apartments. The Massachusetts legislature designated Beacon Hill as a historic district in 1955, and the federal Department of the Interior gave it landmark status in 1963.

Alexander Graham Bell

As everybody knows, Alexander Graham Bell invented the telephone, but not everyone knows that he did it in Massachusetts. Born in Edinburgh, Scotland, on March 3, 1847, he was the son of a speech teacher. Young Bell became entranced with speech and worked with his brother on speaking devices involving telegraphy and tuning forks. These endeavors inspired him to become a teacher for the deaf, and to experiment with sending signals over wires. He emigrated to Boston in 1871 to teach deaf students to speak. Although he lacked academic credentials, Bell's success earned him a job at Boston University as a professor of vocal physiology in 1873.

Alexander Graham Bell at the unveiling of a plaque commemorating the invention of the telephone, Boston, 1916. Photo by Richard Sears. Library of Congress, Prints and Photographs Division.

Assisting Bell in his sound research was a young electrical worker, Thomas A. Watson. On March 10, 1876, Bell communicated to Watson on a primitive telephone from the next room, speaking famous words: "Mr. Watson, come here, I want to see you." Bell and Watson improved their invention and publicized its value in demonstrations and lectures. In 1877 Bell organized the Bell Telephone Company. As it succeeded, Bell became interested in other research and left the company for others to run for him. He spent many years on new scientific projects, though none reached the same level of fame as the telephone. He died on August 2, 1922, in Nova Scotia.

Edward Bellamy

Edward Bellamy was a social reformer made famous by his utopian novel *Looking Backward, 2000–1887.* His book offered a tantalizing solution to the abuses of industrialization and the capitalist system, and hit home in a nation undergoing massive changes that challenged the bucolic ideal of a rural society.

Born in Chicopee Falls in western Massachusetts on March 29, 1850, Bellamy was the son of a Baptist minister. He went to local schools and attended Union College in Schenectady, New York, but did not graduate. Witnessing the transformation of Chicopee from a village to a depressed mill town, he became sensitive to the cycles of unemployment and poverty that had become the norm during the rising industrial revolution. For a short time Bellamy worked as a journalist and edited and ran newspapers in Springfield. He also wrote short fiction and tried his hand at novels, including one supporting the cause of **Shays's Rebellion.**

Still largely unknown, Bellamy decided to write a futuristic novel that would gain the attention of a wide audience while at the same time preaching his gospel of equality and an end to the depredations of an unfettered capitalism. He published *Looking Backward* in 1888, and it became an immediate success. The protagonist is a young man who falls asleep in 1887 and awakens in 2000 in a society that has eliminated poverty and class differences. In this utopian world there are no rich or poor. The government owns the means of production, and a centralized economy has eliminated competition and unregulated individualism. This revolutionary transformation has come about without violence, by means of evolution and the application of common sense. The new bureaucratic government skillfully distributes wealth in a rational manner. Unemployment, hunger, child labor, unsafe working conditions—all are a thing of the past, as the central government works only for the general welfare, not for profit.

Translated into twenty languages, the novel became a national and international best-seller. Hundreds of Bellamy Nationalist clubs sprang up all over America so that devotees could discuss the novel's vision and work for its realization. But the realities of an individualistic society predicated on the free enterprise system soon eclipsed the Bellamy movement, and by the mid-1890s it had ended. Bellamy tried to keep his ideas alive by publishing a sequel in 1897, *Equality,* but it had little success. He died the following year of tuberculosis, on May 22, 1898, in Chicopee Falls.

Although Bellamy's futuristic society was anti-democratic, it appealed to followers because it seemed the best solution to the many problems facing modern America. The novel's popularity gave evidence of the growing apprehension in the nation about the baneful impact of the industrial revolution and its lack of regulation. Bellamy's ideas contributed to a rising tide of social criticism promoting the need to reform society in a more just manner, and helped lay the foundation for the reform movements of the Progressive Era in the early twentieth century.

Berkshires

The Berkshires Hills, located in Berkshire County in western Massachusetts, first attracted vacationers in the nineteenth century, when Boston's literati and wealthy families made the area their summer destination. Since that time, visitors from all over the world come to enjoy these hills in all seasons. In fall, the "leaf peepers" admire the magnificent foliage. Winter visitors enjoy a wide array of snow sports. In spring and summer, vacationers meander the region's wooded hillsides, winding roads, and pristine villages. The Berkshires are also the setting for a unique concentration of cultural activities which draw large numbers of tourists. Hotels, theaters, private schools, and resorts now inhabit the former grand old mansions and country houses of the Boston elite.

The main attraction is the **Tanglewood** Music Festival at Lenox, which is the summer home of the Boston Symphony Orchestra. Famous for its concerts in the Shed while music lovers picnic on the lawn, it is also a place where young musicians undergo rigorous training. In nearby Becket, America's most innovative dance companies perform at **Jacob's Pillow.**

Theater is abundant, from the Berkshire Theater Festival in Stockbridge in the south to the Williamstown Theater Festival in the north. While Williamstown boasts a first-class art collection at the Clark Institute, Stockbridge is home to the popular **Norman Rockwell** Museum. Not far away at Chesterwood is the estate of sculptor Daniel Chester French. A major museum of modern art, **MASS MoCA,** is situated in a former factory building in North Adams. For those who prefer natural beauty, part of the Appalachian Trail runs through the Berkshire Hills.

Big Dig

State and Boston officials conceived of the Big Dig, or Central Artery/Third Harbor Tunnel Project, as a means to relieve traffic congestion in downtown Boston and provide easier access to Logan Airport. The project called for demolishing the old elevated section of I-95, the Central Artery, to allow for construction of an eight- to ten-lane underground expressway and a new third tunnel beneath Boston Harbor leading to the airport. Aboveground plans called for acres of new parkland. All the dirt excavated from the project would contribute to capping landfills and creating parks and recreation areas. Project completion was scheduled for 2005.

The Big Dig, the largest such construction project in the nation's history, had its origins in a highway and transit bill passed in Congress by one vote over President Ronald Reagan's veto in 1987. The projected cost in 1991 was $5.2 billion, though by 1994 costs were already $7.7 billion and rising, and street traffic was perpetually snarled by construction delays and ever-shifting detours. The Third Harbor Tunnel, the **Ted Williams** Tunnel, opened to commercial traffic and emergency vehicles in 1995. By 2000 costs had soared to $14.4 billion, with the federal government capping its contribution at $8.5 billion. This shortfall raised the state's contribution, originally 15 percent, considerably. Suggestions for finding the funds to cover the increased costs included the sale of state lands, higher tolls, and "creative financing." In the spring of 2003, two major sections of the project, the northbound lanes of the underground expressway and the Leonard Zakim Bunker Hill Bridge, were opened to the public.

E. B. Bigelow (Carpets)

Making low-cost carpets available to the general public was the work of Erastus Brigham Bigelow, the inventor of the carpet loom. In the mid-nineteenth century, Bigelow helped lead the way from reliance on hand labor to the efficiency and productivity of the new age of machines.

Bigelow was born April 2, 1814, the son of a farmer and mechanic. The family's poverty deprived Bigelow of the chance for any formal education. Between the ages of ten and twenty he drifted through various jobs—farm worker, clerk, musician, teacher of penmanship, and author of self-help pamphlets. But his chief skills were as an inventor. This was quite surprising, since he had little training in drawing or drafting. Nonetheless, in 1837 he produced his first successful invention, a power loom to produce lace. Bigelow soon formed his own company to build looms. Over the next twenty years, numerous mechanical improvements brought him fame and prosperity. His many notable inventions included power looms for weaving tapestry and carpets and a wide variety of machines for producing fabrics and cloth of all kinds. He built factories throughout Massachusetts and Connecticut, but the most famous was the Bigelow Mills in Clinton, Massachusetts. He died in Boston on December 16, 1879, a pioneer in the textile manufacturing industry and an innovative inventor who contributed to advancing the industrial revolution in the United States.

Blackstone Canal

A vestige of the early industrial revolution in Massachusetts and Rhode Island, the Blackstone Canal marked an attempt by Worcester and Providence businessmen to cut the costs of shipping freight overland to Boston. The canal was in the Blackstone River Valley, on the border between Massachusetts and Rhode Island. With capital mainly supplied by the Providence merchant Edward Carrington, the canal opened in 1828, allowing barges to move up and down the forty-nine granite locks, each one eighty feet long by ten feet wide, between the two cities. Operating problems resulting from freezing winter weather, insufficient water supply, and disputes over water rights plagued the canal. Finally, in 1847 the newly completed Providence and Worcester Railroad eclipsed the canal with cheaper freight rates. The Blackstone Canal with its horse-drawn barges went out of business within a year. Visitors can view restored sections of the canal at the Blackstone River and Canal Heritage Park in Uxbridge, Massachusetts.

Alice Stone Blackwell

Alice Stone Blackwell, a pioneer suffragist, feminist, and social reformer, was born in Orange, New Jersey, on September 14, 1857, the daughter of two prominent members of the suffrage movement, **Lucy Stone** and Henry Blackwell, who were the founders of the American Woman Suffrage Association. Young Alice's home was a meeting place for many reformers, such as **William Lloyd Garrison** and **Julia Ward Howe.** She attended Boston High School while the family lived in Dorchester, then went to Boston University, graduating in 1881. She then joined her parents in their suffrage endeavors and began to work on their periodical, the *Woman's Journal.* In 1893, after the death of her mother, she served as editor of the journal until 1917. Between 1887 and 1905 she was also editor of a weekly suffrage newspaper, the *Woman's Column.*

Alice Blackwell played an important role in the formation of the National American Woman Suffrage Association in 1890, which formally ended divisions among suffrage leaders. She served that organization as recording secretary for over two decades and was a member of many other reform groups, including the Women's Trade Union League, the Woman's Christian Temperance Union, the Anti-Vivisection League, and the National Association for the Advancement of Colored People. Blackwell helped found the League of Women Voters and worked on several projects to end the oppression of women all over the world. She was an activist in the movement to free **Sacco and Vanzetti** in the 1920s. In 1930 she wrote a biography of her mother. She died in Cambridge on March 15, 1950, after a long and fruitful career.

Body of Liberties

The Body of Liberties signified the first statutory step toward democracy in the fledgling **Massachusetts Bay Colony.** Under the auspices of the royal charter granting rights to the Massachusetts Bay Company, in 1630 the **Puritans** established a government encompassing a legislature of deputies—the Great and General Court—a governor, deputy governor, and assistants. The deputies in the General Court considered establishing some sort of legal code to restrain overzealous magistrates from violating civil rights and liberties. After years of discussion, in 1640 they appointed Nathaniel Ward of Ipswich to create such a code. There were one hundred provisions that amounted to both a bill of rights and an attempt to codify the ideas of governance for the colony. In addition to the right to trial by jury, the code gave freemen the right to elect all government officers, and set up governance procedures for towns, creating the unique **town meeting** form with its "select persons." The General Court accepted this Body of Liberties in 1641, principles that were later embodied in the Bill of Rights of the U.S. Constitution.

Lizzie Borden

Lizzie Borden (July 19, 1860–June 1, 1927) was the famed ax murderess of Fall River who was accused of killing her father and stepmother. The case, with its gruesome details and Freudian overtones, brought Borden and her town instant national notoriety. Her father, Andrew Borden, was a self-made investor of some wealth. Lizzie and her sister Emma resented, probably with good cause, their stepmother, Abby Gray. Unmarried, Lizzie Borden lived in an oppressive household, though she spent much of her time out of the house on religious activities. On the morning of August 4, 1892, an attacker killed both Abby and Andrew Borden, apparently with an ax. Lizzie and a servant were the only others at home at the time, though both claimed they hadn't seen or heard anything. The authorities arrested Lizzie when she could not provide a coherent account of her activities.

Her trial in 1893 in New Bedford proved to be the event of the year. The prosecution had a weak case with no murder weapon and no direct evidence connecting her with the murders. Her lawyer played up her defenseless femininity, speaking of her as a "little girl," even though she was thirty-three at the time. Her father was known in the community to be miserly and cold, while his wife was thought to be a bullying stepmother. All the testimony worked in Lizzie Borden's favor, and the jury acquitted her. Life back in Fall River was not easy, however, so she moved away and changed her name to Lizbeth. This local murder case became part of American folklore, memorialized in the famous children's rhyme:

Lizzie Borden took an ax
And gave her mother forty whacks;
When she saw what she had done
She gave her father forty-one!

The murder was never solved.

A scene from the Borden murder trial as depicted in *Frank Leslie's Illustrated Weekly,* June 1893. Library of Congress, Prints and Photographs Division.

Boston Associates

At the turn of the eighteenth century, wealthy Boston merchants led Massachusetts's transition toward a large-scale industrial society. Seeking to overcome the high risks inherent in overseas maritime trade, they chose to invest instead in a more secure high-technology activity—textile manufacturing. In preserving their wealth by moving to industrial production, they transformed the state and eventually the nation. This merchant elite came to be known as the Boston Associates, brought together in a mutual investment enterprise that was the first corporate monopoly in the nation. Coming from a background that focused on commerce and the commercial life, and imbued with the values of diligence, order, thrift, prudence, personal restraint, and self-improvement, they were perfect models of capitalist striving.

Because of the restrictions placed on trade by the War of 1812, these merchants redirected their surplus capital, starting up new industries on a large scale. They developed modern techniques of manufacturing and devised an efficient system to sell their products. The Boston Associates recruited, trained, and housed a large labor force, sometimes building new communities, such as Lawrence and Lowell, in the process. They contributed to the construction of a transportation system of canals and railroads vital to their own needs. By 1850 the Boston Associates, including Edmund Dwight, Kirk Boott, Patrick T. Jackson, William Sturgis, **Harrison Gray Otis,** T. H. Perkins, Israel Thorndike, Amos and **Abbott Lawrence, Nathan Appleton,** the Lowells, the Cabots, the Quincys, and the Eliots, owned most of New England's large cotton mills. These men controlled production by exchanging information on costs, posting similar bids for raw cotton, and attempting to fix the price of finished goods. They monopolized regional water power sites, had substantial interests in the subsidiary manufacture of textile machinery, and often built and rented out the houses their workers lived in. They had impressive holdings in banks and insurance companies.

Their control over politics and the professions led to their domination of culture as well, and they later became known as the Boston Brahmins. The term "Brahmins," referring to the highest caste of Indian society, was first used by poet Oliver Wendell Holmes Sr. to characterize the well-to-do families who became the aristocrats of nineteenth-century Boston. Those family members who were not attuned to business and politics soon dominated the arts and professions. Cultural celebrities of Boston such as **James Russell Lowell, Amy Lowell,** Francis Parkman, **Oliver Wendell Holmes Jr.,** and Charles Eliot Norton came from wealth, and **Henry Wadsworth Longfellow** married into it. Descendants of this ruling elite still influence the culture of Boston.

Boston Brahmins

(See **Boston Associates**)

Boston Bruins

In 1924 the Boston Bruins became the first United States hockey team in the previously all-Canadian National Hockey League. Over the years they won five Stanley Cups, with forty-two team members inducted into the Hockey Hall of Fame, including the great Bobby Orr. The Bruins started out playing at the Boston Arena, but moved to the Boston Garden, a multipurpose sports arena, in 1928. They called the Garden home until 1995, when they moved to a new facility, the Fleet Center.

The man behind the team's development was Boston businessman Charles F. Adams, who owned the First National Stores. The Adams family owned the Bruins for five decades and witnessed all five Stanley Cup victories.

Adams's choice for the Bruins' first coach and general manager was the versatile Art Ross, former player and hockey innovator. It was Ross who created the modern-day hockey puck, the standard net, and the metal stick. With Ross at the helm and hockey great Eddie Shore, who joined the team in 1926, on the ice, the Bruins became one of the outstanding teams of the 1920s and 1930s. The Bruins won Stanley Cups in 1929, 1939, and 1941. They then reached the finals in 1943, 1946, 1953, 1957, and 1958 but lost each time. By the 1960s the Bruins were playing poorly, but the fans kept coming. It is interesting to note that during this period the Boston Celtics were playing outstanding basketball, but the cellar-dwelling Bruins drew bigger crowds. The great Bobby Orr joined the team in 1966 at age eighteen, and the Bruins' fortunes changed. In 1968 they made the playoffs but lost to their nemesis, the Montreal Canadians. Finally, they won their fourth Stanley Cup in 1970, and their fifth and last one of the twentieth century in 1972. The Bruins again reached the finals in 1974, 1978, 1988, and 1990, only to lose. Nonetheless, Boston fans remain loyal to the team that made Boston the nation's first hockey town.

Boston Celtics

Boston Celtics basketball is one of the major reasons why the Hub is renowned as a dedicated sports community. Boston businessman Walter Brown founded the Boston Celtics basketball team in 1946. Brown was president of both the Boston Garden and the Boston Arena, and by the early 1950s he was running both the Celtics and the **Boston Bruins,** and was co-director of the **Boston Marathon.** But it was basketball that was Brown's passion. The Celtics won seven National Basketball Association championships under Brown's leadership, and between 1946 and 1992 the team had thirty-eight winning seasons. Brown chose the Celtics name to entice the area's large Irish Catholic population to attend basketball games in the face of the overwhelming popularity of the Bruins hockey team. The symbol he chose, a white shamrock on a field of green, spoke to many ethnics of the rise to power of the Irish Catholics over the Yankee Protestants. For many in the black community, however, the symbol represented racism and exclusion.

Brown was among those who established the Basketball Association of America in 1946, made up of eleven teams, including Boston. The Celtics played their first game in Providence, Rhode Island, on November 2, 1946, where they lost to the Providence Steamrollers. They played their home opener on November 5, the same day **John F. Kennedy** was elected to Congress, in the Boston Arena because the Garden was booked for a rodeo. In their first season they finished in last place. They made the playoffs in 1948, but lost to the Chicago Stags in championship play. In 1949 the Basketball Association gave way to the National Basketball Association.

In 1950, after four losing seasons and much lost money, Brown hired a new coach, Arnold "Red" Auerbach. Along with the aggressive Auerbach came basketball greats Bob Cousy and Chuck Cooper, the first African American player in the NBA. In 1956, with the arrival of the "big man," Bill Russell, Auerbach's brand of fast-break basketball heralded the beginning of a new era of good fortune for the Celtics. They won their first championship in the 1957 season and went to the finals in 1958, losing to St. Louis. The Celtics bounced back to win the title in 1959. In 1964, the Celtics were the first team to field five black players at the same time.

After leading the team to eight consecutive championships, Auerbach stepped aside as coach in 1966 to become general manager. He appointed Bill Russell to the job, the first black coach in the NBA, who led the team to championships in 1968 and 1969. By then the Celtics had won eleven NBA championships. Further victories followed in 1974, 1976, 1981, 1984, and 1986, with players such as Dave Cowens, John Havlicek, Jo Jo White, and one of basketball's greatest players, Larry Bird. With Bird's retirement in 1993, the team began to slide. A succession of new coaches and new management, and some talented young players, rekindled fans' hopes that the Celtics might yet repeat their invincible years of the past century in the new century.

Boston Common

Located in downtown Boston, the Boston Common comprises forty-five acres of parkland that serves as a place of recreation and respite from the stimulus of urban life. In 1634 the newly settled town of Boston purchased this land from the Reverend William Blaxton, the first English inhabitant of what was then known as the Shawmut Peninsula. Over the years, Bostonians used it as a place to pasture their cattle, to muster their militias, to celebrate holidays with parades, and even to execute those charged as wrongdoers. The Common was a vital area for patriots to gather in order to promote their Revolutionary activities. Among the monuments erected on the Common is the **Robert Gould Shaw** Memorial, a frieze by sculptor Augustus Saint-Gaudens showing Shaw leading the all-black Fifty-fourth Massachusetts regiment off to battle in the Civil War. Across Charles Street to the west of the Common lie the Public Gardens, with European-style formal walks, flowerbeds, and a pond used for boating in the summer. When work began in the 1850s to fill in the land of the **Back Bay,** some twenty-four acres were set aside for this public park. This is the home of the popular swan boats, which have provided an enjoyable moment on the pond for generations of local residents and visitors. The "Emerald Necklace," a band of parkland and open spaces laid out by the famed nineteenth-century landscape architect Frederick Law Olmsted, winds its way westward from the Public Gardens through several miles of urban neighborhoods.

Boston Marathon

The Boston Marathon is the nation's oldest marathon. It is run on Patriot's Day, the Monday in April closest to April 19, which commemorates the battles of **Lexington and Concord.** Contenders race in several divisions: men, women, and wheelchair participants. The course, based on Olympic standards, covers 26 miles and 385 yards.

In 1896, the Olympic games held in Athens, Greece, the first in the modern era, inspired Boston Athletic Association member John Graham and Boston businessman Herbert H. Holton to organize a marathon for Boston. The first one, held on April 19, 1897, was run from Metcalf's Mill in Ashland to the Irvington Oval in Boston, a measured distance of 24.5 miles. There were only fifteen entrants, and the winner was John McDermott of New York with a time of two hours, fifty-five minutes, and ten seconds. By 1903 there were over one hundred runners entered. By 2000, some quarter million men and women had run the Boston Marathon, with over thirty-seven thousand competing on its one-hundredth anniversary in 1997. The course has varied over the years, but its present route begins in Hopkinton and moves on to Ashland, Framingham, Natick, Wellesley, Newton (with its "Heartbreak Hill"), and Brookline, to finish near the Prudential Center on Boylston Street in Boston. Runners from all over the world come to Boston each April to compete.

For many years the marathon was strictly a male affair, until 1966, when Roberta Gibb ran the race unofficially with a respectable time of three hours and twenty minutes. Other women followed, unofficially entering the race, until the Boston Athletic Association reluctantly agreed in 1972 to allow women to participate officially. Wheelchair competition began in 1975 and has progressed from conventional wheelchairs to high-tech models specially designed for racing.

Over the years the marathon has had its share of cheaters—those who enter the race, drop out, use cars to get close to the finish line, and then slip back in. The most notorious case was that of Rosie Ruiz in 1980, who entered the race in the last mile and was crowned the women's champion by the BAA. After uncovering the gambit, the BAA disqualified Ruiz and demanded that she return the medal. She refused to do so.

Boston Massacre

The Boston Massacre was one of the seminal events leading to the American Revolution. Because of continued unrest in Boston after the **Stamp Act** riots of 1765, the British government in 1768 sent four regiments of troops to be quartered in the town to maintain the peace. The dispatching of troops enraged **Sam Adams** and other patriots and created widespread animosity among the townsfolk in general. The citizens harassed and hindered the troops both on and off duty. On the snowy night of March 5, 1770, a group of young boys threw snowballs and perhaps stones at a British sentry on guard duty at King Street. When a crowd gathered, the leader of the guard, Captain Thomas Preston, arrived on the scene with reinforcements. The crowd grew ugly and menaced his troops, uttering insults and keeping up a barrage of snowballs and other missiles. It appears that by accident, one soldier's musket went off. The fearful troops, thinking that they had received an order to fire, shot into the crowd. The volley of gunfire killed three, including **Crispus Attucks,** an African America, and wounded eight, two of whom died later. Local authorities had Preston and the soldiers arrested and ordered an immediate investigation.

The shootings raised the level of dissatisfaction with British rule and brought many moderates over to the radical side. Silversmith **Paul Revere** quickly worked up a popular engraving of the event that helped keep emotions high throughout the city and province. Sam Adams saw the value of flaunting Boston's martyrdom to the rest of the colonies while at the same time putting on a semblance of evenhanded justice for the arrested troops. To ensure a fair trial, the patriot leaders prevailed on two of their own supporters, and Boston's best legal minds, **John Adams** and **Josiah Quincy,** to defend Preston and the soldiers in court. The jury acquitted Preston at trial in October 1770, and in a later trial jurors acquitted all the soldiers but two, whose punishment was branding on the thumbs. The massacre and the subsequent trials kept alive the sentiment among Massachusetts patriots that they must resist British imperial despotism. (See also **Boston Tea Party**)

Boston Post Road

The Boston Post Road took its name from the first dispatch of mail in the colonies via post rider on January 22, 1673. The 250-mile route ran from New York to New Haven, Hartford, Springfield, Brookfield, Worcester, and Cambridge to Boston. After some disruption during **King Philip's War,** mail delivery resumed in 1679, when the Massachusetts legislature established the residence of one Richard Fairbanks as the house "appointed to receive all letters."

Known as the Old Boston Post Road, this was the route **Paul Revere** took to carry the **Suffolk Resolves** of the Massachusetts Congress in 1774 to the Continental Congress in Philadelphia. Ebenezer Hurd rode from Boston in 1775 delivering the news to the same congress of the battles of **Lexington and Concord.** The first post road in the colonies, it was sometimes also called the Upper Road, the King's Highway, or the Great Road. Travelers entering or leaving New England went by the Old Post Road.

The original Post Road should not be confused with two others of the same name. One runs from Boston along the Connecticut shore to New Haven, where it joins the original Old Post Road. This Lower Road (270 miles) passed from Boston through Dedham, Walpole, Attleboro, Providence, Warwick, Bristol, Newport, New London, Saybrook, Guilford, and Brandon to New Haven. The Middle Road (225 miles) left Boston, crossing Massachusetts westward by way of Dedham, Medway, Uxbridge, Douglas, Pomfret, Berlin, Meriden, Wallingford, and North Haven to New Haven, connecting there with the original road. It is often thought, though incorrectly, that the Lower Road, now U.S. Route 1, is the original because at New Haven all three roads merge into Route 1 and follow the shoreline to New York.

In 1840 it took two days by stagecoach to travel from Boston to New York. This changed with the coming of the railroads, which moved along different routes. Then a century later, with the decline of the railroads, the U.S. Post Office switched to postal vans, which once again used the route of the post roads to deliver the mail.

Boston Red Sox and Fenway Park

Boston is and has long been a fervent baseball town, having a team as early as 1871—the Boston Red Stockings. The successful Red Stockings became the Boston Beaneaters in 1876, when the team joined the newly organized National League. By 1901 the team became known as the Boston Braves. Meanwhile, rival team owners organized an American Association in 1881, which later merged with the Western Association to form the American League in 1899. A Boston team was one of the four new teams to engage in American League play in 1901. Owners found a site for a new playing field on Huntington Avenue on land leased from the New York, New Haven, and Hartford Railroad Company. The team, which had no official name, was called variously the Boston Americans, the Pilgrims, the Puritans, the Plymouth Rocks, and the Somersets, either by sportswriters or by the public.

The team's first manager, Jimmy Collins, was the former third basemen from Boston's National League team. Collins lured from the National League pitching legend Cy Young, who went on to win more games (511) than any other pitcher before or since. The Boston team played their first game in Baltimore on April 26, 1901, and then opened at home for the first time at the Huntington Avenue site on May 8, 1901, in a game they won against Philadelphia. That season Boston ended up in second place, losing out to the Chicago White Sox. They won the league championship in 1903

Fenway Park. Photo by Jim Davis via www.Merlin-Net.com.

and went on to defeat Pittsburgh in seven games in baseball's first World Series.

In 1904 the owner of the *Boston Globe,* Charles Henry Taylor, bought the team. Run by his son John, the team won the pennant that year. John Taylor put red stockings on the players in 1907, and that is when they became officially known as the Boston Red Sox. In 1912 Taylor sold the team just as a new ballpark opened in the Fenway area of Boston. Even then, Fenway Park, now one of the oldest still in use in the nation, was small and intimate, with walls jutting in and out at various angles and providing limited room to catch foul balls. The high wall in left field turned many a home run into a single. At the base of the wall was a ten-foot sloping embankment called "Duffy's Cliff" for outfielder Duffy Lewis, who learned how to play it well. The first Red Sox game held at Fenway was an exhibition game against the Harvard University team on April 19, 1912. The first league play game the next day saw Boston beat the New York Highlanders 7 to 6. Any excitement about opening day was vitiated by the news of the sinking of the *Titanic* on the same day.

The Sox had an excellent year in 1912, winning the World Series against the New York Giants, behind pitching great Smoky Joe Wood (34 and 7), and outfielders Tris Speaker, Harry Hooper, and Duffy Lewis. After a mediocre 1913 season, a new owner in 1914 brought in a left-handed pitching ace, George Herman "Babe" Ruth. Ruth pitched some superlative seasons: in 1915 he went 18 and 8, in 1916, 23 and 12, and in 1917, 23 and 13. He soon began pitching less as his hitting prowess became apparent and fans poured into Fenway Park in the hope of seeing a Ruth home run. With Ruth and Wood leading the team, the Sox won the pennant and the World Series in 1915 and again in 1916.

The next year New York theatrical manager Harry Frazee bought the team. Again in 1918 the Red Sox won it all. After a poor season in 1919, Frazee, who was desperate for cash to pay off his debts, sold Ruth in January 1920 to the New York Yankees. The "Bambino," as Ruth was called, went on to become one of the greatest baseball players of all time, leading the Yankees to victory after victory. The foolish move by Frazee is seen by superstitious fans as a curse that has prevented the Red Sox from ever winning another World Series. This "curse of the Bambino" lasted throughout the entire twentieth century and into the twenty-first.

The years after Ruth's departure were dismal for the Red Sox, who did not win a division title until 1934 under the aegis of a new owner, Thomas Yawkey. Yawkey, a millionaire, bought the team in order to build a winner. He acquired many good players, a move that paid off in the 1934 win. Over the next two years he reconstructed the stadium, adding concrete bleachers and increasing the size of the grandstand, and he built a new left field wall 315 feet from home plate and some 37 feet high, topped by a 23-foot screen to prevent home runs from flying onto Lansdowne Street. In 1947 Yawkey installed lights and had the many advertisements plastered on the left field wall painted over in green, thus leading to the sobriquet the "Green Monster." When the National League Braves decamped for Milwaukee, the Sox had Boston to themselves. As much as Yawkey attempted to improve the team, it faltered over the years largely because of lackluster pitching. Indeed, from 1919 to 1945, with the exception of 1934, the Red Sox won nothing.

Since 1945 they have come close several times, winning the pennant in

1946, 1967, 1975, and 1986, but losing the World Series to, respectively, the St. Louis Cardinals twice, the Cincinnati Reds, and the New York Mets. In 1948 they tied for the pennant but lost in a single playoff game to the Cleveland Indians. They won their division three times, in 1988, 1990, and 1995, but then lost the pennant to Oakland twice and to Cleveland once. The Sox earned the new wild card position in 1998 and 1999, but lost playoff series to Cleveland and the Yankees. Despite the efforts of some of the greatest players in baseball since 1940—Ted Williams, Bobby Doerr, Mel Parnell, Jackie Jensen, Carl Yastrzemski, Dick Radatz, Rico Petrocelli, Jimmy Piersall, Jim Lonborg, Jim Rice, Fred Lynn, Carlton Fisk, Dwight Evans, Luis Tiant, Roger Clemens, Nomar Garciaparra, Pedro Martinez—a World Series win has remained elusive.

Boston Tea Party

Like the **Boston Massacre,** the Tea Party incident heightened tensions and led to the violent overthrow of British rule by the colonies. After several encounters between Massachusetts's colonists and Parliament over the argument that taxes could not be levied without the consent of the governed, the British aggravated the turmoil by passing the Tea Act on May 10, 1773. Its purpose was to provide profits for the failing East India Company, to raise revenues in the colonies, and once again to demonstrate Parliament's imperial right to tax the colonists without their consent. The act also provided that the East India Company could ship tea directly to the colonies, thus avoiding the English tax and thereby increasing its profits. Instead, the colonists would pay the tax, thus promoting a stable source of revenue for the Crown.

The Tea Act infuriated the colonists. Boston merchants joined with Boston radicals in opposing what they saw as an act of imperial despotism. Indeed, all those who drank tea became incensed at the violation of their liberties as Englishmen by the British government. When three ships carrying tea docked at Griffin Wharf, Bostonians demanded that the tea be sent back. On December 16, 1773, faced with opposition by the local Crown authorities, the townspeople took action. That evening a small group of men, members of the **Sons of Liberty,** disguised as Mohawks by painting their faces and carrying blankets and hatchets, boarded the vessels. In front of a large, approving crowd on the dock, the "Mohawks" dumped the tea chests into the harbor. Among the group was a sprinkling of gentlemen and merchants, but most were artisans, the most famous being **Paul Revere.** The patriot instigators of the tea dumping, such as **Sam Adams** and **John Hancock,** did not participate but looked on.

Word of the successful Boston resistance spread throughout the colonies, and other patriot groups began preventing tea ships from unloading their cargoes. **John Adams** correctly summed up the significance of this protest when he wrote in his diary, "This destruction of the Tea is so bold, so daring, so firm, intrepid, & inflexible, and it must have so important Consequences and so lasting, that I cannot but consider it as an Epocha in History." Events soon proved Adams right. The Crown ministers became furious at this flagrant breach of the law, and Parliament passed the **Coercive Acts.** These harsh and punitive laws closed the port of Boston, quartered troops on its townspeople, and generally abrogated all rights of self-government in the colony. These actions led to the beginning of colonial armed resistance and the finality of the "shot heard round the world" at **Lexington and Concord.**

William Bradford

William Bradford, for many years the governor of Plymouth Colony, epitomizes the will and tenacity of the Pilgrims in their struggle to gain their religious freedom in an uncharted wilderness. Born in 1590 (the precise date is unknown), son of a farmer in Yorkshire, as a teenager Bradford turned to the Pilgrims' separatist faith, joining them in their journey to Holland, where the sect settled in Leyden in 1609. By the time he was nineteen, his piety was so well known that Pilgrim leaders chose him as a ruling elder in their church. While they settled in at Leyden and began to prosper, church members worried about maintaining their faith and feared that their children would become assimilated into the Dutch culture. Bradford and the other Pilgrims reasoned that it was necessary to start a new community where they could control religious practice and bring up their children free from outside influences. They decided to build that community in the New World.

Bradford and his family sailed on the *Mayflower,* and he was one of the signers of the **Mayflower Compact.** When the first elected governor of Plymouth Colony, John Carver, died of sunstroke, the Pilgrims quickly elected Bradford to take his place. For some thirty years he held the post of governor or assistant, serving as a major stabilizing force in keeping the settlers committed to their religious goals. Under his judicious governance, the colony was able to overcome its precarious beginnings and to flourish. Bradford died on May 19, 1657, just at the point when more and more newcomers were arriving and beginning to challenge the Pilgrim domination of the colony. (See also **Pilgrims and Plymouth Colony**)

Anne Bradstreet

Anne Dudley Bradstreet (1612–September 16, 1672) was one of America's first settlers and also one of its first poets. She arrived in Massachusetts in 1630 aboard the *Arbella* with her husband, Simon Bradstreet, and her father, Thomas Dudley, both of whom would become governors of the **Massachusetts Bay Colony.** Anne Bradstreet played no significant role in governing the colony. It was her poetry that was to bring her recognition. She wrote privately, with no intention or expectation of being read by others. Her purpose was rather to express her feelings about nature, her family, and her religion. For Puritans, poetry had a religious purpose very similar to that of their sermons—to instruct and extol religiosity. Although Bradstreet's poems had religious themes, this was so simply because she was a Puritan, and her writing was therefore representative of her society. Her intent was not to proselytize but rather to express how her piety affected her and her relationships. One of her earliest poems speaks of her love for her husband, beginning with the famous line, "If ever two were one, then surely we." Another tells of her deep satisfaction as the mother of eight children:

I had eight birds hatcht in one nest;
Four Cocks there were, and Hens the rest,
I nursed them up with pain and care,
Nor cost nor labor did I spare,
Till at the last they felt their wings,
Mounted the trees, and learn'd to sing.

In 1650 her brother-in-law published her poems in England, without her knowledge, as *The Tenth Muse Lately Sprung Up in America.* Her poetry became quite popular. Six years after her death a second edition of her poems reached the public, enshrining her words as part of the Puritan legacy.

Louis D. Brandeis

Louis D. Brandeis rose to fame as a public interest attorney, a social reformer, an adviser to President Woodrow Wilson, and a justice of the U.S. Supreme Court. Born in Louisville, Kentucky, on November 13, 1856, he was the son of a successful Jewish businessman. After some schooling abroad, he entered Harvard Law School, earning his degree in 1877. Brandeis first practiced law in St. Louis, but returned to Boston in 1879, where he clerked for a state Supreme Court justice and then opened a law practice. As a lawyer he became quite successful and was asked to teach courses at Harvard Law. Brandeis was concerned that large organizations, such as the insurance companies, exploited the common people and then sought protection by hiring the best attorneys to defend them. He began to write articles condemning inequities in the law that favored the rich over the poor. In doing so, he became known as "the people's attorney." He worked on public issues, gave lectures, and began a long-term attack on monopolies, which he saw as denying individuals equality of opportunity.

One of his most famous cases was *Muller v. Oregon* in 1908, in which he defended Oregon's right to establish a maximum ten-hour workday for women workers. Using statistical data documenting that long hours were detrimental to the health of women workers, he persuaded the U.S. Supreme Court to take into consideration evidence of societal abuse in addition to the usual weight of legal precedent. He won the case, and his famous "Brandeis Brief" set its own precedent for years to come. Brandeis also supported child labor laws, old age pensions, and anti-monopoly legislation. It was his belief in the need to restore competition to the economy that led him to support presidential candidate Woodrow Wilson in 1912, becoming his intellectual adviser. Wilson's "New Freedom" doctrine called for a return to a free and equitable society liberated from the power of monopolies.

At the outbreak of World War I, Brandeis set his sights on advancing the cause of Jews throughout the world. He became a leader in the American Zionist movement, eventually founding the American Jewish Congress. In 1916 Wilson came under political attack for not being progressive enough. To counter this criticism he promulgated progressive legislation and nominated the Jewish social reformer Brandeis to the Supreme Court. Despite acrimonious hearings that were both anti-Semitic and anti-reform, Brandeis was elevated to the Supreme Court, where he served as a justice for twenty-three years.

Throughout his career on the bench, Brandeis upheld his pragmatic view of legality and insisted on the need for courts to promote the well-being of the many over the demands of the rich. He was a crucial ally of President Franklin D. Roosevelt's New Deal, helping turn the Court from its obstructionist position to look with favor on social reform legislation such as Social Security and the Wagner Labor Act. Because of poor health he resigned from the Court in 1939. Brandeis died in Washington, D.C., on October 5, 1941, leaving behind a rich legacy of judicial interpretation advancing protection of the individual from the predations of large corporations. Brandeis University in Waltham, founded in 1948, is named in his honor.

Bread and Roses Strike of 1912

The strike of textile workers in Lawrence was symptomatic of troubles arising from the growing chasm between acquisitive capitalists and the nascent labor movement in the early twentieth century. In 1912 Lawrence was an immigrant industrial city of textile mills and worker housing. Among its population of 86,000, 74,000 were either foreign-born or the native-born children of foreign-born parents. The largest population groups were the French Canadians, Italians, Irish, Russians (including many Jews), and Syrians. As textile laborers they received poverty wages that were inadequate to support a family. Their strike for "bread and roses" exposed the intolerable conditions under which so many worked.

When the state legislature, in an effort to protect families, mandated that women and children under eighteen could work no more than fifty-four hours a week, employers responded by cutting wages proportionately. On January 11, 1912, women weavers, who had been accustomed to working fifty-six hours per week, found less pay in their envelopes. Largely illiterate and powerless, they courageously went on strike demanding higher wages. The men, whose wages were also intolerably low, joined in the protest. Within a few days the strike had spread throughout the city, closing most of the mills. Workers organized strike committees along ethnic lines, while resisting the approaches of unions. Organized picketing and parading led to ugly confrontations, especially when the police brutally attacked prominent women picketers. The resulting publicity created widespread support for the strikers, but the employers refused to meet with them, and daily protests brought violence and increasing property damage. Hoping to keep the peace, Governor Eugene Foss called out the militia.

Throughout the winter months the workers and their children suffered, lacking money to buy food. By early March, Governor Foss had grown angry with the obdurate mill owners and their refusal to negotiate. He threatened to remove the militia. At the same time, orders for textile goods were piling up. Finally, the mill owners agreed to meet the demands of their employees. The workers received pay increases and promises that the strikers would not be punished. Ethnic solidarity among the working poor had won the day for the Lawrence strikers—but only for the moment. The owners would later retaliate by moving their plants to the South, where unions could be suppressed, thus killing off the once thriving Massachusetts textile industry.

Broad Street Riot

The constant violent attacks on the newcomer Irish became a lurid symbol of **anti-Catholicism** in nineteenth-century Boston. The Broad Street riot of June 11, 1837, involved over fifteen thousand people, almost one-fifth of the city's population. The circumstances of the riot reflected the ongoing animosity Boston's Yankee workers felt toward the Irish immigrants. A volunteer fire company made up of Yankee Protestants had just returned from a fire when one of their members became involved in a shoving match with some members of an Irish funeral procession of four or five hundred that was forming on the same street. Firemen rushed out of the firehouse to help their colleague but were no match for the large group of Irishmen. After the procession started on its way, the firemen began ringing the firehouse bells, calling for reinforcements, as one fireman ran to other firehouses exclaiming, "The Irish have risen upon us, and are going to kill us!" As the funeral moved along, it collided with a fire company looking for a fire. Then several other fire companies arrived on the scene and began to attack the mourners.

The fighting escalated when the Irish moved as a group toward their homes on Broad Street. Word of the violence spread throughout the heavily populated North End, and scores migrated to the contested area. After two hours the more numerous firemen won the day; the Irish had either fled or returned to their homes. At that point the looting and vandalism began. The mob emptied houses of their furnishings, set fire to their contents, and continued the assault on Irishmen. The violence ended with the appearance of Mayor Samuel Eliot, who arrived with the sheriff and eight hundred militiamen. The troops dispersed the crowds and then patrolled the neighborhood.

Since detailed hospital and police records are lacking, it is impossible to determine the extent of physical injuries or if anyone died as a result. Property damage was in the thousands of dollars—a great deal of money at the time. Many Irish families lost their homes. The authorities indicted several rioters, and a Yankee jury found four Irishmen guilty, but the firemen emerged unscathed. The rowdiness of the volunteer firemen had so frightened city leaders, however, that in September they disbanded the volunteer fire forces and established Boston's first full-time professional fire department. (See also **Know-Nothings** and **Ursuline Convent Riot**)

Brook Farm

In the mid-nineteenth century, nostalgia for a lost agrarian way of life and growing disgust over the crass commercialism of modern society led idealists to seek alternative communities that would promote brotherhood and a more aesthetic existence. One such experiment was Brook Farm, a utopian community established at the town of Roxbury, later West Roxbury, near Boston in 1841. The main organizer was George Ripley, a former minister and Transcendentalist, who wished to create a community based on equality, where all shared the work and combined their income to promote the general good. Each member would get the same day's pay, whether for manual labor or creative work. It was conceived as an attempt to demonstrate that collective living could be the means both to eliminate poverty and to promote culture.

The commune, on two hundred acres, attracted teachers, artisans, and writers. One of the fifteen original members was **Nathaniel Hawthorne,** and many other famous figures of the day—**Ralph Waldo Emerson,** Bronson Alcott, **Margaret Fuller, Elizabeth Peabody,** Theodore Parker—were lecturers or visitors there. Brook Farm also started an experimental school to promote intellectual liberty by eliminating the rote learning and harsh discipline then common in education. In 1844 the commune converted to Fourierism, a movement predicated on the principle of collective socialism and the rejection of private property. The colony never became financially secure, and its members eventually dispersed in 1849. As an attempt at creating a more just form of living, the experiment failed, but it did help establish Massachusetts at the time as a center of social reform thinking. (See also **Transcendentalism**)

Edward W. Brooke

Edward W. Brooke III was the only major African American figure in Massachusetts politics during the twentieth century. Born in Washington, D.C., on October 26, 1919, he was the son of an attorney in a middle-class family. He grew up in the segregated capital, where he went to all-black schools. He graduated from Howard University in 1941, and then served in Italy during the Second World War in a black regiment. Returning from the war, he enrolled at Boston University Law School, then began practicing law in the black community of Roxbury in Boston. Brooke entered politics by running as a Republican for state representative in 1950, but lost. He ran again in 1952, and lost again. With more blacks migrating to Boston, he tried for elective office once more in 1960, running for secretary of state, but lost again to a popular young Democrat, **Kevin H. White.**

Throughout Brooke demonstrated his loyalty to the Republican Party and was rewarded with the nomination for state attorney general in 1962. While most Republicans suffered defeat that year, Brooke won, becoming the first black in the nation to win statewide office in a popular election. He ran for reelection in 1964 and won. Then in 1966 he was elected to the U.S. Senate, beating a former governor, Democrat Endicott Peabody. He became the first, and so far only, black man to be elected to the Senate from Massachusetts. Brooke was reelected in 1972. In 1978, however, beset by rumors of scandal, he lost to the reformer Paul Tsongas, the Democratic congressman from Lowell. Reminding voters that he was the only black in the Senate and campaigning with the support of Coretta Scott King and Jesse Jackson were to no avail. Republicans were now a small minority in Massachusetts. Returning to private life, Brooke nevertheless remained a voice for moderation and social responsibility in the Republican Party.

Charles Bulfinch

Charles Bulfinch was Boston's foremost architect of the late eighteenth and early nineteenth centuries. He was born on August 8, 1763, the son of a Boston doctor. After graduating from Harvard in 1781, he took an extended tour of England and the Continent and came back imbued with the English and French style of architecture, which he transformed into his own, classically influenced Federal style. His first building was a church in 1788, designed in the English style. He built elegant Federal-style mansions and town houses for Boston's elite, including three homes for the wealthy and powerful politician **Harrison Gray Otis,** and countless churches and public buildings. His most famous creations were the new State House, opened in 1798, his enlargement of Faneuil Hall, and the unusual design for a block of connected town houses called Tontine Crescent. So numerous were his architectural contributions that he left a lasting personal imprint on the city of Boston.

In spite of his architectural eminence, Bulfinch was not a good businessman and was constantly in debt. At one point in 1811 he spent a month in debtor's jail. Throughout his years in Boston he was also a devoted public servant, elected as a selectman in 1791 and as chairman of the board of selectmen on and off for twenty-three years until 1799. That year, while maintaining his seat as a selectman, he received an appointment as superintendent of police, an office he held for several years. Always facing financial difficulties, he finally left Boston in 1817 when President James Monroe appointed him architect of the Capitol. With a good salary he stayed on in Washington for twelve years before returning to Boston, where he died on April 15, 1844. One architectural historian has credited him with leaving "a lasting mark upon the buildings and topography of Boston."

Bunker Hill and Monument

The shots fired at Charlestown made indelibly clear that the point of no return had arrived and American colonials were now in armed revolution against the British. It was at the Battle of Bunker Hill on June 17, 1775, that, though forced to retreat, the **Minute Men** learned that they could stand up against British regulars and fight. The battle, which actually occurred at nearby Breed's Hill, was fought by militia from Massachusetts, Connecticut, and New Hampshire under the command of Colonel William Prescott. Two months earlier the Minute Men had stood against the British at **Lexington and Concord,** and now once again they stood their ground until circumstances forced them to retreat. The British commander, General Thomas Gage, made the decision to attack the colonial contingent on Breed's Hill so as to free the Charlestown heights of rebel artillery that could imperil English control of Boston. The redcoats made three frontal assaults on the hill, finally succeeding on the last when the Minute Men ran out of ammunition. The British suffered more losses than the colonials, however, giving them an empty victory.

They learned a lesson as well. The following year, colonial troops sur-

Bunker Hill Monument. Courtesy of the National Park Service.

rounded the city and moved artillery brought from Fort Ticonderoga onto the Dorchester heights, overlooking Boston. Feeling vulnerable from the cannons on the hill above the city, the British contemplated a frontal assault on the heights. But remembering the losses of Breed's Hill, they did the only thing they could: they evacuated the city.

At the fifty-year celebration of the victory at Bunker Hill, Bostonians decided to commemorate the spot by building a memorial. Constructing the monument called for granite to be transported from the Quincy quarry, a difficult task. Planners solved the problem by constructing a horse-drawn railway in 1826, the first in the nation. They covered wooden rails with iron plates to move the granite four miles over land to the nearest water site where it could be shipped to Charlestown by barge. The Bunker Hill Monument, an obelisk 220 feet high and 15 feet square, with 295 spiral steps to the top, was completed in 1843. It is maintained today by the National Park Service.

Vannevar Bush

Vannevar Bush was an electrical engineer and inventor, an academic, business innovator, and venture capitalist in the field of electronics. He was also a government consultant who brought together university research laboratories and private venture capitalists, with funds supplied by the federal government.

Born March 11, 1890, in Everett, he was the son of a Universalist minister. After graduating from high school in Chelsea, he earned his way through Tufts University by tutoring other students in mathematics and physics. After working briefly for General Electric in Schenectady, he returned to Tufts to teach, and in 1916 wrote a Ph.D. dissertation in electrical engineering in a joint Harvard-MIT program. Subsequently he became a consultant to a fledging radio equipment company. Working with a design for a thermostat, he formed his own company with partners, and eventually in 1925 created **Raytheon,** a company producing power vacuum tubes for radio. In the same year Bush, along with H. B. Stewart and Frank Gage, two colleagues at MIT, built the Intergraph, the first of four analog computers.

By 1932, Bush was serving MIT as both dean of the School of Engineering and university vice president. As a professor, consultant, and business entrepreneur in the dynamic new field of electronics, he gained national prominence. In 1939, as chair of the National Defense Research Committee, he set about reorganizing the procedures for new weapons development for the federal government. His main contribution was the idea of funneling federal funds through grants to private research facilities, both in business and at the universities, to conduct the necessary research and development for weapons promotion. This approach became the standard for all American scientific technology research and inspired the creation of new laboratory and science programs throughout the nation. Bush died on June 28, 1974.

Busing Riots

The ferocity of the anti-busing riots that broke out from 1974 to 1976 was unique to Boston. Even the *Boston Globe* called the city "the Little Rock of the North." The controversy was the result of many converging forces. Since the 1950s, large numbers of blacks had migrated to Boston in the hope of finding jobs; instead they encountered discrimination in hiring and housing. At the same time, during a period of national recession, Boston's lower-class and working-class ethnic whites faced unemployment and poverty. Ethnic segregation and restricted economic opportunity created a "fortress" mentality, especially among the Boston Irish and Italians, who accused the blacks of competing for their jobs and trying to move into their all-white ethnic neighborhoods. For blacks, lacking sufficient numbers to make an impression on local politics dominated by the Irish and other ethnic groups, the first attempt to achieve equality was through school desegregation.

Boston's all-white school committee maintained a purposefully segregated system in order to please their constituents and advance their own political goals. The black community, led by the NAACP, fought this racial injustice by suing the school committee. A federal judge, W. Arthur Garrity, found for the plaintiffs and ordered the immediate remedy of busing students to schools throughout the city. The plan, however, called for transporting students between two of Boston's most polarized neighborhoods, black Roxbury and white South Boston, an area with a history of animosity toward blacks. The plan was seriously flawed, but the refusal of the school committee to cooperate, and the wholesale defiance of many public officials, left Judge Garrity with few options. Most school districts accepted the busing plan, but a virulent resistance sprang up in three white neighborhoods—South Boston, Hyde Park, and Charlestown—centered on their local high schools.

What followed, from September 1974 to the fall of 1976, was an outpouring of staggering violence, continuing almost daily in those three neighborhoods. In retaliation for white depredations in Roxbury, blacks rioted. A strong stand by Judge Garrity, as well as the forcing of the public schools into federal receivership, the stationing of state troopers, police, and finally federal marshals in the schools, and the failure of the anti-busing forces to achieve any legal victories, finally brought an end to the violence. But federal control over Boston schools did not cease until 1985. The results of the busing controversy were felt in heightened racial conflicts that went on for years, as white flight from the city to the suburbs increased. Over time, hostility faded and the Boston schools became more integrated, even though white students are now a minority in an increasingly diverse urban school system.

Benjamin F. Butler

Benjamin F. Butler was a colorful Civil War general and maverick politician who served both in the U.S. Congress and as governor of Massachusetts. Born in Deerfield on November 5, 1818, he was the son of a seaman who died while Benjamin was still an infant. The boy spent his early years in Lowell, where his mother kept a boarding house for mill workers. After attending Colby College, he studied law and returned to Lowell to practice in 1840. As an attorney he built a reputation for taking on unpopular cases, and he amassed a fortune by investing in real estate. He joined the Democratic Party, and after several unsuccessful attempts to achieve elective office, he won election as a state representative in 1853, going on to the state Senate in 1859.

After two unsuccessful runs for the governorship, with the outbreak of the Civil War, Butler rallied to the Union cause. Republican governor John A. Andrew appointed him a brigadier general in the state militia. Butler led troops in several important battles, relieving Washington, D.C.'s, isolation by sending troops to occupy Annapolis and capturing Baltimore—without permission from the army. His greatest military feat was the capture and occupation of New Orleans in 1862. Butler's harsh but efficient administration of the city earned him widespread admiration, though Southerners dubbed him "Beast Butler." His military career ended in 1864 when his forces suffered an embarrassing defeat in North Carolina.

Butler went on to serve in Congress from 1867 to 1874. As a Radical Republican and foe of President Andrew Johnson, he played a major role in the House impeachment proceedings. In 1871 and again in 1873 he lost bids for the Massachusetts governorship. Then, because of his association with various Washington scandals, he lost his House seat in 1874. Rejecting the Republican Party, he ran as an independent for governor in 1878 and 1879, but lost again. In 1880 he rejoined the Democratic Party, and in 1882 finally won the governorship. After a single one-year term, in 1884 he ran for the presidency on the People's Party ticket, but received few votes. Retired from politics, he died on January 11, 1893. Flamboyant and outspoken, a political opportunist and individualist, Benjamin F. Butler is remembered as a political gadfly and a constant irritant to the Massachusetts political establishment of his day.

The Fishermen's Monument Statue by Leonard Craske, Gloucester.
Photo © Arlene F. Taliadoros Photography.

C

Cape Ann

The Cape Ann peninsula juts out into the Atlantic in the outermost northeastern portion of the state. Its only city is Gloucester, a working-class port with an industrial waterfront focused on deep-sea fishing off the Grand Banks. Sebastian Junger's book *A Perfect Storm,* and the movie of the same name, immortalized the vicissitudes of life among Cape Ann fishermen and their families. Just north of Gloucester is the town of Rockport, famed as an artists' colony—the nation's oldest. Located on a picturesque harbor lined with small boats and yachts, its village streets full of art galleries and craft shops, Rockport is the perfect setting for the tourist trade. What distinguishes Cape Ann, and differentiates it from Cape Cod with its sandy beaches, is its rocky spine of granite ledges and boulders washed by thunderous waves, providing vantage points that offer breathtaking views, particularly at sunset.

Cape Cod and the Islands

Seventy miles from end to end, Cape Cod is the L-shaped peninsula that juts out into the Atlantic Ocean, separated from the Massachusetts mainland by the **Cape Cod Canal.** Two bridges connect this famous summer resort to the rest of the state, allowing its millions of visitors to bask at its beaches, ponds, and river estuaries. The Cape had its geological origins in glacial drift that occurred over fifteen thousand years ago during the Pleistocene Ice Age. Now waves and wind are slowly eroding this fragile land mass, and it is estimated that in five thousand years it will be gone.

In shape Cape Cod resembles an outstretched arm, bent at the elbow and with a clenched fist at the end. The Upper Cape forms the meaty part of the arm, beginning at Sandwich in the north and Woods Hole and Falmouth in the south. The arm extends eastward to the Mid-Cape, from Barnstable, Hyannis, and Harwich to the "elbow" in Chatham, the link to the Outer Cape, which runs from Orleans through Truro to the "fist" at Provincetown.

With its staggering population growth, the Cape and its fifteen towns are home to masses of summer tourists and a growing number of full-time residents, including many retirees. Route 6, the main road through the Cape, snakes down the center of the bent arm. One of the area's many attractions is the Cape Cod National Seashore, controlled by the federal government, which preserves miles of magnificent ocean beaches for the enjoyment of the public. Here the surf pounds and the water is cold. Those who prefer more tranquil swimming seek out the warmer waters of Cape Cod Bay, or the many kettle ponds left by retreating glaciers. The Cape offers a multitude of summer activities, but the traffic and crowds call for patience. Visitors hoping to avoid the teeming summer scene can travel by ferry to the two main islands off the Cape, Martha's Vineyard and Nantucket.

Martha's Vineyard, measuring over 100 square miles, lies just south of the Cape, a short ferry ride from **Woods Hole.** The English explorer Bartholomew Gosnold discovered Martha's Vineyard in the early seventeenth century while on an expedition in search of the sassafras plant, believed to be a cure for many diseases. The island's name at that time was Capawack. It was at first the home of **Algonquins,** who were displaced by English farmers and sheepherders. Soon the sea became the main source of livelihood for fishermen and whalers. But they did not prosper. By the 1830s Methodists began holding revivalist tent meetings on the island, setting up camp and eventually building the fantastic gingerbread cottages of Oak Bluffs.

By the end of the nineteenth century summer vacationers discovered the island, and tourism has been the main attraction ever since. Vineyard Haven, Edgartown, and Oak Bluffs, on the island's north and east, are the most populous communities. To the west lie West Tisbury, Chilmark, and Aquinnah, or Gay Head, areas mainly of private homes, some populated by the rich and famous. Most of the magnificent beaches are open only to residents, summer renters, or those willing to travel by bicycle. A curious sightseer might even stumble across the grave of entertainer John Belushi in Chilmark and its curious mementos left by fans. The most infamous portion of the island is the sparse area to the east of Edgartown, almost a separate island in itself, Chappaquiddick. This isolated rural area reached national prominence because of the automobile accident involving Massachusetts's junior senator, **Edward M. Kennedy,** in 1969. Between Martha's Vineyard and the southeast coast of Massachusetts runs the small and sparsely populated chain of the Elizabeth Islands.

Nantucket, lying thirty miles southeast of Hyannis, is another summer playground, but largely for the upscale visitor. The long ferry ride and the scarcity of public beaches make Nantucket a place of lavish summer homes and visiting yachts. The fifty-four-square-mile island rose to economic prominence in the late eighteenth century because of its whaling industry. The whalers would go out for years at a time to bring back the precious oil used to light lamps. The introduction of a cheaper fuel, kerosene, ended whaling by the 1860s, and the island eventually developed into a summer resort. Now many beautiful homes and secluded residential districts abound. The main focus of the island is the harbor town of Nantucket, with its cobblestone streets and quaintly elegant homes, as well as its expensive boutiques and restaurants. What makes this hard-to-reach island particularly attractive is the intense desire of its inhabitants to preserve as much as possible the original flavor of this antique whaling community.

Cape Cod Canal

For over two hundred years Massachusetts residents struggled to make the sea and land journey from Buzzards Bay, off the southeastern coast of the state, to Cape Cod Bay, lying between the Outer Cape and the mainland. By sea a ship had to circumnavigate the entire Cape to reach the eastern shore of the mainland. A valley with two rivers, the Manomet and the Scusset, flowing in opposite directions, separated the Cape from the rest of the state. The Pilgrims followed the example of the Natives by portaging across. As time went on, many recognized the need for a canal to connect the two bays. Finally, in 1884 a commercial venture was undertaken to dig one. Because of a long history of contract disputes, lawsuits, and political interference, the project did not reach completion until 1909, and it was not until 1914 that vessels were able to make the journey between the two bays.

As a strictly moneymaking proposition the Canal proved a bust. The narrow channel made navigation difficult and resulted in many accidents as ships rammed into drawbridges. Investors welcomed the takeover of the canal in 1928 by the federal government. Concerned not with profits but with easy access to the Cape, the government widened the canal and built two highway bridges that continue to provide automobile traffic access to Cape Cod. At 17.4 miles long and 480 feet elevation, the Cape Cod Canal is the world's broadest such canal. (See also **Cape Cod and the Islands**)

Charles River Bridge Case

In the early nineteenth century a landmark Massachusetts legal case arose that affected the development of transportation throughout the nation. This was a period of growing infrastructure demands, and older corporations, such as turnpikes and toll bridges, were facing competition from new entities being granted state charters. The opening of new toll bridges and turnpikes diminished the monopoly, and thus the income, of the older corporations. In some cases the state granted compensation to existing chartered companies when they granted new charters to competing ones, but not as rule, and only under special circumstances.

In 1829 the proprietors of the Charles River Bridge in Boston claimed that when the legislature granted a charter to a nearby competing bridge—the Warren Bridge—the state was in violation of its contract with them. They argued that since this new charter had resulted in "injurious competition," it amounted to a "confiscation of property" and was therefore unconstitutional. The state court, considering the case too important to decide, sent it on to the U.S. Supreme Court.

In *Charles River Bridge v. Warren Bridge* the federal court ruled against the Charles River Bridge Corporation, maintaining that progress would require grants of additional charters in the future. Loss was part of business and was not integrated into the contract idea. This decision made constant progress and innovation possible, stimulating further business investment in infrastructure while making it clear that state charters were subject to the perils of market demands. In looking to the future, the decision had a lasting national impact on the issue of property rights.

"City on a Hill" (See **John Winthrop**)

Clipper Ships

The clipper ships were new designs of sailing craft in the mid-nineteenth century meant to increase speed of vessels far beyond any then in use. With their sleek design and many more sails they were expensive to build and costly to maintain. They had a relatively small cargo space, yet required a large crew to control the many sails. Merchants paid higher freight rates on clippers to get their specialty goods shipped faster. Passengers, such as those eager to go to the gold fields of California, also paid higher rates for a speedier journey.

Massachusetts became famous for the building of these ships. The first Bay State clippers—the *Surprise* and the *Gamecock*—went to sea in 1850, designed and built by Bostonians. Other Massachusetts builders constructed clipper ships as well. But the master of clipper ship–building was Boston's Donald McKay. His first ship, the *Staghound,* in its maiden trip from New York to San Francisco in 1851 ran a new record of 1,256 miles in eighty-nine days. He followed with the *Flying Cloud,* which broke the record on a trip from Boston to the equator. McKay built twenty-one other majestic greyhounds of the sea, with names such as *Mastiff, Flying Fish, Westward Ho!,* and *Lightning.*

The clipper trade prospered for only a short time, however. The costs of maintaining and building the ships were high, and they could not compete with simply built, slower vessels that were cheaper to keep up and yielded higher profit margins. By 1855 the era of the graceful and speedy clipper was over, a casualty of pragmatic economic need.

Cod Fishing

The Massachusetts legislature recognized the importance of cod fishing for the prosperity of the state on March 17, 1784, when it was decided to hang a wooden codfish in the chambers of the House of Representatives.

Cod fishing began in earnest in Massachusetts and the Plymouth colonies after the mid-seventeenth century, when it became clear that prospects for agriculture were limited. Fish became their largest export well into the next century. Cod fishing flourished especially in North Shore and Cape Ann communities such as Marblehead and Gloucester. The fish from these northern waters and from the Grand Banks proved perfect for salting and drying. Three types of cod were used for export. The dun fish was considered the best type because its longer drying time made it most acceptable for the tastes of Portugal, Spain, and France. In trade for the dun fish, the fishermen returned with salt, wine, iron, grapes, and oranges, which they carried to English and colonial markets. The next highest grade of codfish became the winter staple of the colonial farmer, while the lowest grade went to the West Indies as food for slaves.

Cod fishing became the linchpin that in turn promoted shipbuilding and a variety of maritime products, all of which enhanced the lucrative **triangular trade.** Fishing and shipbuilding dominated the prosperous seaport towns of colonial Massachusetts, while the interior communities remained largely rural subsistence economies. When cod fishermen suffered bad times after the Revolution owing to British trade restrictions, Congress granted them a federal subsidy of five cents for every barrel of exported pickled fish. These subsidies were increased from time to time, and cod fishing once again enjoyed prosperity and rising export tonnage—until the disastrous 1807 Embargo and the War of 1812. After the war, cod fishing no longer played an important role in the Bay State's maritime trade, though cod export to the West Indies continued for many years.

Coercive Acts

The British Parliament passed a series of harshly punitive laws in 1774 known as the Coercive Acts, or Intolerable Acts, to punish Bostonians for the **Boston Tea Party.** This foolish attempt to force the aroused colonials to mend their ways only served to increase resistance to imperial authority. The most egregious parliamentary blunder was the order to close the port of Boston to all traffic, a death blow to a town whose prosperity depended on commerce. Two statutes attacked and virtually nullified all the self-governance that represented a long tradition in Massachusetts. The Administration of Justice Act required that officials charged with capital crimes must be tried in England. The Abrogation of the Royal Charter Massachusetts Government Act nullified in its entirety the 1692 charter establishing a **royal colony** in Massachusetts, calling instead for royal appointment of the Governor's Council, until then chosen by the popularly elected House of Representatives. In addition, the governor was now given authority to appoint and remove judges, while sheriffs, not towns, were to appoint jurors and **town meeting** was limited to a single yearly session. In addition, the Quartering Act stationed troops in Boston, to be put up if necessary in local homes, at the expense of the town. The harshness of these laws so enraged Massachusetts and the other colonies that a call for resistance and revolution was the result. Bostonians began to stockpile arms in the outlying towns of **Lexington and Concord,** setting the stage for the "shot heard round the world."

Committees of Correspondence

Looking for ways to communicate his ideas about British repression, Boston radical **Sam Adams** came up with the idea of creating colonial Committees of Correspondence. After the 1770 **Boston Massacre** and the **Boston Tea Party** of 1773, Adams contacted Virginia patriot Arthur Lee, asking if they could organize committees in the colonies to correspond with one another as a way to stay informed about local incidents of British transgressions. Within these fledgling Committees of Correspondence, colonists would be able to share their grievances and thus keep alive a spirit of resistance to parliamentary tyranny.

The issue that brought things to a head was the new imperial decree that judges would no longer be paid by the Massachusetts General Court but from the Civil List, thus thwarting colonial control over judges. When Governor **Thomas Hutchinson** denied Boston's **town meeting** the right to discuss the issue, also refusing to call an assembly of the General Court for the same purpose, Adams decided to invoke the Committee of Correspondence procedure. He got the Boston town meeting to establish such a committee to let the other colonies know of the Crown's rejection of the "Rights of Colonists." This "Boston Declaration of Rights" fanned the flames of revolutionary ardor by reiterating everywhere the long-held view of the colonists that they had the right to govern themselves. Committees of Correspondence became the norm in the colonies and served the purpose of maintaining close contact among the patriots in their resistance to British arbitrary rule.

Calvin Coolidge

Calvin Coolidge, or "silent Cal," was the thirtieth president of the United States, vice president, and governor and lieutenant governor of Massachusetts. Born in Vermont on July 4, 1872, the son of a farmer and merchant, he graduated from Amherst College in 1895, read for the law, and began practicing in Northampton in 1897. As a young man he quickly turned to local politics, holding several municipal jobs as a Republican until elected mayor of Northampton in 1909. In 1911 he won a seat in the Massachusetts Senate. Noted for efficiency and diligence, the taciturn Coolidge was a favorite of the Republican majority. He became lieutenant governor in 1915, and in 1918 won the governorship. Coolidge was a rugged individualist who was concerned mainly with saving the taxpayers money. He had no interest in the rising tide of political reform called Progressivism that was sweeping the nation in the first two decades of the twentieth century.

His would have remained an unremarkable career had it not been for the **Police Strike Riots of 1919.** Violence broke out in Boston when the police went on strike, and the incompetent Republican police commissioner, Edwin Curtis, was unable to restore order. The Democratic mayor, Andrew Peters, took over and called out the Boston area militia, and after three days of battles the riots ended. It was then that Governor Coolidge acted. Fearful of a Democratic Party upsurge, he upstaged the mayor and called out the entire state militia to take control over the already resolved situation. Even though the violence had ended, Coolidge's action, which restored the Republican police commissioner to power, gave the Republicans the credit for bringing law and order to a chaotic city. On the strength of this political sleight of hand, Coolidge earned the Republican nomination as vice president on the national ticket in 1920.

Coolidge, like other vice presidents before him, would likely have gone on to political obscurity if not for the intervention of fate. Incumbent Warren G. Harding died suddenly, making Coolidge president of the United States in August 1923. Coolidge then easily won election to his first full term in 1924 under the slogan "Keep cool with Coolidge." During his administration he ignored the growing evidence of severe problems in the nation's economy, preferring a presidency of little or no action. Though a skillful administrator, he believed that government should act only when forced to do so, and that the economy was best left alone. Coolidge championed the venerable Republican program of cutting taxes, reducing the national debt, and instituting high protective tariffs and favors for special interest groups—policies that brought on the Great Depression. He approved of Congress's restriction of immigration in 1924. Although he encouraged American exports and overseas investments, many of these investments were dubious and would come back to haunt the administration of his Republican successor, Herbert Hoover.

Choosing not to run again in 1928, Coolidge retired to Northampton, where he died on January 5, 1933, during the Great Depression and just before the Democratic presidential candidate Franklin D. Roosevelt came to power to save the country with his New Deal. Although Coolidge did little as president, it appears that he was reflecting the wishes of the great majority of Americans of that prosperous era, and can thus be considered a successful follower, if not a great leader.

John Singleton Copley

John Singleton Copley was a noted American-born artist of the eighteenth century who went on to achieve fame in England. Born in Boston on July 3, 1738, to a family of Irish immigrants, he began his career as an engraver before taking up history painting and portraiture. His gained success, becoming the most sought-after portrait painter of the colonial elite. In 1766 the English Society of Artists elected him a member, a rare distinction for an American colonial. Now a rich man, Copley settled into a mansion on Beacon Hill.

In 1774, in the turmoil of the American Revolution, Copley, the Tories' favorite painter, became discontented and sailed for England, never to return. Painting London's nobility brought him even greater fame, and he became a member of the exclusive Royal Academy of the Arts in 1779. In addition to portraits, he continued to explore history painting, often depicting battle scenes featuring victorious British generals and the naval engagements of famous English admirals. After a celebrated forty-year career in England, he died on September 9, 1815, in London, the first artist from the American colonies to achieve such stature.

Copley Square

Originally called Art Square, the site of Boston's first art museum, Copley Square, at the edge of the Back Bay, stands today as one of Boston's most admired open spaces. Built totally on landfill, the buildings of the square are supported by wooden pilings driven deep into the spongy ground and kept moist by a regulated source of water. In 1883 Art Square was renamed for the painter **John Singleton Copley.** Totally unplanned, the area began to take its present form with the construction of Henry Hobson Richardson's Romanesque Trinity Church, completed in 1877, followed in 1895 by the remarkable neoclassical Beaux Arts Boston Public Library designed by the firm of McKim, Mead, and White. These two astonishing architectural triumphs face each other across the square, giving this open space a majestic grandeur reminiscent of European cities. Adding to the monumental urban design, however controversially from the point of view of style, is Boston's tallest skyscraper, the 1975 John Hancock Tower, designed by I. M. Pei. With its sleek glass exterior reflecting the stone facade of Trinity Church, the modern tower marks the skyline as it stands sentinel over Copley Square.

Covenant and Half-Way Covenant

The **Puritans** expressed their connection to God and their vision of redemption or salvation through the concept of covenant, based on their interpretation of the Book of Genesis, in which Abraham, by his act of obedience, contracts with God for eternal salvation, but with the obligation of maintaining his virtue. Only those few chosen by God for salvation, the elect, were to be admitted to the covenant. Puritan religious belief based all relationships on a series of contracts. Thus Puritans had obligations to one another and to society in general. They worked out rules of behavior to maintain a godly and orderly society, and these became the basis of government, resulting in a consolidation of church and state. Only the elect could vote or assume positions of governance. Individuals had to provide proof of a virtuous life and give testimony of the experience of salvation in order to be received as church members. For newcomers to enter the select circle, Puritans set up religious tests based on biblical interpretation and on the piety of one's actions. Women could be among the elect, but they were not allowed to participate in governance or to vote.

Trinity Church and Copley Square, Boston. Photo © Peter Vanderwarker, used by permission of Trinity Church in the City of Boston.

Believing they were God's chosen people, Puritans thought of themselves as "saints" with responsibilities to their families and the community. These religious principles were the impetus for their emigration to New England and their desire to establish a pure religious society that would be a model for the rest of the world. To preserve the family unit, Puritans promoted collective responsibilities that gave governing bodies the right to ensure morality and stability in the community and to intervene with "problem" families. From these communal concerns arose political bodies that created laws to promote and maintain the general welfare.

A restrictive code of church membership and political participation became problematic for Puritans as the years passed and the **Massachusetts Bay Colony** attracted more immigrants. Many of these newcomers did not fit the Puritan definition of "saint," yet they wished to participate in community life. By the middle of the seventeenth century, it had become difficult for the Puritans to justify both the monopolization of the means to salvation and their tight control over governance. To cope with increasing demands for inclusion, a group of ministers met in 1662 and relaxed the rules of the covenant, giving political rights to children of church members even though they did not experience a personal conversion. This Half-Way Covenant also allowed newcomers to vote, but their church participation would be limited until they proved themselves.

Continued immigration further strained the religious monopoly of the Puritans. The rise of an elite class of merchants fostered the notion that wealth was a temporal sign of salvation, which led to a widespread secularization of society and a heightening of religious tensions. The revocation of the charter of the colony and the installation of a **royal colony** in 1692 ended the covenant as a system of community control and political governance.

Cranberry Bogs

Cranberries are one of the state's best-known crops, grown in bogs in southeastern Massachusetts and **Cape Cod and the Islands.** Cranberry plants feature a distinctive pink flower on a long stem. At harvest time, the berries are beaten off the vines by a water wheel, creating crimson ponds of floating berries. They are then vacuumed up and processed into the juices, jellies, and sauces that grace the nation's dining tables, especially at Thanksgiving. There is an entire museum devoted to the fruit, Ocean Spray's Cranberry World in Carver, which displays how the crop is grown, harvested, and made into a salable consumer product. Visitors can also ride the Edaville USA train through a cranberry plantation theme park in Carver.

James Michael Curley

The dominant force in Boston politics from the 1920s to the 1940s was the irrepressible James Michael Curley (November 20, 1874–November 12, 1958), "mayor of troubled times." The son of impoverished Irish immigrants, without a formal education he worked his way out of the slums of Roxbury to become one of the most memorable Massachusetts politicians of the twentieth century. In 1902, while he was serving on the Common Council, one of Curley's constituents asked him to take the civil service test for the post office for him. Curley agreed but was recognized and indicted for fraud. Under indictment in 1903, he ran for office as an alderman and won. In 1904, after several appeals, he ended up in jail. While there he ran again for alderman on the slogan "He did it for a friend" and won easily. The voters of Ward 17 in Roxbury loved Curley's antics, especially when he manipulated the Yankee establishment in their favor. To them, Curley personified service and humanitarian concern, and they rewarded him for these qualities.

Curley served as alderman from 1904 to 1909 (including the sixty days he spent in jail), and won election to the city council in the latter year. In 1910 he went on to the U.S. Congress. As a local politician with a political club, Curley was in a position to provide services to his poor working-class constituents. He wrote orders for butchers, grocers, and fuel suppliers, he called doctors, wrote to creditors, went to police stations and courthouses to plea for those in trouble. In the afternoons he would meet groups of the unemployed and walk them around his district seeking work. While in office he used the patronage system to give his followers jobs. This vision of the humanitarian purpose of government ran counter to that of the Yankee business community of Boston and earned him their undying hatred.

When Curley announced that he would run for the mayoralty in 1913, a group of rival Irish ward bosses and the Yankee establishment coalesced to oppose him. Despite their efforts, he won by a large margin. His first administration was to set the standard for those that followed. People lined the corridors of City Hall every day to ask him for favors. As mayor he focused on public works projects—hospitals, neighborhood health clinics, playgrounds, parks, subways, tunnels, highways. He'd overspend and then go to the state legislature to borrow more. In 1917, because of his opposition to World War I based on Irish nationalist hatred of the British, Curley lost favor with many non-Irish voters and lost his bid for reelection. He won again in 1921, but this time the Republican state legislature took aim at him, amending the Boston city charter so that incumbent mayors could not succeed themselves.

Seeking other opportunities, he ran for governor in 1924, but lost to Yankee Republican Alvan T. Fuller. Five years later, following the stock market crash of 1929, the voters of Boston elected him mayor once again on the promise that he would help ease unemployment through public works projects. Unable by law to succeed himself, he ran for and won the governorship in 1934. Taking advantage of New Deal deficit spending allotted for digging the gigantic **Quabbin Reservoir,** he hired three thousand Boston Irish unemployed as tree cutters. He ran for the U.S. Senate in 1936 only to lose to a Yankee Republican, **Henry Cabot Lodge Jr.,** then lost the mayoral race in 1937 to another Irish Catholic, Maurice Tobin. The Republican legislature so feared Curley that in 1941 they amended the Boston city charter again so that an incumbent mayor *could* run, and the popular Tobin defeated Curley that year.

The indefatigable Curley ran for and won two terms in the U.S. Congress in 1942 and 1944. By 1945, the Boston economy was in trouble again as a result of postwar recession and massive defense layoffs. At the age of seventy, and under federal indictment for mail fraud, Curley won the mayor's office for a fourth time. Two weeks after the election, however, he went on trial, was found guilty, and was sent to prison. He served five months before being pardoned by President Harry S. Truman, then returned to Boston in triumph to take up the mantle of mayor.

By now, times were changing. Rising postwar prosperity, shifts in residential voting patterns, and the development of high-tech, financial, and service industries had created a new electorate that rejected Curley's old patronage politics. He lost his bid for reelection in 1949, then again at age seventy-six in 1951, and at age eighty in 1955. Long scorned by his enemies as corrupt, he died in 1958 at eighty-four, leaving an estate valued at $3,768—proof that personal enrichment was never his goal. Curley was a city builder, a man who used patronage as the one vehicle available for the ethnic working classes to get a fair shake in a society still controlled by nativist Yankees. He well deserved the sobriquet "Mayor of the Poor."

Richard Cardinal Cushing

Richard Cushing (August 23, 1895–November 2, 1970) was the Roman Catholic archbishop of Boston from 1944 to 1970. Born in South Boston the son of a workingman, he went to Boston College and St. John's Seminary, and was ordained a priest in 1921. He first worked for the Society for the Propagation of the Faith as a fund-raiser, an interest he maintained throughout his career. Known to be very personable and down-to-earth, Cushing projected a populist image. A series of promotions brought him the rank of archbishop of Boston in 1944, which he held until his death. In 1958 he was elevated to cardinal.

In postwar Massachusetts rapid population growth made Catholics the majority in the state. Cushing spent these years supervising the expansion of church activities and buildings to accommodate these new members. He also worked to promote good relations between Catholics and those of other faiths and took an active part in politics when it affected the church. For example, in 1948 he organized a successful campaign to defeat a referendum that would have legalized birth control devices. By 1966, however, parishioners had made clear their desire for legal contraception, and a new law passed without his opposition.

Like most Catholic leaders of the time, he was a cold warrior who supported Joseph McCarthy and other right-wingers during the Red Scare. He was also a confidant and friend of the Kennedy family. Cushing proved a poor financial manager, however, and retired in 1970 leaving church finances in turmoil. Despite these shortcomings, his outgoing manner and his willingness to spend money made him a folk hero among local Catholics.

The Dwight House in Old Deerfield. Photo by Amanda Merullo. Courtesy of Historic Deerfield.

D

Deerfield Village

Operated by the Historic Deerfield Corporation, Old Deerfield Village is a preserved eighteenth- and nineteenth-century rural village in the town of Deerfield in western Massachusetts, just off I-91. A total of fifty-three buildings on ninety acres recreate in detail a typical pristine New England village and illustrate how people led their lives over two hundred years ago. Fourteen preserved buildings on the main street are open to the public, where interpreters demonstrate a valuable collection of original furnishings, including clocks, textiles, silver, needlework, and ceramics. Also on the grounds is Deerfield Academy, a prestigious private boarding school.

The preservation of the village came about through the patronage of Henry and Helen Flynt, who became acquainted with the area when their son entered Deerfield Academy in 1936. Entranced, the Flynts bought a home on Main Street and restored it and its contents. Then they bought the Deerfield Inn, restoring it and opening it to travelers once again. Their generosity led to the incorporation of the village as Historic Deerfield in 1952, to preserve the old houses and open them to the public in order to keep alive a part of New England's colonial past.

Emily Dickinson

The "Belle of Amherst," Emily Dickinson, though little known in her own time, was one of America's great poets of the nineteenth century. Born in Amherst on December 10, 1830, she was the daughter of a local lawyer. A recluse, she spent most of her life in the Dickinson family home, doting on her family and a few intimate friends. She wrote her poems in solitude either in her upstairs bedroom or in the kitchen pantry. These short, precise poems were products of her imagination and inner self, as she had little experience in the outside world. Her genius lay in her ability to take common things—family relationships, the natural world, religious faith, dreams—and imbue them with an aesthetic spirit that still deeply touches many readers.

She published her poems anonymously in a variety of newspapers and journals from 1852 to 1878 and died in relative obscurity in the Dickinson Homestead on May 15, 1886. It was not until after her death that friends first began publishing her poems in book form, in 1890 and 1896. Other volumes appeared in 1914 and then in 1945, belatedly gaining the poet worldwide recognition that has grown over the years, restoring her to her rightful place in American literary history.

Dorothea Dix

Dorothea L. Dix was one of the nineteenth century's leading social reformers, distinguished for her work with the mentally ill. Born in Hampden, Maine, on April 4, 1802, she was the daughter of an itinerant minister whose family lived in genteel poverty. She became a schoolteacher in 1816, eventually opening a school for girls in Boston in 1821. One of her students was the daughter of her minister, William Ellery Channing, the noted Boston clergyman and reformer. Channing took her under his wing and introduced her to the progressive leaders of Boston society. While traveling in Europe she developed an interest in penal reform, and upon her return she began to visit jails in Massachusetts.

The treatment afforded the mentally ill, who were housed in prisons even though they had not committed any crime, shocked and dismayed her. With the support of several Boston reformers, such as **Horace Mann, Samuel Gridley Howe,** and **Charles Sumner,** she embarked on a career of helping the mentally ill. She spent years visiting prisons and poorhouses, and began publishing and lecturing on the results of her research in order to awaken complacent Americans to the barbaric conditions faced by these unfortunates. She succeeded in getting the Massachusetts state legislature to build a special facility in Worcester for the mentally ill. Sixteen other states followed suit.

During the Civil War the government appointed her superintendent of U.S. Army nurses. After the war ended, she continued to promote the cause of the mentally ill until her retirement at age seventy-nine. She died on July 17, 1887, in Trenton, New Jersey. As a one-woman army she fought to enlighten the nation, and initiated the movement for mental health reform that continues to this day.

Frederick Douglass

Frederick Douglass. Library of Congress, Prints and Photographs Division.

Born a slave, Frederick Douglass became a world-famous abolitionist and author. He spent his life devoted to awakening white northern society to the evil of slavery. Born in Maryland in February 1818, he was the son of a slave mother and an unknown white man. He secretly taught himself to read and write, and then began teaching his fellow slaves. For these illegal acts and his open resistance to slavery, his owners repeatedly punished him, and he was sold to a series of harsh masters. In 1838 he escaped from slavery by disguising himself as a sailor in Baltimore and signing on as a hand on a ship bound for New York City. Newly married, he settled in New Bedford, where he worked as a ship fitter.

There Douglass became active in the antislavery movement and began attending meetings of **abolitionists,** where he would dramatically reveal himself to be a runaway slave. Because of his talents as an orator, he attracted the attention of the famed Massachusetts abolitionist **William**

Lloyd Garrison. Recognizing the propaganda potential of a well-educated escaped slave, Garrison hired him in 1841 as a speaker for the American Anti-Slavery Society. Douglass moved to Lynn and began to travel extensively on the abolitionist lecture circuit. His 1845 autobiography, *Narrative of the Life of Frederick Douglass, Written by Himself,* became a national and international best-seller.

Fearful of slave catchers once he revealed his identity, Douglass fled to England, where he continued to speak to sympathetic audiences. His supporters collected enough money to buy his freedom, thus enabling him to return home. He set up his own abolitionist newspaper in Rochester, New York, in 1847. By this time he had grown apart from Garrison and his followers, rejecting their pacifist and moralist views. Instead he espoused the use of political activism and even violence to end slavery. Douglass denounced the Fugitive Slave Law of 1850 and preached disobedience to its enforcement. He took an active part in the Underground Railway, assisting many slaves to escape to Canada. He also helped plan and finance John Brown's abortive raid on Harpers Ferry in 1859. Because of his role in this episode, Douglass himself had to flee to Canada to elude arrest.

The Civil War brought him back to the United States, where he appealed to President Lincoln to emancipate the slaves and helped recruit blacks into the Union Army. After emancipation, he concentrated on gaining blacks equal rights with whites. He remained a loyal Republican and continued his fight for civil rights for the rest of his life. He died on February 20, 1895, after returning to his home in Washington, D.C., from a lecture tour. The most famous black man of his century, Douglass established the shift from freedom to equality that would typify the struggles of African Americans in the twentieth century. (See also **Fugitive Slaves)**

W. E. B. Du Bois

William Edward Burghardt Du Bois was one of the leading African American activists and scholars of the twentieth century, who devoted his life to promoting equality and civil rights for blacks in America. Born in Great Barrington on February 23, 1868, the son of a servant and an itinerant laborer, he went to local schools and excelled, coming to the attention of the local white community, who supported his further education. He attended all-black Fisk University in 1885, which prepared him for his acceptance to Harvard College in 1888. He received his diploma two years later and went on to graduate school, earning an M.A. in 1891 and a Ph.D. in history in 1895, the first African American ever to do so at Harvard. His dissertation on the slave trade was published as a book in 1896. Du Bois immersed himself in the new field of sociology, writing a statistical study, *The Philadelphia Negro,* in 1899. He would write many books during his lifetime, while also lecturing on the race problem and teaching at Atlanta University and other institutions.

His position as spokesperson for legal equality for blacks put him at odds with other African Americans, such as Booker T. Washington, who preached accommodation and acceptance of second-class status. He joined with black leaders such as **William Monroe Trotter** and sympathetic whites such as Oswald Garrison Villard to found the National Association for the Advancement of Colored People (NAACP), an organization established to fight for the legal rights of black citizens. He became editor of the NAACP newspaper, *The Crisis,* which he used as a platform to attack racists and advance NAACP policies. Du Bois published widely, attended conferences worldwide, and generally devoted his energies to the cause of civil rights. From a new chair in sociology at Atlanta University he wrote several books, including the significant study *Black Reconstruction in the United States* (1935) and his memoir, *Dusk of Dawn: The Autobiography of a Race Concept* (1940).

During the Great Depression of the 1930s, after visiting the Soviet Union and Africa, Du Bois rejected the legalistic approach of the NAACP as inadequate to remedy the depths of racism in the United States. As a communist sympathizer, he was forced out of the NAACP in 1948. In 1958 he traveled to the USSR and China, and in 1961 he accepted a job in Ghana overseeing publication of an African encyclopedia. He joined the Communist Party that year, left the United States permanently, and two years later became a Ghanaian citizen.

During his productive life he wrote seventeen books, edited four journals, and pursued successful careers in both academia and journalism. Throughout, he aided black Americans in their efforts to gain full citizenship in a racist society. Du Bois died on August 27, 1963, in Ghana, never living to see the flowering of the civil rights movement that he had done so much to achieve.

Michael Dukakis

A three-term governor of Massachusetts and candidate for the presidency in 1988, Michael Dukakis was born November 3, 1933, in Brookline. The son of Greek immigrants, Dukakis went to public schools and graduated from Brookline High in 1951. That same year he ran in the **Boston Marathon,** finishing with a respectable time. He went on to Swarthmore College, where he majored in political science. When he graduated with top grades in 1955, he confided to others his ambition to become governor of Massachusetts. He served in the U.S. Army in Korea, and then entered Harvard Law School, graduating in 1960. While at law school he made his first bid for public office in 1958, running for a seat on the Brookline Redevelopment Authority. He lost by a wide margin, but in 1959 he won election to Brookline **town meeting** and became active in the state Democratic Party. He then made a successful bid in 1962 for election as a state representative and won reelection in 1964, 1966, and 1968.

Dukakis gained prominence in Democratic circles as a reformer concerned with improving the process of governance. His major achievement in the Massachusetts House of Representatives was the design and passage of the nation's first no-fault auto insurance law. In 1970 he achieved the Democratic nomination for lieutenant governor, but lost to Theodore Dwight. Biding his time, he joined a law firm but remained in the spotlight by hosting a local current events show on television.

His reputation for personal integrity and his position as a fiscal conservative stood him in good stead when he ran for the governorship in 1974 in an atmosphere tainted by the Nixon administration's Watergate scandal. He was willing to attack not only his Republican opponent, Governor Francis Sargent, but corrupt Democratic politicians as well. In doing so he created a rift in the Democratic Party, but he attracted the support of liberal reformers and large numbers of independents in the suburbs. Dukakis won the election handily, but he now faced serious economic problems caused by runaway inflation, high unemployment, and falling revenues. Initially he swore to avoid tax increases by cutting public spending for services such as public higher education and social programs. But with no end in sight to budget deficits, he went back on his pledge and instituted a series of tax increases, thus undermining his political support. These actions led to his downfall in 1978, when, as incumbent governor, he could not win renomination from his own party. Instead, Democrats nominated conservative Edward King, who went on to win the election.

Thanks to King's poor performance, Dukakis rallied suburban voters behind him in his bid for renomination in 1982. He won the election for governor easily, and again in 1986. By this time the nation's economy had rebounded, and under Dukakis the state's economic revival became known as "the Massachusetts miracle." Spiraling prosperity won him enormous popularity and nationwide renown. He seized upon his new national image to gain the Democratic nomination for the presidency in 1988. But his personal standoffishness and reputation as a chilly technocrat proved unattractive to voters. He ran a largely confused and lackluster national campaign, succumbing to the aggressive tactics of the incumbent vice president, George H. W. Bush. Nonetheless, Dukakis ran well in urban areas, taking 46 percent of the popular vote nationwide and 112 electoral votes—a result that is, perhaps unfairly, recalled as a debacle for the Democrats. Two months after his defeat, he announced that he would not be a candidate for reelection as governor in 1990, thus ending the Dukakis era in Massachusetts politics.

Christian Science Center, Boston.

Mary Baker Eddy

Mary Baker Eddy was the founder of the Christian Science faith. Born in New Hampshire on July 16, 1821, to a family of strict Calvinists, she had an irregular education. As a young woman she married twice, with one husband dying and the other marriage ending in divorce. She had little financial means and was always dependent on others for support. Sickly as a child, she remained in poor health throughout her life, constantly seeking remedies that went beyond traditional medical practices, including religious healers of one kind or another. After a bad accident affected her spine, she began reading accounts of Christ's healing practices—and she recovered. This experience inspired in her the notion of using faith to cure the sick.

Becoming a faith healer, she spent years in poverty. In 1875, while she was living in Lynn, a small group of followers paid for the publication of a book based on her beliefs, *Science and Health.* In 1877 she married her third husband, Asa Eddy, a sewing machine salesman. He died a few years later in 1882. In the meantime, her book was attracting disciples. With their support, in 1879 she founded the Church of Christ, Scientist. Through the 1880s and early 1890s she refined her healing philosophy. She envisioned God and the spirit as real and material things as an illusion. Thus healing would come, she believed, through communion with God, not from medicine. She wrote several more religious tracts espousing these views, which gained her many more followers, largely disaffected Methodists and Congregationalists.

In the 1880s Eddy founded a Christian Science church in Boston which became the seat of all Scientist authority. In 1889 she went into semi-retirement in Concord, New Hampshire. By this time her words in *Science and Health* had become church scripture, thus eliminating the need for pastors. The church kept expanding, and offered up many new publications, including, in 1908, the *Christian Science Monitor* newspaper. That same year Eddy moved to Chestnut Hill, outside Boston, where she died on December 3, 1910. Throughout this period many critics, including Mark Twain, ridiculed her church and its ideas. Nonetheless, Eddy built up a large and enduring following, a unique accomplishment for a woman in nineteenth-century American society.

Jonathan Edwards

Jonathan Edwards, a Congregational minister from Northampton, was one of the leaders of a religious revival in the colonies in the 1740s known as the **Great Awakening.** He preached the need to revive and return to the theology of the **Puritans,** which a more secularized society had diluted over the years. Born in Connecticut on October 5, 1703, the son of a minister, he entered Yale at age twelve as a divinity student, graduating in 1720 and receiving an M.A. in 1723. While serving as a tutor at Yale, he suffered several bouts of illness which led to spiritual crises. He left New Haven in 1726 to become co-pastor of his grandfather's church in Northampton.

After his grandfather's death, Edwards began what for him was a lifelong struggle to urge sinners out of their apathy and back to the true spirit of the church. As a revivalist he preached and wrote about the dire impact of a life of sin and the need for all to experience a spiritual conversion. Edwards revitalized the Puritan notions of human evil and depravity and the requirement that people lead pure Christian lives. In 1740 he invited other revivalist preachers, including the English minister George Whitfield, to Northampton, which became the center of the Great Awakening, a new spiritual movement based on public conversions that spread throughout the colonies and Britain.

Edwards preached and published sermons calculated to provide a strict theoretical model for all to follow. His refusal to sanction the more liberal **Half-Way Covenant** and baptize his parishioners' children without the child's spiritual conversion led to his dismissal in 1752 from his ministry. Desperate for a living, he became a missionary to the Indians in Stockbridge. In 1758, because of his voluminous theological writings, he was made president of the College of New Jersey (now Princeton). After only one month in office, he died from a smallpox inoculation on March 22, 1758. Although the Great Awakening he inspired was an influential movement in colonial America, his vision of a strict and harsh Calvinism could not withstand the growing materialism, secularism, and toleration that came with the American Revolution.

Ralph Waldo Emerson

Ralph Waldo Emerson was one of the leading writers, thinkers, and poets of the nineteenth-century American Renaissance. He was also the central figure of the intellectual movement known as **Transcendentalism.** Born in Boston on May 25, 1803, to a liberal Congregational minister and his wife, he graduated from Boston Latin in 1817 and entered Harvard College, graduating in 1821. Emerson taught school, studied theology, and became a Unitarian minister, although he suffered from ill health all his life. He was pastor at several Boston churches, but resigned from the ministry in 1832 and spent the next year traveling in Europe. In 1834, living off some stocks willed to him, he moved to Concord. There he began a career as a lecturer on general subjects and succeeded in attracting large audiences, thus earning a good living.

In 1836 he became involved in the Transcendentalist movement, joining a group of discontented Unitarian ministers and Harvard graduates who rejected organized religion, objected to the materialism of the age, and believed in nature as a liberating force that would bring a personal spiritual awakening. That same year Emerson published his first book, *Nature,* which would become the foremost Transcendentalist tract, preaching that nature was the spiritual teacher of mankind. His motto could be summed up: Know nature, know thyself, and know God.

Emerson was the movement's guiding force. He organized the Transcendentalist Club and then its journal, *The Dial,* in 1840, which he edited from 1842 to 1844. His friends included the literary elite and social reformers of the day: Bronson Alcott, **Margaret Fuller, Henry David Thoreau, Elizabeth Peabody,** Theodore Parker, William Ellery Channing. The publication in 1841 of Emerson's first two volumes of essays, including "History," "Self-Reliance," and "Love," among others, established him as a major literary figure. Another volume of essays followed in 1844, comprising "Nature," "Experience," and "The Poet." Emerson published a book of his poems in 1847, adding to his reputation as "the Sage of Concord." He spent the next twenty years successfully lecturing and writing.

In the 1850s he became involved in the struggle against slavery, excoriating the slaveholders in orations that attracted large crowds. After the Civil War, he continued a busy literary life as lecturer and writer of many books, essays, and poems. His health declined, and he died in Concord on April 27, 1882. He lies in Sleepy Hollow Cemetery in Concord, next to **Nathaniel Hawthorne,** Thoreau, and the Alcotts on Author's Ridge. Emerson's views on the bounty of nature became part of American culture, and he influenced generations of writers by giving voice to his quest for individual fulfillment through a personal spiritual experience encompassing the transforming power of nature.

Essex Junto

This was the name given to the political opponents of **John Hancock** and **John Adams,** some of whom came from Essex County north of Boston and were supporters of Federalist Alexander Hamilton. This group, also known as the Boston Junto, represented a small contingent of very conservative Federalist merchants and lawyers who became a sort of privy council to Hamilton from 1789 to 1799. Their major concern was the promotion of New England maritime fortunes, good relations with Great Britain, and rule by an aristocratic elite. Notable among them were George Cabot, Fisher Ames, Jonathan Jackson, John Lowell Jr., and Timothy Pickering. They were from Massachusetts's leading families, and many were interrelated by marriage. A keystone of their policy was close affiliation with British capital, and they feared the French Revolution and Jefferson's democratic ideals. This position brought them into great jeopardy when their opposition to the War of 1812, which caused them to suffer financially from the severely restricted maritime trade, cast them as traitors.

Explorers

The first recorded voyage from Europe to Massachusetts was in 1524 by Giovanni Verrazano, who explored the northeast coast and met with Natives on several occasions. Verrazano, who sailed for Francis I of France, published the first report on what would become known as New England. During the sixteenth century, European deep-sea fishermen came to the New England coast to dry their catches on the shorelines, making frequent contact with the Natives, which resulted in casual trade. Trade became more systematic after the 1580s, when the European demand for furs, particularly the beaver pelts used for men's hats, stimulated French and Dutch rivalries. The French and Dutch were followed by English traders and shipmasters, some of whom treated the Natives badly, going so far as to kidnap and enslave those they encountered.

In 1602 and 1603 adventurers such as Bartholomew Gosnold and Martin Pring sailed down the Gulf of Maine and around Cape Cod seeking fishing grounds and sassafras (believed in Europe to be a cure for syphilis). In 1605–6 Samuel de Champlain made two voyages of exploration, charting the waters around Plymouth, which he called Port St. Louis. Captain John Smith sailed north from Virginia in 1614 to trade for furs and fish. Exploring the coast and Massachusetts Bay, he remarked on the "well populated" villages with many large gardens and corn fields, renaming a Wampanoag village "Plimouth" and the region "New England." He produced a map in 1616 that became a very popular reference in Europe and was probably used by the Pilgrims in their voyage to the New World.

Evacuation Day

Evacuation Day is a Massachusetts holiday that commemorates the British evacuation of Boston on March 17, 1776—a date that also marks Saint Patrick's Day. By early March 1776, patriot troops under George Washington had fortified the Dorchester Heights overlooking Boston with artillery brought from Fort Ticonderoga in New York. The British general Sir William Howe recognized the futility of maintaining the occupation of Boston, and his army vacated the town on March 17. Years later, when the Irish controlled the city of Boston, they made an effort to celebrate the feast day of Saint Patrick on March 17. Still facing powerful Yankee opposition in the legislature, city authorities artfully designated an official holiday in 1901 on the occasion of the British evacuation of 1776, which from that time forward would always fall on March 17, Saint Patrick's Day. This little deception persists every year.

Faneuil Hall, Boston.

F

Famine Irish (See **Immigration**)

Faneuil Hall and Quincy Market

Among the symbols of the "new Boston" and the rejuvenation of its downtown are colonial Faneuil Hall and the adjacent nineteenth-century Quincy Market. Faneuil Hall's origins, however, tell a tale of class conflict amid sharp economic disagreements. In the early eighteenth century, Bostonians preferred to purchase goods from the many traveling vendors who came through the town by boat or cart. Several attempts by rich merchants to establish regulated markets similar to those in New York and Philadelphia failed to pass at **town meeting.** In 1733, in a close town meeting vote, the merchants won approval for three public markets. But the populace in general did not use them, and in 1737 they were destroyed by resentful rioters who took the wood for fuel. The merchants continued to press for a controlled public market but could make little headway.

In 1740 merchant Peter Faneuil offered to build a public market at his own expense and donate it to the town. Town meeting accepted the gift in a vote of 367 to 360. Because of the close vote, members made sure to specify that the market would be strictly voluntary, thus allaying any public fears of merchants' monopolizing food supplies. The building opened in 1742, but for many years Bostonians ignored the now famous Faneuil Market.

The town closed and opened it intermittently between 1747 and 1753. After it burned down in 1761, the town rebuilt it with private subscriptions. It was not until after **Charles Bulfinch**'s architectural adaptation in 1805 that Faneuil Hall began to earn its reputation as a popular local attraction.

Boston's "great mayor" **Josiah Quincy** sponsored the creation of a new market directly behind Faneuil Hall in 1825. In addition to becoming Boston's main market district, Faneuil Hall and Quincy Market became the place where people gathered to hear some of the country's most famous orators. Over the years, the area has maintained its function as both a market and a meeting place, recently adding a museum as well. Throughout the years speakers for all sorts of causes used the meeting hall to present a wide range of views from antislavery, temperance, pro-union, and charitable causes to political debates and even history lectures. With urban renewal changing the face of Boston in the mid-1970s, the Rouse Corporation transformed the site. The result was an updated Faneuil Hall–Quincy Market area, with the market facilities expanded and restaurants and retail stores added. It now attracts a wide variety of suburbanites and tourists to the commercial hub of a revitalized Boston.

Fenway Park (See **Boston Red Sox**)

Fidelity Trust Corporation

Fidelity Trust Corporation, or Fidelity Fund of Boston, has become one of the largest and most successful investment firms in the world. The firm's founder and prime mover was Edward C. Johnson, who joined with others to invest in common stocks as corporate investors rather than as individuals. Johnson then conceived and helped originate his own fund. The model followed was that of a freestanding fund whose trustees hired a separate investment company, owned by some of the same trustees, to invest large sums across the board. Fidelity Fund opened in the midst of the Great Depression in 1930 with only $44,000 in assets. Through shrewd buying, by 1933 the firm was worth $3.5 million, and $4 million by 1940. World War II brought national prosperity, and by the time it ended, the company was worth $5 million.

By 1946 Johnson was in complete control of Fidelity Fund's board of directors and its investment arm, the Fidelity Management and Research Company. Under Johnson, Fidelity Fund reached $20 million in assets. He went on to develop new funds, such as the Puritan Fund, Fidelity Capital Fund, and Fidelity Trend Fund. Capitalization by 1958 was over $416 million. As the years passed, many more funds accrued, like the enormously successful Magellan Fund, which alone was worth $12 billion in 1989. By 1996 Fidelity managed funds worth more than $400 billion on behalf of over 8 million individuals and numerous companies, governments, and financial institutions. Given the fund's national and international prominence, Fidelity's location in Boston helped maintain that city's position as the financial center of New England.

Fifty-fourth Regiment (See **Robert Gould Shaw**)

John F. Fitzgerald

John Francis Fitzgerald helped transform Boston from a Yankee stronghold to a more equitable community for its majority immigrant population. The first Boston-born Irish Catholic mayor, he was the grandfather of John, Robert, and Edward Kennedy. Born in Boston on February 11 or 12, 1863, he grew up in the North End in a family of twelve children whose father was a grocer and liquor dealer. He went to Boston Latin and then to Harvard Medical School, but had to drop out after his first year because of his father's death in 1885. Fitzgerald went into the insurance business and opened a successful weekly newspaper, then entered politics in 1892 with his election to the Boston Common Council. The undisputed boss of his district, the "Napoleon of the North End," he organized a political club, scanned the death notices every morning and went to funerals, made it his business to help people find jobs, and attended dances and social functions, all in order to make himself indispensable to his constituents.

Beginning in 1892, Fitzgerald served for three terms in the state Senate, then ran for U.S. Congress in 1894 and won, serving until 1901. Despite the opposition of other Democratic ward bosses, in 1905 he ran a vigorous campaign for nomination as mayor. He won, going on to defeat his Republican opponent for the mayoralty. While stumping for election, he often sang renditions of "Sweet Adeline," earning him the sobriquet "Honey

Fitz." As mayor he created jobs and expanded his patronage power, which enabled him to challenge Yankee control over the city. His two years in office (1906–7) produced reform but also patronage, ward politics, and corruption. While the city was mysteriously losing large sums of money, Fitzgerald built new facilities for the harbor and constructed new schools, playgrounds, bathhouses, and municipal swimming pools for his working-class constituents. But with several of his appointees under indictment and facing trial for corruption, Fitzgerald lost his bid for reelection in 1907 to Republican George Hibbard.

He ran again in 1910, this time eking out a narrow victory against Republican James Jackson Storrow by emphasizing the contrast between "an Irish boy from the slums and a wealthy encrusted Harvard blueblood." With the mayor's term now expanded to four years, Fitzgerald's administration (1910–14) was characterized by brazen spending on handouts to his friends and more public works projects to help the poor. Boston benefited, gaining a new tuberculosis hospital, the Franklin Park Zoo, a city aquarium, and public holidays for municipal workers. In 1913, however, facing disclosure of an illicit affair with a showgirl, he decided not to run again.

Fitzgerald would run for political office many more times (1916, 1922, 1942, 1948), but without success. He did win a congressional election in 1918, but was unseated three months into office on charges of illegal registration and ballot stuffing. In 1946 he helped elect his grandson, **John F. Kennedy,** to Congress. The lasting legacy of Honey Fitz was his ability as a politician to reach out to voters directly through the use of the mass media; he fought the ward bosses and pioneered new methods of voter mobilization based on service to constituents, all the while embodying the drive for civic respectability among the city's ethnic working classes. He died the beloved elder statesman of Boston Irish politics on October 3, 1950.

Freedom Trail

Boston's historic Freedom Trail leads visitors on a walk through early American history as they follow the red line in the pavement beginning at the **Boston Common** and threading through downtown Boston across the Charles River to Charlestown. The idea for a walk through the historic sites of the city originated during the mayoral administration of John Hynes in 1949. Since then, with private and public support, the Trail has become part of the federal government's Boston National Historical Park. Sixteen historic sites along a 2.5-mile walk constitute this patriotic ramble.

Walkers can start wherever they please, but the Trail begins at the Boston Common, one of the oldest parks in America and the site of many prerevolutionary gatherings of patriots. From there it is an easy stretch to site number two, the **State House** on **Beacon Hill,** designed by architect **Charles Bulfinch.** Built in 1795, the State House with its resplendent golden dome houses the executive and legislative branches of the state government. Nearby is site three, the 1809 Park Street Church at the corner of Park and Tremont streets. Here on July 4, 1831, abolitionist leader **William Lloyd Garrison** inaugurated the antislavery movement with a speech delivered from the balcony.

Close by on Tremont Street is site four, the Granary Burying Ground, where one discovers the graves of **Paul Revere, John Hancock, Sam Adams,** Robert Treat Paine, and the five patriots killed in the **Boston Massacre.** Down the street is King's Chapel, site five, America's first Anglican church, founded in 1689, though the present structure dates from 1754. The churchyard includes the graves of sixteenth-century luminaries such as Massachusetts's first governor, **John Winthrop.** Around the corner on School Street is site six, a plaque marking the original location of America's first public school, the Boston Latin School.

Sites seven, eight, and nine include the Globe Corner Bookstore, built in 1712, the Old South Meeting House of 1729, and the Old State House, built in 1713. Next to the Old State House at State Street and Congress is number ten, the site of the Boston Massacre. Just down Congress Street the Trail leads to **Faneuil Hall,** site eleven, long known as the meeting place for debates on many issues pertinent to American history. In the North End are sites twelve and thirteen, the home of Paul Revere and the **Old North Church,** from which the two lanterns were hung signaling Paul Revere's ride. Also in the North End is Copp's Hill Burying Ground, site fourteen, a cemetery dating from the seventeenth century that overlooks Boston Harbor and Charlestown, where the British bombarded the **Minute Men** at **Bunker Hill** in 1775.

To view sites fifteen and sixteen, the walker must take the longer journey across the Charles River to Charlestown. Here one finds the tall obelisk that commemorates the Battle of Bunker and Breed's hills, and the Charlestown Navy Yard, home to the oldest commissioned U.S. Navy warship, the **U.S.S. *Constitution*.** Along the Trail are other sites of interest relating to the history of African Americans and of Boston's immigrants.

Robert Frost

Robert Frost is known as one of America's greatest and most beloved poets of the twentieth century. Born in San Francisco on March 26, 1874, he was the son of a journalist. The early death of his father led his mother to move the family east to Salem, New Hampshire, in 1885, where she became a schoolteacher. They then moved to Lawrence, Massachusetts, where Frost attended high school. It was then that he began writing poetry. After graduation he tried one semester at Dartmouth, but he soon dropped out and went to work in a Lawrence mill. Next he taught school while continuing to write poems. He shuttled back and forth between teaching and journalism, all the while successfully publishing his poems. From 1901 to 1911 Frost lived with his family on a farm in New Hampshire, where he immersed himself in nature and rural life, writing profusely.

During these early years he published several books of poetry, including *A Boy's Will* in 1913, *North of Boston* in 1914, and *Mountain Interval* in 1916. He traveled in Britain, returning in 1914 to find himself a renowned poet. Frost moved to Amherst in 1917, where he spent the rest of his life. He taught at Amherst College, as well as many other colleges and universities, writing poetry all the while. One book of poems, *New Hampshire,* won the Pulitzer Prize in 1923; he won a second Pulitzer in 1930 for his *Collected Poems,* and a third in 1937 for *A Further Range.* Heaped with honors, he continued publishing throughout the 1940s, becoming America's favorite and most famous poet. His last collection of poems, *In the Clearing,* appeared on his eighty-eighth birthday. He died on January 29, 1963, in Boston.

Fugitive Slaves

Many slaves who managed to flee the bonds of slavery in the South came north to seek refuge from slave catchers. Boston, with its African American and abolitionist communities, provided a sanctuary for escaping slaves. Opposition to slavery was so widespread that Boston, and Massachusetts in general, became national havens for these fugitives. In order to free runaways from recapture, many Bostonians were willing to use violence and break the law. A decisive episode took place on August 11, 1836, when a slave agent had two black women arrested as runaways. In court, outraged bystanders overcame the bailiff and removed the women to safety. When the judge tried to prevent the rescue, crowd members knocked him to the floor and made good the escape.

The arrest of one fugitive slave in 1842 did not cause any violence, as members of the community paid for his freedom. But the incident raised the question whether the legally constituted Massachusetts authorities should participate in capturing runaway slaves for Southerners. This debate led to the passage of the 1843 Liberty Act, which forbade Massachusetts officials from arresting or apprehending fugitive slaves, and disallowed the use of state facilities for that purpose.

The passage of a national Fugitive Slave Law in 1850 made the Liberty Act moot, and led to more serious confrontations in Boston. The new law put the responsibility for returning runaways solely in the hands of federal agents, with no jury trial for the fugitives. Judges and federal commissioners thus made administrative decisions without recognizing the rights of the accused or the antislavery sentiment of the community. Two runaway slaves, a married couple, William and Ellen Craft, had lived in Boston since 1848. On October 25, 1850, their slave owner hired agents to effect their capture. Local blacks and white **abolitionists** organized a rescue based on intimidation. A crowd of over two thousand harassed the owner and the slave catchers, who fled the city in fear, forcing the release of the couple. When, on February 15, 1851, federal agents seized a fugitive named Frederick "Shadrack" Minkins, who was working as a waiter in the city, a crowd of blacks stormed the courtroom and whisked away Minkins, who made his way safely to Canada. The municipal authorities sorely regretted these incidents and promised they would not be repeated.

The next time federal authorities arrested a fugitive, Thomas Sims, on April 3, 1851, the mayor ordered the entire police force to guard him and prevent his rescue. Sims was escorted to the docks, where he was put aboard a ship and sent back to the South. The last major attempt to rescue a fugitive slave in Boston occurred in 1854, when police arrested the runaway Anthony Burns. On May 26, while a large abolitionist meeting took place in **Faneuil Hall** to decide what to do, a small band of abolitionists and mechanics, led by minister **Thomas Wentworth Higginson,** attacked the jail where Burns was being held. After much fighting, in which a federal marshal was killed, the federal officers repulsed the abolitionist attackers. Large contingents of army, militia, and police took over the streets of Boston using violence against protesters and bystanders, and Burns was shipped south, while the city went into mourning. The brutality of the Burns ab-

THE

BOSTON SLAVE RIOT,

AND

TRIAL

OF

Anthony Burns,

CONTAINING THE

REPORT OF THE FANEUIL HALL MEETING; THE MURDER OF BACHELDER; THEODORE PARKER'S LESSON FOR THE DAY; SPEECHES OF COUNSEL ON BOTH SIDES, CORRECTED BY THEMSELVES; VERBATIM REPORT OF JUDGE LORING'S DECISION; AND, A DETAILED ACCOUNT OF THE EMBARKATION.

BOSTON:
FETRIDGE AND COMPANY.
1854.

Press of J. S. Potter & Co., 2 Spring Lane and 130 Washington Street.

Portrait of Anthony Burns, published shortly after the last major attempt to rescue a fugitive slave in 1854. Library of Congress, Prints and Photographs Division.

duction finally convinced a majority in Massachusetts that slavery had to end. By now it was clear that only an army of occupation could prevent Bostonians from freeing fugitive slaves. The outcome of the Civil War finally resolved the issue.

Margaret Fuller

Margaret Fuller was a feminist, Transcendentalist, author, and journalist. She was a champion of women's rights whose successful writing career influenced other women writers, such as **Louisa May Alcott,** Edith Wharton, and **Emily Dickinson.** Born in Cambridgeport on May 23, 1810, she was the daughter of a lawyer and politician. Largely self-schooled, she was an omnivorous reader who taught herself to become proficient in German. She met **Ralph Waldo Emerson** when he engaged her to teach him German pronunciation. She soon became involved with the Transcendentalist movement, teaching at Bronson Alcott's experimental school in Boston while beginning a writing and publishing career. In 1840 Emerson and the Transcendentalists invited her to become the editor of their journal, *The Dial,* a job she held for two years. In the process she wrote many pieces on the condition of women, emphasizing their oppressed position and the need for creative liberation.

In 1844 she became the first woman literary editor of a major newspaper, the *New York Tribune.* Fuller's 1845 book, *Woman in the Nineteenth Century,* elaborated on her feminist program of equality with men, particularly in the literary sphere. Her book, editorials, and newspaper articles gained widespread appreciation and popular attention. She traveled to Europe as the *Tribune*'s foreign correspondent for an extended stay, where she had an affair with an Italian nobleman and gave birth to a son. She was in Rome during the abortive Revolution of 1848. The father of her son fought on the side of the revolutionaries, and Fuller wrote articles persuading Americans to support his cause. When the French retook the city, she and her family set sail for New York, only to be drowned in a shipwreck off Fire Island on July 19, 1850. (See also **Transcendentalism**)

Great Fire of 1872, Milk Street opposite the Post Office, Boston. Photo by J.W. Black, November 1872. Boston Pictorial Archive. Courtesy of the Boston Public Library.

G

Isabella Stewart Gardner

Boston's most eccentric socialite of the late nineteenth and early twentieth centuries, Isabella Stewart Gardner left her mark by establishing a superb collection of European art in a unique setting and then leaving it to the people of Boston. The Isabella Stewart Gardner Museum is a fifteenth-century Venetian palace that was transported stone by stone to Boston's Fenway to house an eclectic personal collection of treasures from the Italian Renaissance, as well as later French, German, and Dutch masters. Gardner's mania for collecting art was her way of dealing with personal tragedy and with the scorn of Boston's stodgy upper-class Brahmins, who never fully accepted her.

Born April 14, 1840, the daughter of a rich New York City dry goods merchant, in 1860 she married the impeccable Boston Brahmin John Lowell Gardner, heir to maritime and industrial fortunes. Refusing to conform as a Boston matron should, she created a new social circle in the city including artists, scholars, poets, and writers. She shocked the bluebloods by smoking in public, wearing ostentatious jewelry, walking with a pet lion, flirting with various religions, and holding infamous parties. Known as "Mrs. Jack," she began collecting art under the tutelage of connoisseur Bernard Berenson.

After the death of her husband in 1898, which was a great blow, she took up collecting in earnest. Her dream was to build herself a new home that would itself be a work of art as well as a place to house her collection. The most prominent feature of the palace she built is the open courtyard in the center, lush with seasonal plants, on which three floors of galleries gaze down. When it was completed in 1903, she organized a grand opening, inviting major figures from society and the art world to listen to the Boston Symphony Orchestra while they viewed some of the greatest art treasures of Europe. When she died on July 17, 1924, she left her home to the people of Boston as a museum, with strict instructions to maintain the exhibit space exactly as she had planned it—a request honored to this day.

William Lloyd Garrison

William Lloyd Garrison. Library of Congress, Prints and Photographs Division.

William Lloyd Garrison, editor of the *Liberator,* was one of America's foremost **abolitionists.** His voice was the clarion call that awakened a dormant North to the evils of slavery in the years before the Civil War. He prepared the nation for conflict and convinced many that the time had come to make a stand. Born in Newburyport on December 10, 1805, he was the son of a seaman and of a housekeeper. Raised in a deeply religious but poverty-stricken family, the young Garrison became an apprentice in 1818 to the owner of the Newburyport *Herald,* thereby beginning his lifelong career as a newspaperman and editor. After finishing his apprenticeship he tried to establish several newspapers on his own but failed largely because he supported moral issues—such as temperance, abolition, and women's rights—that were not popular.

In 1828 he co-edited a newspaper in Baltimore, Maryland, a slave state. In his editorials he attacked a slave trader as a murderer. The man sued him for libel and won. Garrison refused to pay the fine imposed, and on principle went to jail. By spending forty-nine days in jail for fighting slavery, he became a national figure and began receiving financial support from abolitionist leaders such as Arthur and Lewis Tappan. It was then that he enunciated his moral doctrine of immediate emancipation to end a practice that was anti-Christian and immoral. He eschewed using political or violent means to achieve an end to slavery, claiming that once the American people were persuaded of its immorality they would demand its abolition. Thus he took it upon himself to convince the nation of the urgency for a moral crusade to end slavery immediately.

To do so, he founded what would become the major abolitionist newspaper in the nation, Boston's *Liberator,* in 1831. His opening editorial, rejecting gradual approaches, proclaimed his unswerving opposition to slavery: "I *will be* harsh as truth, and as uncompromising as justice. On this subject, I do not wish to think, or speak, or write, with moderation. . . . I will not equivocate—I will not excuse—I will not retreat a single inch—AND I WILL BE HEARD." From that moment on, Garrison became the bellwether of the antislavery movement, founding in Boston's **African Meeting House** on **Beacon Hill** the New England Anti-Slavery Society, and with others in Philadelphia the American Anti-Slavery Society. He bombarded the nation with strident editorials that worked their way throughout the Northeast and the South. Garrison's stand so infuriated many well-to-do Bostonians, who had investments in textile mills that required Southern cotton, that in 1835 they mobbed him, threatening his life.

Besides being a passionate abolitionist, Garrison pressed for women's rights, and he received widespread support from women abolitionists such as Lucretia Mott, Angelina and Sarah Grimke, and Abbey Kelley, even though his feminist position split the American Anti-Slavery Society. Garrison lost many other supporters when, in 1842, he proclaimed that the Constitution—and thus the Union—should be annulled because it legalized slavery. When he publicly burned a copy of the Constitution in 1854, many looked upon him as an extremist.

Throughout his life he championed freedom for African Americans, spoke out against segregation in the North, and assisted **fugitive slaves.** But he never preached violence or the extension of political equality to blacks. The Civil War accomplished what Garrison could not, for it took violence to end slavery in the United States after all. He spent the postwar years in semi-retirement. He died in New York City on May 24, 1879, and was buried in Massachusetts.

Judge W. Arthur Garrity (See **Busing Riots**)

Theodore Seuss Geisel ("Dr. Seuss")

Theodore S. Geisel, or Dr. Seuss, was the beloved author of children's books that became the standard for the literature in the field. Combining fantasy with figures speaking in artful rhyme, Dr. Seuss explored the rich and complex imaginative world of children as few had done before. Born in Springfield on March 2, 1904, the son of a brewer, he was educated at Dartmouth, where he worked on the campus humor magazine. Graduating in 1925, he toured Europe, returning in 1927, when he began working as a writer and illustrator for a New York City weekly humor magazine. In 1928 he conceived of the pen name "Dr. Seuss." At the same time, Geisel became successful drawing advertising cartoons for large corporations and a variety

Theodore Seuss Geisel at work on a drawing for *How the Grinch Stole Christmas,* 1957. Photo by Al Ravenna, for World Telegraph & Sun. Library of Congress, Prints and Photographs Division.

of national magazines. He put this skill to work in 1937, publishing his first book of children's verse and imaginary characters, *And to Think That I Saw It on Mulberry Street.* He also tried writing adult fiction, but with disappointing results.

Geisel returned to writing and illustrating books for children with *Horton Hatches the Egg* (1940), about a conscientious elephant sitting on a bird's nest, which became very popular. During the Second World War he penned anti-German and anti-Japanese cartoons for the newspaper *PM,* then went into the service and produced training films for soldiers. After the war, living in California, he produced a documentary film denigrating the Japanese, *Design for Death,* which won the 1947 Academy Award for best documentary. Geisel continued writing for the movies, including an acclaimed documentary on Hitler, and penning children's books, but he achieved national prominence with his 1957 best-seller, *The Cat in the Hat.* The success of this book alone made him a worldwide celebrity. The Grinch was introduced that same year in *How the Grinch Stole Christmas.* He went on to create many other characters that delighted children—and their parents—receiving a Pulitzer Prize for lifetime achievement in 1984. He died in La Jolla, California, on September 24, 1991.

General Court (See **Massachusetts Constitution**)

Elbridge Gerry and the Gerrymander

Elbridge Gerry was a prominent eighteenth-century politician best known today as the father of the "gerrymander," a political device for creating electoral districts that benefit one party over another even though the resulting district's shape makes little sense. Gerry was born July 17, 1744, to wealthy parents in Marblehead; his father was a merchant and his mother the daughter of a merchant. After graduating from Harvard in 1762, he went to work in the family business. He entered politics, came to know **Sam Adams,** and was soon a member of the Massachusetts **Committee of Correspondence.** In 1776 Gerry was a delegate to the Continental Congress and served as a representative in the Congress from 1783 to 1785.

As a delegate to the Constitutional Convention of 1787, he originally opposed ratification of the Constitution because it did not contain a bill of rights. He subsequently changed his mind, and in 1789 won election to the first U.S. Congress, leaving office in 1793. By 1800 Gerry was a member of the Democratic Republicans, archfoes of the powerful Federalists. He ran for governor more than once between 1801 and 1803 but lost each time, then finally won in 1809, serving from 1810 to 1812. During his tenure the Democratic legislature redrew a congressional district in Essex County so as to benefit their party. The meandering shape of the district reminded some people of a salamander, so Federalist punsters dubbed it a "gerrymander." Entering national politics, he was elected vice president of the United States under James Madison in 1812 but died in office on November 23, 1814.

Robert H. Goddard

Known as the "rocket man," Robert H. Goddard was a physicist and a visionary who was the first to conceive and carry out experiments in space rocketry. His development of liquid fuel rockets provided the means to power space flight. Born in Worcester on October 5, 1882, the son of a businessman, he attended local schools and then Worcester Polytechnic Institute, graduating in 1908. Goddard went on to receive an M.A. and a Ph.D. from Clark University in 1910 and 1911. He then taught at Clark until retiring in 1943. In 1914 Goddard began his experiments with rockets, publishing theoretical articles on the possibility of space flight. In 1919 he published a book, *A Method of Reaching Extreme Altitudes,* arguing that a rocket could reach the moon. From that time on he was known as the rocket man, though skeptics labeled him a "moonie."

On March 16, 1926, in a farm field in Auburn, he successfully launched the first liquid propellant rocket. Ten feet long and weighing ten and one half pounds, it reached an altitude of forty-one feet. He continued his research on rockets, though his own experimental devices never soared higher than ten thousand feet. During World War II he worked on rocket engines for the U.S. Navy and continued to contribute scientific papers. He died on August 10, 1945, in Baltimore and was buried in Worcester, having conducted thirty-five successful rocket tests. Two NASA centers are named after this pioneer whose innovative work served to inspire others in the field of rocketry and space travel.

Great Awakening

The Great Awakening was a religious revival movement of the 1730s and 1740s that took hold throughout the colonies. Secularism and a move toward worldliness and liberalism had whittled away at the old-time religious fervor of the seventeenth-century **Puritans.** Ministers such as Northampton's **Jonathan Edwards** preached a return to strict Calvinist principles as the only way to achieve salvation. The movement's followers believed that the millennium was at hand, and this notion excited waves of religious enthusiasm among many Congregationalists as well as Baptists and Presbyterians. This religious movement sparked a host of revivals, with schools and colleges springing up to train a new generation of ministers to act as missionaries for the propagation of the old faith restored. By 1744, however, the Great Awakening had begun to decline as renewed materialist drives emerged and congregations tired of their ministers' constant chastisement for the sinfulness.

Great Fire of 1872

On November 9, 1872, fire gutted downtown Boston from the harbor to Quincy Market and the Old South Meeting House. Downtown in the 1860s consisted of five- to seven-story buildings with wooden roofs and wood-lined stairwells and elevator shafts. The area where the fire began contained many retail stores, businesses, and some factories. These wooden structures were filled with flammable goods, and the blaze soon got out of hand. At the time, many of the fire department's horses happened to be suffering from some sort of equine epidemic. In addition, there were not enough working fire engines, ladders could not reach the top floors of the buildings, and few hydrants were available. As a result, the fire consumed sixty-five acres, demolishing 776 buildings at a cost of $75 million. Business interests and local officials quarreled over the best approach to rebuilding, the result being a haphazard redevelopment lacking all planning.

Shaker interior, Hancock Shaker Village. Courtesy of Hancock Shaker Village.

H

Half-Way Covenant (See **Covenent and Half-Way Covenant**)

John Hancock

John Hancock, one of the nation's founding fathers, was born in Braintree (now Quincy) on January 12, 1737, the son of a minister. He graduated from Boston Latin in 1750 and then Harvard College in 1754. After entering the Boston merchant house of his rich uncle Thomas Hancock, he took over the business on his uncle's death in 1764, becoming very rich in the process. Hancock resented British interference with American trade with the Sugar Act of 1764 and the **Stamp Act** of 1765. A moderate, he nevertheless joined the patriot group because he felt that the mother country had violated his rights as an Englishman.

Bostonians showed their confidence in him by electing him both a town selectman and a representative to the General Court during the pre-Revolutionary years. His patriot reputation increased when British customs officials impounded his sloop, *Liberty*, accusing him of smuggling. The charge was true, but the **Sons of Liberty** staged riots, forcing the customs officials to flee and allowing Hancock to retrieve his property. He was in Lexington with **Sam Adams** when word came of the impending approach of British troops. Hancock served as a delegate to the Continental Congress in Philadelphia and was elected president of these momentous proceedings.

Thus on July 4, 1776, he became the first to sign the Declaration of Independence.

Back in Massachusetts, after approval of a new state constitution in 1780, the people overwhelmingly elected him the first governor of the Commonwealth. He resigned in 1785 because of ill health. After the abortive **Shays's Rebellion** of 1786–87 he came out of retirement and was reelected governor. Amid great controversy, he and Sam Adams supported ratification of the federal Constitution in 1788, which aided its ultimate passage. He remained governor until his retirement in 1793 and died in Boston on October 8 of that same year, his name enshrined forever as one of the leaders of the American Revolution. (See also **John Adams**)

Hancock Shaker Village

Hancock Shaker Village, on the western border of Massachusetts, was the third of nineteen utopian communities founded in the United States between 1783 and 1836 by the United Society of Believers in Christ's Second Appearing. Originating in England in 1747 as believers in religious visions and revelations, the Shakers came to the United States in 1774 seeking a more tolerant environment. The adherents of the church became known as Shakers because of their emotional prayer meetings in which they shook themselves, trembled, and whirled around. Their founding leader, Mother Ann Lee, emphasized faith in the Second Appearing, or Second Coming of Christ. They believed in celibacy, communal farm life, confession, gender equality, pacifism, and the notion of creating heaven on earth.

The Shakers founded Hancock Shaker Village in 1783. After peaking in the 1830s, with three hundred families and over two thousand acres, the village began to decline owing to pressures of the industrial revolution, the impact of universal celibacy on the community, and practices that troubled many new adherents, such as bowing down to prominent elders. Decline in communal and church membership continued until the village finally dissolved in 1959, when only three aged sisters remained. A group sympathetic to the movement restored Hancock Shaker Village in 1960 as a historic community to preserve the Shaker memory and present a living representation of a past age.

The Shakers have become known for their style of building construction and for the design of their furniture, which exhibited a unique simplicity yet with a stylish pristine aesthetic. Shaker-style furniture and artifacts are still much in demand today. With its twenty buildings, including a visitor center, library, gift shop, and café, on over 1,200 acres, the village, located at the junction of routes 41 and 20 in Hancock, preserves for posterity a vanished communitarian way of life.

Hartford Convention

The War of 1812 so disrupted New England's maritime trade that many Federalist merchants and politicians considered seceding from the Union and creating a federation of states that would maintain good relations with Great Britain. This secessionist sentiment came about as a result of the hated Embargo of 1807–9 and the ruinous war, which were seen as the work of Jeffersonian Republicans, now led by the incumbent president, James Madison. The depressed region sought relief for its severe economic problems. Federalists in the General Court of Massachusetts called for a convention of New Englanders at Hartford in late 1814, to confer on matters of defense and to defy the Republican administration.

Delegates to the convention included Massachusetts's Timothy Pickering and John Lowell, who presented arguments defending New England's right to secede from the Union. The convention report that was published on January 6, 1815, however, was more moderate. It criticized the Republican government and threatened nullification should conscription be introduced, but ruled out secession. The end result, nonetheless, was the generally held view that the Hartford Convention was "traitorous," a source of shame and embarrassment to the Federalist Party as the war soon ended. The convention ruined the Federalists as a national party, and its members hastily beat a retreat in search of new political venues, which would eventually result in the launching of the Whig Party.

Harvard University

Since its founding as the nation's first institution of higher learning, Harvard University has developed into one of the premier centers of scholarship in the world. It became the model and progenitor for America's private colleges and universities, especially in Massachusetts. The original Harvard College, named after minister John Harvard, arose out of the need felt by the **Puritans** of the **Massachusetts Bay Colony,** according to historian

Bernard Bailyn, to instill a religious "Puritan culture" in the young gentlemen who would become the future leaders of the colony. Moreover, the colony was in need of a local school to train the ministers who would man and supervise the Puritan Congregational Church system.

Thus, the Massachusetts legislature provided the money for the Cambridge college in 1636, making it a public institution. A charter of 1650 created a board of overseers and a powerful presidency as integral parts of the new Harvard Corporation. The legislature levied a tax to pay the president's salary and allowed the college to support itself by granting it the income from the Charlestown ferry. The state's new constitution of 1780 officially recognized Harvard as a university. A medical school was established in 1782 and a law school in 1817.

The decline of Puritan values in the early nineteenth century led to a more secularized Massachusetts society. A leader in this secularization process was Harvard, whose faculty and leaders turned, after a struggle, to the more liberal religious views of Unitarianism. Aggravating this religious controversy was a major riot among the student body in 1823 which led the more conservative General Court to sever the public connection. By that time the school had already become the recipient of large endowments from its alumni. Well up to the end of World War II, Harvard students were drawn largely from the ranks of the upper classes, and their beneficence made the university one of the world's richest institutions.

Harvard was transformed into a modern university under the leadership of President Charles W. Eliot (1869–1909), who introduced innovative educational techniques—setting up departments based on academic disciplines, revising the curriculum to limit requirements and institute an elective system, creating an honors program, steering the university toward a new focus on scholarly research, and building a world-class library. Harvard became the premier center for graduate study in the nation.

The Harvard example inspired others in the state, and as a result Massachusetts became home to an unusually large number of private institutions of higher education. While the many small colleges focus on undergraduate teaching, the large universities stress graduate research and the recruitment of leading scholars in addition to undergraduate education. Liberal arts colleges, including colleges for women, proliferated in the state: Williams in 1791, Amherst in 1825, Mount Holyoke in 1837, Wellesley in 1870, Smith in 1875, Radcliffe (the women's college of Harvard) in 1894, Simmons in 1899, and Hampshire in 1970, among other well-known institutions.

The emerging Catholic population found it necessary to develop their own colleges, such as the College of the Holy Cross in 1843 and Boston College (really a university) in 1863. Tufts (1852), Massachusetts Institute of Technology (1861), Boston University (1869), Clark (1887), Northeastern (1898), Suffolk (1906), and Brandeis (1948) round out the list of prominent private universities in the state. No other state in the nation has such a profusion of private colleges and universities. (For a list of all institutions of higher learning in Massachusetts, see the appendix).

Childe Hassam

Frederick Childe Hassam was a well-known impressionist painter who gloried in street scenes and the variety of urban life. Born on October 17, 1859, in Dorchester, the son of an antiques merchant, he spent his formative years in Boston and then went to live in Europe and New York City for the remainder of his life. He went to local schools but never graduated from high school. The **Great Fire of 1872** destroyed his father's store, and Hassam was forced to become an apprentice to a graphics designer. His artistic abilities blossomed, and he soon advanced to watercolor painting, beginning a successful career as an illustrator for a number of periodicals.

After travel abroad in 1883, he returned and began a series of remarkable paintings depicting Boston street scenes. His work was well received. He returned to Paris in 1885 and became a devotee of the impressionist school, launching a series of paintings of Paris, as well as garden paintings, all of which burnished his reputation and enabled him to support himself as an artist. He relocated to New York City in 1890, continuing his work with urban motifs. Hassam spent the remaining years of his life drifting back and forth between the Continent and New York, his career continuing to flourish. He died in East Huntington, New York, on August 27, 1935.

Nathaniel Hawthorne

The works of Nathaniel Hawthorne, written in the nineteenth century, are well known to generations of American public school students. Hawthorne used New England settings and popular legend to focus on the darker side of human nature. Born in Salem on July 4, 1804, the son of a ship's captain, he graduated from Bowdoin in 1825 well versed in literature. Among his fellow students were two close friends, **Henry Wadsworth Longfellow** and Franklin Pierce, who were to prove helpful to him later on. Determined to become an author, Hawthorne returned to his family home, where he struggled for twelve years to gain recognition. Although he succeeded in getting some books published, they received almost no attention.

He began to publish stories in periodicals, and gained some fame with his *Twice-Told Tales* (1837), which Longfellow praised in the *North American Review,* comparing him to Washington Irving and commending his use of New England locales. In 1836, pressed to earn a living, he accepted the first of several political appointments, this time at the Boston Custom House. In 1841 he became an original investor in the utopian community **Brook Farm** and lived there for a short time, but left discouraged by the strictures of collective living. Settling at the Old Manse in Concord, he continued to write well-received stories, including the noteworthy "Rappaccini's Daughter" and "The Birthmark." In 1846 his Democratic political connections got him a job as surveyor of customs in Salem, which again relieved him and his family from their straitened circumstances. Three years later the triumphant Whigs came back to power, and Hawthorne was fired.

That year he began work on his most famous novel, *The Scarlet Letter.* This attack on both Puritan society and his own, published in 1850, brought him a worldwide audience. He moved to Lenox that year, where he wrote *The House of the Seven Gables,* as well as stories and children's books. At Lenox he met and befriended **Herman Melville,** who dedicated *Moby Dick* to Hawthorne when it appeared in 1851.

In 1852 Hawthorne returned to Concord after residing for a short time in West Newton, where he completed *The Blithedale Romance,* a novel ridiculing the Brook Farm experience. In 1853 his old friend and now president, Franklin Pierce, appointed him to the lucrative position of U.S. consul in Liverpool, where he spent the next four years. His last novel, written in Concord, *The Marble Faun* (1860), derived from his European travels, focuses on the relationship between an Italian couple and an American couple living in Italy. Ill health overcame him, and he died while on a pleasure trip with Pierce in New Hampshire on May 19, 1864. His remains are interred on Author's Ridge at Concord's famous Sleepy Hollow Cemetery.

Louise Day Hicks

Louise Day Hicks stands alone as the foremost female political personality in the history of Boston and of Massachusetts. Although she served as chair of the Boston School Committee and city councilor, her chief claim to fame, or notoriety, was as a leader of the staunch opponents of racial integration in the public schools. Her many elected positions demonstrated the widespread support she enjoyed among the working-class voters of Boston's ethnic neighborhoods, a level of political success achieved by no other woman before or, arguably, since.

Born in 1916 to a middle-class family in South Boston, she was the daughter of a part-time judge, lawyer, banker, and real estate man, John Day. In 1932 her mother, Julia, died, and the teenage Louise became the woman of the house to her father and three brothers. She married John Hicks, who promptly moved into the family home. After graduating from Wheelock College with a teaching certificate, she taught and then spent ten years as a law clerk in her father's office. By now a mother of two, she entered Boston University Law School, a rare occurrence for a woman in 1952. She passed the bar examination in 1956 and opened a practice with her brother. Then in 1961 she ran for school committee.

The Boston School Committee had shifted from a bastion of Protestant Yankee values in the nineteenth century to an Irish-dominated political pork barrel. By the time Hicks sought a seat on the committee, it was recognized as a good place to launch a political career. Committee members controlled large numbers of jobs in the school department, from custodian to administrator, and issued lucrative city contracts; they openly used their position to raise money for political campaigns by selling tickets to so-called testimonial dinners. Hicks won easily and in 1963 was elected chair.

At that time Boston's black community was seeking to redress the overt segregation and inequality that black students faced in the schools. Hicks and her school committee refused to recognize any such problems. Her steadfast support for neighborhood schools increased her reputation as the protector of the white neighborhoods. Her opposition to desegregation propelled her into the race for the mayoralty in 1967, though she lost to **Kevin H. White** in a very close election. She ran for and won election to Congress in 1970, and the voters gave her strong majorities for city council victories in 1969, 1973, and 1975, but she again lost the mayoralty race in 1971 and her bid for reelection to Congress in 1972. The refusal of Hicks and other anti-busing leaders to compromise with the federal judicial decision desegregating the Boston schools resulted in increased hostility and led to the **busing riots** that racked the city from 1974 to 1976. Regardless of the eventual outcome, Hicks was Boston's most famous woman politician and a force to be reckoned with. She died in Boston on October 21, 2003.

Thomas Wentworth Higginson

Thomas Wentworth Higginson led an active life as a minister, abolitionist, soldier, author, and editor. As editor of the *Atlantic Monthly,* he served as the first mentor to the Amherst poetic genius **Emily Dickinson.** One of the leading social reformers of nineteenth-century Massachusetts, he was born in Cambridge on December 22, 1823, the son of a Boston merchant and descendant of a long line of Boston gentlemen who played a part in the colony and the Revolution. He entered Harvard at the age of thirteen, graduating at seventeen, and later trained in its Unitarian-leaning divinity school, becoming a minister in 1847. He kept few pulpits for long because of his impassioned opposition to slavery as well as his outspoken commitment to women's suffrage and temperance. He finally found a safe pastorate in the "Free Church" of Worcester, where he remained from 1852 until 1861.

Higginson was a radical abolitionist who, like **William Lloyd Garrison,** saw the U.S. Constitution as evil for tolerating slavery and called for its dissolution. His blunt rhetoric, however, and his penchant for using violence to advance his cause, branded him as a fanatic, and he was generally scorned by the Boston aristocracy. Nonetheless, when the authorities began to arrest **fugitive slaves,** Boston antislavery leaders invited Higginson to come aid in the cause. In 1851 he and two black ministers planned a forcible rescue of the apprehended fugitive slave Thomas Sims, but the authorities got wind of their activities and Sims was sent south under heavy guard. Undaunted, Higginson and a small contingent of mechanics and black **abolitionists** attempted another rescue in 1854, when they attacked the Boston courthouse where runaway slave Anthony Burns was being held. Federal marshals repulsed this violent foray, and the authorities arrested Higginson, but then released him, fearing that his trial would further incense antislavery sentiment in Boston.

In 1856 he journeyed to "bleeding" Kansas, where he met the fiery abolitionist John Brown. Higginson was one of the "Secret Six" backers of Brown's raid on Harpers Ferry in 1859, along with two other Boston abolition leaders, the Reverend Theodore Parker and **Samuel Gridley Howe.**

During the Civil War, Higginson's reputation as a fighter against slavery earned him the rank of colonel and command of an all-black regiment, the First South Carolina Volunteers. Wounded in battle, he retired from the military in 1864 and spent the rest of his long and fruitful career fighting for reform causes, as well as writing books and articles and giving speeches. A true Renaissance man, he died in Cambridge on May 9, 1914.

Oliver Wendell Holmes Jr.

Oliver Wendell Holmes Jr. was a jurist and Supreme Court justice whose decisions were to have a weighty impact on the Constitution and the nation. He was born in Boston on March 8, 1841, the son of noted physician and poet Oliver Wendell Holmes Sr. The elder Holmes was also the founder of the *Atlantic Monthly,* and was noted for his collection of essays, *The Autocrat of the Breakfast Table.* Coming from such an illustrious family, young Holmes went to private schools and to Harvard, graduating in 1861. During the Civil War he fought in several major battles, and was twice wounded seriously. He then went on to Harvard Law School and graduated in 1866.

After traveling in Europe, he opened a law practice in Boston. As an independent legal scholar, he also published books and articles on the law, emphasizing the importance of experience over legal precedent. His major legal treatise, *The Common Law* (1881), maintained that the law was not fixed but was continuously evolving, a view that characterized him as a legal pragmatist. In 1882 he became a justice of the Massachusetts Supreme Court, then chief justice in 1889. Three years later President Theodore Roosevelt appointed Holmes to the U.S. Supreme Court in the hope that he would be supportive of Roosevelt's progressive programs grounded in common sense and experience.

Although Roosevelt's Justice Department won its antimonopoly suit against the Northern Securities Company in 1904, Roosevelt was bitterly disappointed with Holmes, who voted with the conservative minority. Holmes's stance, however, was typical of his individualistic interpretation of the law, which produced many ambiguous decisions in the years that followed. He was a moderate who felt that the Court should bow to the wishes of state courts, and that antitrust laws—the work of progressives—should be interpreted in a narrow fashion. He was an advocate of preserving individual liberties from usurpation by the state, but only if the usurpation process itself was unfair. If the state acted in a fair and legal manner, Holmes believed that the individual's rights should be subordinated to the needs of society. This put him in direct opposition to his colleague on the bench from Massachusetts, **Louis Brandeis.**

Holmes did not support the right of African Americans to vote. Conversely, he took a progressive position when he joined the minority contending that states had the right to regulate maximum hours for workers. He took a controversial stance on the right of free speech in the case of the sedition laws passed during World War I, maintaining that free speech could be curtailed if there was "a clear and present danger" to society. But in later decisions he backtracked somewhat, explaining that violations of free speech could be prohibited only if there was evidence that the speech was uttered with the purpose of doing harm, an interpretation that created legal contention and controversy for years to come. Holmes resigned from the Court because of ill health in 1932 and died in Washington, D.C., on March 6, 1935.

Winslow Homer

Winslow Homer was a famous American artist of the late nineteenth century whose superlative watercolors, particularly those combining the sea, the shore, and human figures, continue to delight large numbers of Americans. Born in Boston on February 24, 1836, into a solid middle-class family, he went to high school in Cambridge and then was apprenticed to a lithography firm in Boston. There he honed his drawing skills and became knowledgeable about the use of illustrations in periodicals. At the age of twenty-one he began submitting his drawings and paintings to various journals and publishers and was immediately so successful that he was able to support himself. Two years later he moved to New York City to study painting. He soon attracted attention as a painter, focusing on landscapes and seascapes with figures. He traveled extensively, bringing to life the haunts of fisher folk and others who lived by the sea. Winslow Homer died on September 29, 1910, probably America's best-known painter of the time and an artist who is still revered today.

Hoosac Tunnel

When a prosperous Fitchburg industrialist named Alvah Crocker found he needed access to the Erie Canal for his textile goods, he conceived of building a tunnel through the Hoosac Mountains near North Adams in

Hoosac Tunnel. Courtesy of the North Adams Public Library.

western Massachusetts that would make such access possible. Crocker invested the money, and tunnel construction began in 1851, with the completion expected in three years. By 1861, workers using steam drills and black powder for explosives had cleared only about one-third of the route through the mountain. Crocker gave up. A series of other companies also tried and failed. Finally the project became a state-sponsored effort. Hundreds of workers, many of them immigrants, toiled for years using dynamite and compressed-air drills under very dangerous conditions. By the time the 25,031-foot tunnel was finally completed in 1875, almost two hundred men had lost their lives in accidents. The tunnel was hugely expensive, costing over $14 million to build, but the railroad connection never could compete with the other lines farther south that were already hauling most of the finished industrial goods produced in the state. It remains today, an obsolete reminder of visions gone astray during the heyday of industrial expansion in nineteenth-century Massachusetts.

Elias Howe

Elias Howe is known as the inventor of the sewing machine, an intrinsic component of the new technology that transformed American life during the industrial revolution. Born in Spencer on July 9, 1819, as a young boy he worked on the family farm and in nearby mills. He became a factory apprentice at the age of sixteen, initiating a lifelong fascination with machines. He held various factory jobs, working in a machine shop and for a watchmaker. After much experimentation he succeeded in developing a mechanical sewing machine in 1845, acquiring a patent in 1846. Although the machine worked well, he had great difficulty getting it accepted. Then others found out about his invention and began to produce copies.

One of those who purloined Howe's idea was Isaac Singer, who produced an improved version of the sewing machine in 1850. Howe sued Singer and won the case in 1854. The court forced Singer to pay Howe damages and royalties. Howe then went on to sue others who had copied his machine and won in court each time, finally getting rich on his royalties until the patent ran out in 1867. He opened his own sewing machine company in Bridgeport, Connecticut, in 1863, which prospered. He died in Brooklyn, New York, on October 3, 1867, finally having secured the credit for his remarkable invention.

Julia Ward Howe

Julia Ward Howe was the author who penned the words to the famous Civil War anthem "The Battle Hymn of the Republic." Her own successful effort to break the confines of gender-enforced domesticity set the stage for many other women who followed in her pathbreaking footsteps. Born in New York City on May 27, 1819, the daughter of a businessman, she received some private schooling and tutoring, but for the most part was self-taught. She married the noted Boston reformer **Samuel Gridley Howe,** founder of the Perkins Institute for the Blind, and bore six children. Her efforts at self-improvement and the writing of poetry and drama caused dissension, however, as her husband was adamant that a wife's place was in the home. Finally she became so unhappy that in 1850 she left her family and lived for a while in Rome. After her return, ignoring her husband's demands, she began publishing her poetry, and later plays and a book.

During the Civil War she wrote the words to "The Battle Hymn of the

Republic," setting them to the music of the popular song "John Brown's Body." The *Atlantic Monthly* published the hymn, which soon became the symbol of the Union struggle against the slave South. The stirring song continues to be a rallying cry for freedom and the fight against injustice. Howe's success propelled her to fame, and her writing career prospered. She published a wide variety of books and poems, and lectured extensively over the years. Her particular interest was women's suffrage. She served as president of the New England Woman Suffrage Association from 1868 to 1877, and in 1879, with suffragist **Lucy Stone,** she became co-leader of the American Woman Suffrage Association. Throughout the rest of her life she continued to work for the movement. She died at Newport, Rhode Island, on October 17, 1910.

Samuel Gridley Howe

Samuel Gridley Howe, a social reformer and the founder of Boston's famed Perkins Institute for the Blind, was born in Boston on November 10, 1801, the son of a well-to-do businessman. He graduated from Brown University in 1821 and then entered Harvard Medical School, receiving his degree in 1824. As a young idealist, he volunteered to serve in the Greek war for independence in 1825, as both a soldier and a doctor. After he returned to Boston in 1831, he took on a commission to found the New England Asylum for the Blind. He recruited teachers, obtained donations, and attracted students. One of the school's trustees, the wealthy merchant Thomas H. Perkins, donated his Watertown mansion to be used as the school's permanent quarters in 1838, and the name of the school was changed to honor Perkins's generosity.

Howe believed that the blind could be educated to lead independent lives. He set up other schools for the blind in several states and developed a type system for blind readers using embossed letters which educators used for many years until it was supplanted by the Braille system. Howe later broadened his interests to include the mentally retarded. His best-known student was Laura Bridgeman, who was deaf as well as blind. Howe gained fame when he proved that she could be educated. He helped establish the Clark School for the Deaf in Northampton in 1867 and went on to work in education reform and reform of treatment for the mentally ill. Howe was also an ardent abolitionist. He died in Boston on January 9, 1876, a pioneer in the movement for what is now called special education.

Anne Hutchinson

A forceful woman of great intelligence, Anne Hutchinson was a Puritan settler who was at odds with the established ideas of the **Massachusetts Bay Colony.** Born in England in 1591, she landed in Boston with her husband on September 18, 1634, in what was by now a well-established colony. Proud of her knowledge of theological scholarship, she had made the journey because she believed that she could find a purer church in the colonies than in England. Displeased with Boston's ministers, however, Hutchinson began to enlarge her own interpretations, expanding on religious themes that were contrary to prevailing teachings. She held that human actions gave no clue to whether a person was saved or not—that one's life in this world offered no evidence of the possibility of salvation. Hutchinson believed instead that the Holy Ghost resided in saved individuals, such as herself, who in turn could clearly see whether others were saved as well. She pronounced that with a few exceptions, all the colony's ministers and leading citizens were not so chosen and were thus liars and hypocrites. This vision of personal revelation attracted followers, and soon the colony was racked with dissension.

Hutchinson was espousing a radical dogma. The **Puritans** based their entire concept of life and governance on the principle of "sanctification," which meant that it was possible to discern who were the saved because they were those who knew the Bible and experienced visible conversions. These were the "saints" who ran the colony and ministered to the churches. The notion of personal revelation was anathema to their fundamental belief that God's intent was revealed only in the Bible. Frightened by her eloquence, Governor **John Winthrop** summoned Hutchinson to court to be tried for heresy. At first she triumphed, easily defeating her questioners with her superior knowledge of the Bible. But her arrogance got the better of her when she revealed that she had divine revelations—that God spoke to her. She condemned herself by this admission, and the court excommunicated her and banished her from the colony in 1637.

She left with a small band of followers to take up residence in Rhode Island, where other dissenters, including **Roger Williams,** made their home. In 1643 Hutchinson and some members of her family were killed by hostile Indians in New York, where she had migrated after leaving Rhode Island. Folklore has presented Hutchinson as a hero for upholding the ideal of freedom of religion and religious tolerance, though in fact she was no different from the Puritans in insisting that her beliefs were the only correct ones and imposing them on others. The idea of religious freedom only came later with the Revolution and the ratification of the Constitution.

Thomas Hutchinson

Thomas Hutchinson (September 9, 1711–June 3, 1780) was a Boston merchant, a member of the Tory elite, and governor of Massachusetts in the years leading up to the Revolution. As the foremost leader of Boston's privileged class, he vigorously defended British policies against a rising tide of voices condemning imperial despotism. Born in Boston, he was a direct descendant of religious prophet Anne Hutchinson. But Thomas Hutchinson was more interested in status and money than religion. The scion of a long line of merchants, he went to Harvard and then dove into the world of investments and trade, becoming rich and successful. As a member of both the social elite and the wealthy merchant class, he served in many political capacities: Boston selectman and representative to the General Court (on occasion serving on both simultaneously), speaker of the House of Representatives, governor's councilor, probate judge, lieutenant governor, chief justice of the state supreme court, and finally governor. He was also a historian who took it upon himself to write a history of the colony, which stands today as a valuable source of information about early Massachusetts.

He was personally at odds with major Revolutionary leaders, such as James Otis, **Sam Adams, John Hancock,** and **John Adams.** Throughout the struggle to uphold colonial rights based on the notion of rule by consent of the governed, patriots targeted Hutchinson as the prime example of British repression. On the occasion of the **Stamp Act** protest, the **Sons of Liberty** destroyed his mansion and vandalized his priceless possessions as an expression of their contempt for defenders of the Crown's arbitrary policies. As a supporter of the right of Parliament to tax the colonies, Hutchinson personified upper-class privilege and insensitivity to the rights of the common people. His staunch defense of the hated tea duty pushed colonial moderates into the hands of the radical forces, which culminated in the **Boston Tea Party.** Finally, recognizing his inability to stop the course of events that would lead to independence, Governor Hutchinson fled Massachusetts in 1774 to live and die in exile in England.

Irish emigrants at Queenstown, Cork, in 1852, prepared to embark to Boston and other destinations. From *Illustrated London News,* May 10, 1852. Courtesy of Eugene Worman Collection.

Immigration

Everyone who lives in Massachusetts—or anywhere in America—is descended from ancestors who arrived from someplace else. There have been five main periods of immigration to Massachusetts. The first to arrive were Amerindians, hunter-gatherers from Asia Minor who crossed to the Western Hemisphere over land and ice bridges in the Bering Sea up to forty thousand years ago. Paleo-Indians came to southern New England around 10,000 to 8000 B.C. Around 1000 A.D. native peoples introduced horticulture in the form of maize, squash, and beans. The result was the prosperous and thriving society of the **Algonquins.** European contact began in the early sixteenth century with the arrival of explorers, traders, and fishermen. From 1616 to 1619 a deadly epidemic brought by Europeans decimated the Native population. Through further epidemics and aggressive warfare, the Europeans almost eliminated the Native society, allowing uncontested English settlement to begin in earnest.

From the 1630s well into the late nineteenth century, the English settlers, beginning with the **Pilgrims and Plymouth Colony** and the **Puritans,** then their descendants, the Yankee elite, dominated the political, economic, and cultural life of Massachusetts. In the first two centuries of colonization and settlement they established the mental habits and the political and social basis of their society. With a homogeneous Protestant population, they worked out the standards for social mobility based on a synthesis of prevailing beliefs about success, the general welfare, individual freedom, and the proper role of government. Because subsequent waves of immigration were never sufficient to displace the Yankee majority, their ethical value structure became the standard for the state, as well as for the nation. Newcomers, always in the minority, had to acculturate and assimilate these values in order to survive and prosper.

The third wave of immigration began with small numbers in the 1830s, then vastly increasing numbers after the 1840s, of poverty-stricken Irish immigrants fleeing the ravages of famine in their homeland. The industrial revolution, particularly strong in Massachusetts, paved the way for a warm welcome by manufacturers, but the Irish received a generally hostile response from other Yankee Protestants. Those Irish who came to Boston found a prosperous commercial seaport that had no room for unskilled workers. Many left the city to become the new proletariat of the burgeoning industrial economy of New England. Wherever they settled, these immigrants lived in crowded slums under dreadful sanitary conditions. Their presence inflamed the **anti-Catholicism** of the Yankee host population, and the hapless newcomers faced years of bigotry and even violence.

After the Civil War, French Canadians fled the extreme rural poverty of Quebec and joined the Irish seeking refuge in the new factory towns of the state. These hordes of Catholic immigrants—Irish and French Canadian—working in factories, transformed the state from a rural to an urban society. They lived in densely packed, unsanitary, and socially unstable towns and cities lacking the schools, housing, and transportation necessary for large-scale population growth. Overcoming bitter hatred, the new immigrants worked their way up the ladder of success and became acclimatized to the old Puritan values of hard work and frugality that still dominated. It would not be until the early twentieth century that the Irish achieved political power in Boston, and later across the entire state.

The widespread industrialization of Massachusetts in the post–Civil War era demanded workers. In the 1890s, eastern and southern Europe suffered through a major agricultural depression, which forced the starving peasantry off the land. Those artisans and merchants who depended on an agricultural way of life, especially the Jews of Russia and Poland, also faced dire economic conditions. Added to the fact of widespread political oppression, these deprivations drove millions to leave their homelands seeking salvation in the United States. During this fourth wave of immigration, Italians, Greeks, Russians, Poles, Lithuanians, and Portuguese came in large numbers to industrial Massachusetts where jobs awaited. By 1920 this enormous new presence had transformed the state, ending forever the Yankee dominance and creating a society in which 67 percent of the population were either immigrants or the children of immigrants. The National Origins Act of 1924 ended this massive immigration. In the years that followed, the second generation quickly became acculturated and the third generation became totally assimilated to life in Massachusetts.

In the fifth and latest wave of immigration, two sets of newcomers have arrived in the Bay State. First, after the 1950s, came African Americans from the South. From 5 percent of the state's population they rose to 16 percent by 1970 and 26 percent by 1990. Although they found better jobs in the North, they faced discrimination which held them back from full-fledged social mobility. Bias in housing led to the creation of black ghettos in the state's cities, and thus to school segregation. A powerless minority frozen out by the white ethnic political structure, blacks sought redress in the federal courts. This struggle increased racial tensions and led sometimes to violence. By 1990 blacks were the dominant ethnic group in Boston and Springfield, while the Irish and Italians were now living for the most part in the suburbs. By 2000 the black population of Boston had increased by 2.4 percent, while that of the Irish had decreased by 22.4 percent, leaving Irish Americans only 17 percent of the city they had recently dominated.

The Immigration and Nationality Act of 1965 ended standards based on racial origin and predicated immigration instead on a set of preferences established according to nation. Nations in both the Eastern and the Western Hemisphere were granted equal yearly quotas, with family members of U.S. citizens given preference. This change led to the widespread immigration of Hispanics, Asians, West Indians, Africans, Greeks, Portuguese, Italians, Russians, and even the Irish. But it was largely the Hispanics, most from Puerto Rico, and the Asians, from Vietnam, Cambodia, Laos, China, Korea, and the Philippines, who brought major changes to the cities throughout the state. Once again, immigrants were overburdening the infrastructure, living in slums, crowding the schools, and generating tensions with the host society.

The assimilated immigrants—Irish, Italians, French Canadians, eastern European Jews, and Poles—reacted negatively to the newcomers in almost the same manner as the Yankees had acted toward their parents and grandparents. Language and cultural differences further aggravated the lack of understanding within the host society. Nonetheless, these new immigrants were quickly absorbed into the working world. With increased social mobility, these newcomers should assimilate as easily as their predecessors. Meanwhile, they have added immeasurably to the economic growth and prosperity of the state, as many have been willing to take on the unskilled jobs that no one else wants, while others, of course, add to the brainpower that drives Massachusetts's high-tech and service industries.

Without denying the periodic episodes of hostility and conflict between host society and immigrants, the evidence is abundantly clear that immigration over the long term has proved beneficial to Massachusetts. In time, accommodation and assimilation serve to equalize the differences and to create a more tolerant and ever-enriched cultural environment.

Indentured Servants

To be indentured means to sell one's labor in exchange for some sort of service employment for a predetermined period of time. Two groups of people made up the class of indentured servants in early America: those who wanted to emigrate to the New World but did not have the price of passage, and children whose families contracted them out to learn a skill or a trade. It was a common practice in the colonies during economic hard times or chronic shortages of labor for poor families to indenture their children as servants to other families. Courts recorded the contracts between the parties and stipulated the length of service—anywhere from four to fourteen years—and the skills to be learned. Masters were responsible for the servant's board and health. In Massachusetts, town authorities intervened when host families treated their servants badly. Both Plymouth Colony and **Massachusetts Bay Colony** passed laws governing servants' moral and social behavior, with masters held responsible for violations. Servants had the right to take masters to court for violations of contract or for abusive behavior.

In some cases even well-to-do families sent their children off to live with other families to prevent parents from spoiling them. In the case of troubled families, local authorities often intervened, taking children away from their parents and indenturing them as servants with "good" families so that the children might be cared for and learn moral behavior. There were numerous cases of masters brought to court for abuses, particularly against women and children. For many servants, however, the system worked well. Since the **Puritans** and Pilgrims relied on the notion that one day these indentured servants would become full-fledged members of the community, many of the English settlers committed themselves to their equitable treatment. For the masters, indenturing also served a purpose as a labor source in the shorthanded colonies, where it was clearly preferable to slavery. (See also **Pilgrims and Plymouth Colony**)

The Ted Shawn Theatre at Jacob's Pillow. Photo by Jessica Wickham. Courtesy of Jacob's Pillow.

J

Jacob's Pillow

Jacob's Pillow in the **Berkshires** is one of America's best-known centers for innovative modern dance. Originally a farm on a hilltop in Becket, Jacob's Pillow was bought by the famed dancer Ted Shawn as a retreat in 1930. Shawn and his wife at that time, Ruth St. Denis, were pioneers in the movement to transform classical ballet into a more modern art form by infusing it with themes and styles drawn from folklore and popular tradition. Jacob's Pillow soon became one of the nation's centers for the new modern dance. During the year Shawn and his company would tour extensively, then spend the summer performing at the Pillow. Hard times in 1942 led Shawn to sell the farm to a new group, who formed the Jacob's Pillow Dance Festival Company, with Shawn as the director. The Ted Shawn Theater on the grounds was the first in the nation built especially for dance. Despite years of financial problems, and Shawn's death in 1972, Jacob's Pillow finally prospered, becoming one of the prime cultural attractions of the summer season in the Berkshires. It remains the oldest dance festival in America.

William James

Philosopher, psychologist, and Harvard professor, William James is known for originating the idea of "radical empiricism," or pragmatism, which became the major philosophical tool of reformers of the Progressive Era

(1890–1920). Born on January 11, 1842, in New York City, the son of a prosperous religious author, he was the brother of Henry James, who went on to become one of the greatest of American novelists.

Largely educated by private tutors, William James held no formal degrees until his late twenties. Originally he went to art school, then dropped out to study chemistry at Harvard University but never completed his degree. In 1864 he enrolled in Harvard Medical School, began writing essays on philosophy, again dropped out for a while, then returned and graduated in 1869. It was then that he began seriously to think about the contrast between religious beliefs and scientific truths, so-called. In 1874 he started teaching at Harvard, offering a course comparing physiology and psychology. He then moved into the philosophy department, where he spent his career as both professor of philosophy and professor of psychology until 1907, when he retired.

James published many important works throughout his career, beginning with *The Principles of Psychology,* published in 1890, which took him twelve years to write. It was very well received and became the standard text in the field for many years. His fascination with religion led to the publication in 1902 of *The Varieties of Religious Experience,* in which he analyzed abnormal psychological behavior among religious fanatics. In this popular work, he maintained that religious inspirations based on visions or hallucinations could be said to be true if the recipients altered their lives to follow the precepts presented by the vision. This finding marked the origin of his relativist notion of a truth that varies according to one's experience. From this came his philosophy of radical empiricism, James's answer to Herbert Spencer's deterministic social Darwinism. In *Pragmatism* (1907) James offered a theory of truth based on the commonsense notion that true ideas are those that work and false ideas those that do not. Philosopher John Dewey improved on this idea of functional truth in his notion of instrumentalism, in which methods that prove useful as solutions to problems are true ideas and those that do not are false ideas.

This commonsense reasoning became popular with progressive reformers who were searching for a means to refute the determinism of ideas such as laissez-faire, social Darwinism, and the negative state. With pragmatism as its credo, the state could now intervene in the economy to promote the general welfare instead of leaving matters to work themselves out in the free market. "Practical" political solutions became the watchword among a host of progressive reformers, who were contending with the abuses of an unregulated industrial system. Although most philosophers today shrink from

Jamesian concepts, his notion of the relativity of truth and his application of commonsense reasoning to everyday problems became the dominant popular political philosophy of the nation. James died in New Hampshire on August 26, 1910; he is buried in Cambridge.

The Kennedy family at their summer home in Hyannis Port, 1931. *Left to right:* Robert, John, Eunice, Jean, Joseph Sr., Rose, Patricia, Kathleen, Joseph Jr., and Rosemary. Courtesy of the John F. Kennedy Library, Boston.

K

Edward M. Kennedy

Without doubt the leading senator of his time, Edward M. Kennedy of Massachusetts stands amid the pantheon of the great U.S. senators of the twentieth century. Born on February 22, 1932, in Boston, he was the ninth and youngest child of the famous Kennedy clan, the children of **Joseph Kennedy Sr.** and Rose Fitzgerald Kennedy. He was only twelve in 1944 when two of his brothers became war heroes—John, who survived, and Joseph Jr., an airman killed in action. Ted Kennedy attended private schools, then went on to Harvard like his brothers. At college he became embroiled in the first of several personal failures that would taint his career when he cheated on a Spanish exam. When Harvard expelled him in 1951, he joined the army and served in the military police. After he left the service in 1953, he was readmitted to Harvard and graduated in 1956. His grades were not good enough for admission to Harvard Law School, so he followed his brother **Robert F. Kennedy** to the University of Virginia Law School in Charlottesville.

He entered politics in 1958 working for John's campaign for reelection to the Senate and continued in that capacity when John ran for the presidency in 1960. Both his father and his brother intended that young Ted would take over JFK's vacated Senate seat. The problem was that in 1960 Ted was under the required age of thirty. The Kennedys got Governor Foster Furcolo to appoint a Kennedy loyalist, Benjamin A. Smith, as interim senator until Ted could legally run in 1962. Since a prospective senator needed some political experience, the assistant district attorney for Suffolk County, **Kevin H. White** (later mayor of Boston), was forced to resign his position in 1961 to give Ted his first real political job. Ted Kennedy duly received the Democratic nomination for U.S. Senate in 1962 and won, defeating Republican George Cabot Lodge. The victory over the Yankee Lodge marked the complete ascendancy of the Kennedy family over Massachusetts politics.

What is surprising is that a Senate career launched by chicanery and backstage influence on behalf of a young man with little apparent talent should have become one of the most noteworthy in the history of the United States. Senator Kennedy kept growing in office, beginning as an advocate for civil rights and nuclear arms control, then going on to dominate the Senate as a leader for worthy causes, from fighting for the poor and disabled to working to end apartheid in South Africa. He succeeded in securing increases in the minimum wage and led the way in pushing the Family Leave Act through Congress. His many career highlights speak to his role as champion of universal health care and education reform.

Kennedy made a bid for the presidency in 1980, running for the Democratic nomination against the incumbent president, Jimmy Carter, but he gained little support. Throughout his long and productive career in the Senate he endured the tragedy of his two brothers' assassinations, serious injury in a plane crash, and further personal disgraces, including the notorious incident at Chappaquiddick and a serious drinking problem. Nonetheless, in the eyes of his constituents, and many of his colleagues as well, his substantive political contributions always outweighed these personal failures. For forty years he has remained one of the undisputed masters of the U.S. Senate. (See also **John F., Joseph,** and **Robert F. Kennedy**)

John F. Kennedy

John F. Kennedy was thirty-fifth president of the United States (1961–1963), the first and only Roman Catholic to reach that high office. Born on May 29, 1917, he was the son of multimillionaire and power broker **Joseph Kennedy Sr.** Educated at private schools, he went on to Harvard, graduating in 1940. The year before graduation he spent some time acting as his father's secretary when the elder Kennedy was ambassador to Great Britain. Joseph Kennedy Sr. had had presidential ambitions of his own, only to be thwarted by his isolationist stance in 1940. He then started to groom his eldest son, Joseph Jr., in his stead. But Joe Jr. was killed in the Second World War. **John F. Kennedy,** the next-eldest son, had served with distinction in the navy. His father now turned to him to enter the world of politics and fulfill his dream.

With his father's strong financial backing, John Kennedy won the race for a Boston congressional district in 1946, winning reelection in 1948 and 1950. Throughout, Kennedy suffered from a number of physical ailments, the most serious being Addison's disease, which were to impair his political performance. Though an indifferent legislator, on the strength of his father's support in 1952 he was able to win a U.S. Senate seat by defeating the incumbent Republican, **Henry Cabot Lodge Jr.** In 1958 he was reelected to the Senate, but by now he had set his eyes on the presidency. In 1960 he entered a series of tough primary challenges and won the nomination, even though a segment of the population mistrusted his Catholic background. In the contest against the Republican nominee, Vice President Richard M. Nixon, Kennedy played on cold war hysteria, suggesting that the Eisenhower administration had allowed the Soviet Union to make gains in the missile race, thus reducing the "missile gap" and weakening U.S. defense. This charge was untrue, but combined with his youth, sophistication, and patina of Hollywood glamour, it helped him win a narrow victory over Nixon.

An elegant speaker, and the author of two popular books, *Why England Slept* (1940) and *Profiles in Courage* (1956) (the latter now thought to have been ghostwritten), Kennedy galvanized Americans with his inaugural address. He went on to score only minor victories in his domestic program, including an ambiguous performance in the realm of civil rights. Foreign policy issues became paramount, first when he supported the ill-advised and abortive 1961 Bay of Pigs invasion of Castro's Cuba. After a failed summit meeting with Soviet leader Nikita Khrushchev that led to the erection of the Berlin Wall, Kennedy mobilized the army reserves, heightening cold war tensions even further. At the same time, Kennedy's strident anticommunism led to U.S. involvement in Southeast Asia and the deployment of over seventeen thousand American troops to Vietnam.

The most momentous event of his presidency was the Cuban Missile Crisis of October 1962, when the administration revealed that the USSR had put long-range missiles into Cuba, supposedly for defensive purposes. After setting up a naval blockade around Cuba, Kennedy made it clear that the United States would invade that island unless the Russians removed the missiles. The whole world watched anxiously until a chastened Khrushchev bent to U.S. will to avoid a nuclear war and removed the missiles, gaining Kennedy's promise not to invade Cuba again. Opinion is divided on Kennedy's performance, with many praising his skills at crisis management, while others suggest that he forced the Soviets to capitulate or else suffer nuclear destruction—an unwarranted and risky challenge.

On November 22, 1963, during a trip to Dallas in preparation for his reelection campaign, President Kennedy was assassinated by a gunman or gunmen, a horrific event still shrouded in mystery and controversy. While in death this young and handsome president remains popular with the media—as do his elegant widow, Jacqueline Kennedy Onassis, who died in 1994, and his son, John F. Kennedy Jr., who was killed five years later in a plane crash—some historians criticize JFK's undisciplined personal life and his inconclusive political achievements. (See also **Edward M., Joseph,** and **Robert F. Kennedy**)

Joseph Kennedy Sr.

Public official and multimillionaire businessman, Joseph P. Kennedy Sr. was the paternal power broker behind the political careers of his sons John, Robert, and Edward—the Kennedy clan. Born in Boston on September 16, 1888, he was the son of a Boston politician and ward boss. In spite of his humble lower-middle-class beginnings, he was able to attend Boston Latin and Harvard College. He then went on to become a successful banker, but found his way blocked by the moribund and inhibited Protestant Yankee establishment, who detested the Boston Irish. He became a major player on the New York Stock Exchange and relocated to that city, where he found no prejudicial barriers in banking or investments. He soon made millions, increasing his fortune by investing in Hollywood and the new field of motion pictures. His sense of timing was perfect when he sold his stocks just before the Great Crash of 1929; then he made enormous sums buying up stocks at bargain prices.

Politicians sought his financial backing, and he became a supporter of the presidential bid of Franklin D. Roosevelt. His early and generous aid to FDR resulted in Kennedy's appointment in 1934 as head of the newly created Securities and Exchange Commission, whose purpose was to regulate the stock market. Many were surprised at the appointment, for Kennedy's reputation was shady, but FDR supposedly remarked, "Set a thief to catch a thief." For a short while Kennedy served as chair of the U.S. Maritime

Commission. Then in 1937 FDR appointed him to the prestigious post of ambassador to Great Britain. For an Irish Catholic this was itself a great coup, but Kennedy envisioned himself as nothing less than president, as he waited patiently for the end of FDR's second term.

When the European war broke out in 1939, however, Kennedy revealed isolationist, even pro-German leanings, and he became known as an appeaser. This destroyed any hope he had for the presidency. Yielding to pressure, he resigned in 1940 and returned home under a dark cloud. Recognizing the impossibility of redeeming himself once the United States entered the war, he decided to promote the political career of his eldest son. These hopes died when Joseph Jr. perished in the war. He then set his sights on his second son, John, by now a naval hero, but also an undisciplined playboy. He supplied the funds and engineered his son's successful political rise from congressman to senator to president.

Once John was elected president, the father made sure that his next son, Robert, was appointed attorney general, and he successfully schemed to get his youngest son, Edward, elected to John's former Senate seat. The Kennedy clan by 1962 controlled the White House and held the strings in Massachusetts politics. In 1961 the elder Kennedy suffered a major stroke, but lived on through tragedy—the assassinations of his sons John and Robert—and the scandal at Chappaquiddick. He died November 18, 1969, in Hyannis, the founder of the twentieth century's most powerful political family. (See **Edward M., John F.,** and **Robert F. Kennedy**)

Robert F. Kennedy

A member of the famed Kennedy dynasty, Robert F. Kennedy was born in Brookline on November 20, 1925, the son of public figure and multimillionaire **Joseph Kennedy Sr.** and Rose Fitzgerald Kennedy. Like his two elder brothers, Joseph Jr. and John, he attended private schools and Harvard College, then entered the University of Virginia Law School, graduating in 1951. He worked for the U.S. Department of Justice, and served a stint as legal aide to Senator Joseph McCarthy of Red Scare fame. In 1952 he managed the successful senatorial campaign of his brother **John F. Kennedy** against incumbent **Henry Cabot Lodge Jr.** The next year he returned to senatorial subcommittee work, in 1957 becoming chief counsel for the Senate committee investigating racketeering. Again, he returned to politics, managing his brother's winning bid for the presidency during 1959 and 1960.

In 1961, now president, John Kennedy appointed Robert U.S. attorney general, in which post he had some success preventing the harassment of civil rights advocates and prosecuting criminal activities in the Teamsters Union. Throughout the Kennedy presidency he was his brother's closest adviser, and he played a key role in helping resolve the Cuban Missile Crisis of 1962. The assassination of his brother in 1963 was catastrophic for him, and he had great difficulty bringing himself to stay on in the new Lyndon B. Johnson administration. In 1964 he ran a successful campaign for senator from New York State. With two Kennedys, Edward and Robert, in the U.S. Senate, the family name became nationally prominent once again.

Up to this point Robert had based his career on political expediency, but like his brother **Edward M. Kennedy,** as senator he became increasingly engaged in the fight to help poor and working-class Americans and soon became known as a reformer and a fighter for civil rights. The growing unpopularity of the war in Vietnam galvanized Robert Kennedy and his followers to set his sights on the presidency. The 1968 announcement by President Johnson that he would not run again freed Kennedy to declare for that office. During his campaign, on June 5, 1968, the night of the California primary, he was murdered by a deranged assassin. Many believed that he would have won the presidency instead of Richard Nixon, and that he would have ended the war and ushered in a new era of social justice. Instead, his unfulfilled promise and the anguish of his assassination became part of the political mythology of the nation.

Jack Kerouac

Jack Kerouac was the leading figure of the Beat Generation of the 1950s. His writings about the quest for personal and spiritual freedom reached a large audience, particularly among the young, and he came to symbolize the unconventional life of the bohemian. Born in Lowell on March 12, 1922, he was the son of working-class French Canadian parents. He went to Lowell High School and received an athletic scholarship to Columbia University, but a football injury ended his career. After leaving school he worked at several jobs, reading voraciously all the while. He shipped out as a merchant seaman, served a short stint in the navy, and then reentered Columbia in 1944. There he met poet Alan Ginsberg, who introduced him to author William Burroughs—both of whom were involved in a world of radical lifestyles and innovative literary techniques.

Kerouac spent the next few years writing, wandering, and indulging his appetite for alcohol and drugs. It was Kerouac who invented the term "Beat Generation" for his world-weary companions who aspired to creativity through a mystical daze of drug-induced ruminations about the coming apocalypse. Between 1947 and 1950 he made a series of journeys back and forth across the nation with a new friend, author Neal Cassady. These became the basis for Kerouac's major novel, *On the Road* (1957), a collection of spontaneous improvisations that recall the riffing of jazz musicians. Like all his works, the novel eschewed plot and characters, focusing instead on words as symbols of human feelings.

Much of his written work was produced in the 1950s but was not published until after Kerouac achieved fame with *On the Road.* Becoming immersed in Buddhism, he published his vision of the faith in *Dharma Bums* in 1958, following up with a previously written work about his affair with a black woman, *The Subterraneans,* in the same year. Two more books came out in 1959, *Dr. Sax,* about his childhood, and a book of poems, *Mexican City Blues.* Although his alcoholism was worsening, he kept on writing, publishing another novel, *Big Sur,* about an alcoholic, which came out in 1962. He died of illness related to his drinking on October 21, 1969. Both Kerouac's life and his literary innovations spurred countless imitators, and he had a profound impact on modern literature.

King Philip's War

This colonial war between the English settlers and Native Americans began in June 1675 when a band of Wampanoag Indians attacked the village of Swansea in Plymouth Colony. This act violated the 1620 treaty between the Pilgrims and Chief **Massasoit** of the Wampanoags which had worked so successfully to maintain peace for over fifty years. It was Massasoit's son Metacom, or King Philip as the colonists called him, who broke the treaty and initiated hostilities over what he considered to be the Pilgrims' high-handedness, lack of respect, and continued encroachments on Indian lands. All these charges were true.

The event that triggered the war was the Pilgrims' execution of three Wampanoags for the murder of a Christian Indian, a violation of the treaty agreement that each side would punish its own transgressors. Metacom joined into an alliance with other disaffected tribes, the Narragansetts, Nipmucs, and Pocumtucks, while the **Puritans** in the **Massachusetts Bay Colony** joined with the **Pilgrims and Plymouth Colony.** Massive warfare erupted throughout both colonies.

In the early stages the Native alliance was quite formidable, its warriors attacking English settlements in what seemed an effort to oust the whites once and for all. But with their heavy firepower the settlers soon won several major battles. Late in the summer of 1676, Christian Indians recruited by the settlers helped turn the tide against the Natives. The colonists hunted down the scattered remnants of the Indian tribes, either killing them or sending them as prisoners into slavery. The war ended on August 12, 1675, when during an attack Metacom suffered bullet wounds that proved fatal.

The war resulted in the deaths of many colonists from wounds or disease and a tremendous loss in property, animals, and crops. The economic consequences of the war adversely affected the English settlements for years to come. The impact on the Natives was even more devastating: not only were many more Indians killed than English, but also the disruption of village life completely eliminated them as a significant presence in Massachusetts. Thus, deliberate warfare can be added to disease as one of the main causes for the marginalization of the Indians in New England. (See also **Praying Indians**)

Know-Nothings

In the late 1840s and early 1850s ever-increasing numbers of Irish Catholics were migrating to Massachusetts. In response, **anti-Catholicism** intensified to such a degree that Yankees everywhere began to organize politically to stave off this dreaded incursion. Alarmed nativists organized a national political party called the American Party, but more commonly known as the Know-Nothing Party. This was a grassroots movement whose members promised not to disclose any information about its organization, membership, activities, or rituals. When asked about such things members were supposed to respond, "I know nothing." By the mid-1850s, with the final collapse of the national Whig Party, this movement, largely dominated by the Yankee working and middle classes in coalition with a wide variety of splinter groups, had taken over every major political office in Massachusetts, including the governorship and much of the House and Senate. Once in office, in 1855 the Know-Nothings proceeded according to a rabid nativist agenda. They passed laws that removed Irish paupers and mental patients from state institutions and deported them to England. They disbanded the much-feared Irish militia units and confiscated their arms. The Know-Nothings reduced the role the state courts played in naturalization but failed in a constitutional attempt to pass a law that would have changed the residency requirement for naturalization from five to twenty-one years. They also ordered the daily reading of the Protestant Bible in the public schools. Finally, when a legislative committee created to inspect convents terrorized several Catholic orders, a serious political backlash occurred, contributing to the Know-Nothings' demise.

The party was nevertheless successful in passing a series of measures beneficial to the Yankee working classes—a strict temperance law, tax exemptions for homesteads, a law protecting mechanics from credit liens, abolition of debtor's prison—as well as reform measures forbidding state offcials to return **fugitive slaves** and desegregating the Boston school system. But by 1856 the attention of the nation had turned away from anti-Catholicism to a new, more disruptive issue: slavery in the territories. This burning question resulted in the coming together of a rising political force, the Republican Party, and the Know-Nothings disappeared from view as quickly as they had emerged. (See also **Broad Street Riot** and **Ursuline Convent Riot**)

The gates to Mount Holyoke College, South Hadley, founded by Mary Lyon. Courtesy of Mount Holyoke College.

L

Abbott Lawrence

Boston merchant, industrial investor, politician, and philanthropist, Abbott Lawrence was the principal founder of one of Boston's most prominent elite families. He epitomized those Boston merchants who advanced the industrial revolution in America by establishing interlocking directorates and horizontal monopolies to stabilize markets.

Born in Groton on December 16, 1792, into a farming family, he attended local schools and then went to work in the warehouse firm of his older brother, Amos. After being made a full-fledged partner in 1814, he soon began amassing a large fortune by importing English manufactured goods that had been scarce since the War of 1812. By 1831 the firm had begun to shift portions of its wealth from shipping into investments in the burgeoning textile industry. Joining the ranks of a small but powerful group of industrial innovators called the **Boston Associates,** Abbott Lawrence and his brother emerged as major figures in this new industry and its supporting industries of banking and railroads.

That same year he began a political career, serving first on the Boston Common Council, and then in 1834 and 1838 as a representative in Congress. A leading member of the Whig Party, he favored legislation that benefited his class. He was crucial to the creation of a new industrial center, appropriately named Lawrence in 1845, that was to be a leader in textile manufacturing for many years. From 1849 to 1852 he was U.S. minister to Great Britain. Lawrence died on August 18, 1855, in Boston. Throughout his life he donated money to agencies that supported his elite views, especially **Harvard University.** His efforts in politics and philanthropy were part of his design to gain increased influence over a society undergoing a wrenching transformation from rural to urban.

Lexington and Concord

The gunfire at Lexington and Concord on April 19, 1775, the "shot heard round the world," set in motion a momentous political revolution that transformed not just the colonies but future generations across the globe.

The British response to the **Boston Tea Party** of 1773 had put an end to any possibility of compromises in England's dealings with its Massachusetts colony. The **Coercive Acts,** which included the Massachusetts Government Act, and the Quartering Act of 1774, stripped Boston and Massachusetts of their long-held political rights, created economic havoc by closing the port of Boston, and eroded personal freedoms by bringing in an army of occupation. Throughout Massachusetts infuriated colonists convened to declare their resistance to this British despotism. The result was the formation of a new quasi-government for the colony, which transformed the General Court into a Provincial Congress.

The Congress declared a boycott of British goods and then sought agreement and support from the other colonies. Besides declaring principles that nullified the Massachusetts Government Act and proclaiming their rights as Englishmen, members of the Provincial Congress called for the activation and arming of town militias. Towns were to gather and store military supplies for defensive purposes. The new intercolonial Continental Congress which met in Philadelphia announced its support for these actions.

With the British army occupying Boston, the army commander and now governor, Thomas Gage, thought it prudent to cut off military supplies to the resisting colonists. On April 18, 1775, he ordered a military expedition to Concord to search for and destroy such weapons. Patriot riders, including **Paul Revere,** set out to warn the militia men, now called **Minute Men.** The next day, April 19, British soldiers came upon a militia company at Lexington and opened fire, killing eight. Another skirmish broke out later that day in Concord, at the North Bridge, where the patriots forced the British to retreat. The British nevertheless managed to destroy some supplies before they marched back to Boston, continually under attack by the Minute Men along the way. By the time the British reached Boston, 247 redcoats and 93 militia men lay dead or wounded. Thousands of Minute Men arrived from all over the colony and soon surrounded General Gage and his forces in Boston. The Revolution had begun. (See also **Bunker Hill and Monument**)

Liberator (See **William Lloyd Garrison**)

Liberty Tree (See **Stamp Act**)

Little Women (See **Louisa May Alcott**)

Henry Cabot Lodge Jr.

Henry Cabot Lodge Jr. was a senator and diplomat, scion of a powerful Republican elite family that personified the values of Massachusetts's Yankee upper class. Born in Nahant on July 5, 1902, he was the son of George Cabot Lodge, a poet, and grandson of U.S. Senator Henry Cabot Lodge (thus he was called Jr.). He went to school in France and then graduated from Harvard in 1924. At first he spent some time working as a newspaperman until in 1933, like his grandfather, he won election to the Massachusetts House of Representatives. Three years later he was elected to the U.S. Senate.

Lodge was one of the new Republicans who eschewed their party's rigid conservative positions in favor of a more moderate stance that succeeded in drawing support from a wide range of people, including ethnic Democrats. Though reelected in 1942, he left office to serve in the war, and emerged a highly decorated officer. He ran again in 1946 against long-term Democratic senator David I. Walsh and won, becoming a key player in Dwight D. Eisenhower's campaign for the Republican presidential nomination in 1952. Believing that he could easily defeat the Irish Catholic newcomer, **John F. Kennedy,** who was challenging him, Lodge spent little time on his own reelection campaign. Eisenhower won the nomination and the presidency, but Lodge lost his race to the brilliant campaign strategy of Kennedy and his father, **Joseph Kennedy Sr.**

Eisenhower rewarded Lodge for his loyalty by appointing him ambassador to the United Nations, where he served until 1960. That year he ran for the vice presidency on Richard M. Nixon's Republican ticket, once again losing to Kennedy. Interested in promoting a bipartisan foreign policy, President Kennedy appointed his erstwhile rival to the critical position of ambassador to Vietnam. Lodge served there until 1964, returning when reappointed by another Democratic president, Lyndon B. Johnson, whom he supported in the disastrous program of escalating the war. In 1968–69 Lodge served as ambassador to Germany, and then for a short time he headed the unsuccessful peace negotiations with the Vietnamese. Between 1970 and 1977 he was a special envoy for diplomatic missions under President Nixon and his successor, Gerald Ford. Symbol of an earlier bipartisan era of American foreign policy, Lodge retired to Beverly to write his memoirs and died there on February 27, 1985. (See also **Henry Cabot Lodge Sr.**)

Henry Cabot Lodge Sr.

Henry Cabot Lodge Sr. was a long-term senator from Massachusetts, an imperialist, supporter of **immigration** restriction, and an opponent of Woodrow Wilson's Treaty of Versailles. He was a staunch defender of Republican conservatism and Yankee Protestant superiority. Born in Boston on May 12, 1850, he was the son of a wealthy merchant. Educated at private schools, he graduated from Harvard in 1871. Torn about what to do next, he took a law degree (1874) and then a Ph.D. in history (1876), both from Harvard. He published his dissertation, *Anglo-Saxon Law,* in 1879, worked as an editor for the *North American Review,* and then became an instructor at Harvard, teaching American history. Lodge became a prolific historical author, writing several biographies of famous American politicians.

As a Republican, he served for a short while in the Massachusetts state legislature in 1878 and worked on political campaigns for other Republicans, but he was generally unsuccessful in seeking office for himself. Finally, in 1886, after a previous loss, he won election to the U.S. Congress and served until 1893. In that year the Massachusetts legislature appointed him U.S. senator, a post in which he remained for the rest of his life. Although he was a hard-line conservative on domestic issues, in foreign affairs he agreed with his friend Theodore Roosevelt on the need for the United States to become an engaged imperial power. Lodge took a leadership role in **immigration** restriction, fearing that the new immigrants from eastern Europe would "defile" the Anglo-Saxon race.

The 1912 victory of Democrat Woodrow Wilson, a rival historian (from Princeton) and a progressive reformer, infuriated Lodge. In 1916, with the passage of the Seventeenth Amendment, making U.S. senator an elected rather than appointed office, the voters of Massachusetts made Lodge their first popularly elected senator. Lodge's hatred of Wilson found an outlet when he vowed to defeat the Treaty of Versailles and the League of Nations proposal, which the president had brought to the Senate for ratification. Lodge's policy of obstruction was predicated on his determination not to allow Wilson and the Democrats to take credit for the League, as that might prevent Republicans from winning back the presidency in 1920.

As head of the Senate Foreign Relations Committee, Lodge appended fourteen reservations to the peace treaty in a symbolic refutation of Wilson's own Fourteen Points. Wilson, who also hated Lodge personally, turned ratification into a partisan issue, hoping to run for reelection in 1920 on the League platform. Both men allowed their personal distaste and political ambitions to overcome the best interests of the nation. The Senate failed to ratify the treaty, and a Republican, Warren G. Harding, won the presidency in 1920. Lodge took virtual control over American foreign policy in his role as chairman of the Foreign Relations Committee. He won reelection in 1922, though only narrowly because of his opposition to the League. His last achievement was to help create and shepherd through the Senate the Washington Disarmament Treaty of 1922. He died in Boston on November 9, 1924.

Martin Lomasney

Martin M. Lomasney (nicknamed "Mahatma") was a Boston politician and ward boss who personified the personal politics of Boston's Irish Americans. He championed the needs of the working classes—the Irish first and then the other ethnics. He saw nothing wrong with using politics as a ladder of social mobility, and patronage was his prime tool in carving out a powerful constituency. Born in Boston on December 3, 1859, he was the son of immigrants who had fled Ireland in the Great Famine. He went no further than elementary school, but became a major political force in the gritty local politics of the day. He learned his trade at the hands of another boss and worked his way up through the hierarchy to become boss of Ward 8, Boston's immigrant West End, by the 1880s.

Being a boss meant that Lomasney controlled the majority of votes in his ward, and he could swing those votes to any candidate at will. He was smarter and more adept than the other city bosses, and he ruled with an iron hand. He organized a political club where he promoted a network of ward workers ("heelers") whose task it was to list every voter and potential voter and get them out on election day. His absolute control over the votes in his ward made him a powerful broker among other bosses, including **John Fitzgerald** and **James Michael Curley.**

Taking advantage of his political position, Lomasney enriched himself, particularly in the realm of real estate investments. He occasionally sought office himself, serving on the Boston Board of Aldermen (1893–1895) and two terms in the Massachusetts Senate (1897–98), and he was in and out of the Massachusetts House of Representatives over a thirty-year period. He died in Boston on August 12, 1933.

Long Wharf

Boston merchants built the Long Wharf at the foot of King (now State) Street in 1710. One historian has called it "a dramatic road to the sea." The project required extending the street into the cove and well into Boston Harbor. The wharf was then lined with shops and warehouses, which for the first time permitted direct loading and unloading of large ships. Previously, cargo ships had to drop anchor in the harbor and wait to be unloaded by small boats, a time-consuming and laborious task. The wharf promoted efficiency in the port and increased the volume of imports and exports, enriching maritime traders and providing higher wages and more jobs for a host of port workers. The famed Bonner Map of 1722 depicts the Long Wharf as a finger jutting out into the sea, beckoning ships toward Boston Harbor, the epitome of maritime prosperity.

Henry Wadsworth Longfellow

Henry Wadsworth Longfellow, like **Emily Dickinson** and **Robert Frost,** stands out in the pantheon of American poets whose verse, such as his "Midnight Ride of Paul Revere," has been memorized by generations of schoolchildren and is well known to a large number of Americans. Born in Portland, Maine (still part of Massachusetts at the time), on February 27, 1807, he was the son of a lawyer and legislator. In 1825 he graduated from Bowdoin College alongside his friend **Nathaniel Hawthorne.** After traveling abroad, he returned to Bowdoin to teach modern languages (1829–1835). While there he started publishing scholarly works, and in 1834 he accepted a position at Harvard University as professor of French and Spanish. After more travel in Europe, he ensconced himself at Craigie House on Brattle Street in Cambridge in 1836, where he lived until his death.

In addition to teaching, he now began writing in earnest, first a novel, *Hyperion* (1839), and then several books of poetry, *Voices of the Night* (1839), *Ballads and Other Poems* (1841), and the abolitionist *Poems on Slavery* (1842). After the death of his first wife, he was married for the second time, to **Nathan Appleton**'s daughter Fannie. The wealthy Appleton purchased Craigie House for the couple as a wedding gift. With his fortune secured, Longfellow resigned from Harvard in 1845 to devote himself full-time to writing.

His long career produced many books, poems, and translations. The most noteworthy of his verse epics were *Evangeline: A Tale of Acadie* (1847), about the plight of French Canadians forced to migrate from their homes; the Indian tale *Song of Hiawatha* (1855); and the well-known story of unrequited love, *The Courtship of Miles Standish* (1858). After many years of literary output, he died in Cambridge on March 24, 1882, America's most popular poet. His home is now a national historic site.

Amy Lowell

Amy Lowell daughter of the Boston Brahmin family of Lowells, was a poet and critic, a pioneer in developing a new feminist poetry. Her father was a prominent businessman, her uncle A. Lawrence Lowell went on to become president of **Harvard University,** and her cousin **James Russell Lowell** was also a well-known poet. Born in Brookline on February 9, 1874, educated by tutors and in private schools, she also traveled extensively in Europe. She demonstrated her literary ambitions at age thirteen when her mother supplied the funds to publish two of her short stories. Lowell was an avid learner and book collector, and in this respect was very different from the typical upper-class Boston debutante.

At the age of twenty-eight she decided to become a poet. The *Atlantic*

Monthly printed four of her poems in 1910, and in 1912 she published her first book of verse. The critics savaged it, calling her poetry "lifeless" and lacking in emotion. She expanded her emotional range when she began a relationship that year with another woman in what was then called a "Boston marriage." This attachment lasted throughout her life, and gave birth to a period of poetic outpourings after 1914. Soon her poems began to be well received, and further books of poetry and criticism increased her fame. She published at least a book a year until her death on May 12, 1925, and was posthumously awarded the Pulitzer Prize for poetry in 1926.

Francis Cabot Lowell

If one person could be called the founder of the industrial revolution in the United States, it would be Francis Cabot Lowell, merchant and textile manufacturer, who left a legacy that would transform the United States from a rural to an urban society. Born in Newburyport on April 7, 1775, he was the son of a judge. After graduating from Harvard College in 1793, he became involved in the merchant trade. Though prosperous, Lowell worried about the "hazards" of investing in cargo carried in fragile sailing vessels that spanned the globe. While in England in 1810, he toured British textile factories, in the process closely observing the workings of the Cartwright power loom. He decided that the time was ripe for diversification of his investments into textile manufacturing, which would enable him to avoid the risks of the maritime trade.

Lowell developed a plan to create a single factory that would house all the various processes required to turn raw cotton into finished cloth. Putting together the necessary capital from his own money, that of his brother-in-law Patrick T. Jackson, and other Boston merchants, he created a new industry that would act as the catalyst for the industrialization and urbanization of Massachusetts. These investors, the **Boston Associates,** organized the Boston Manufacturing Company in 1813, using a loom based on Lowell's recollection of the Cartwright prototype, at a site six miles west of Boston on the Charles River in Waltham. The mill, which opened in 1815, was the world's first to use water-powered looms to turn raw cotton into finished goods all under one roof. This was the beginning of the mass production system, heralding the coming of the industrial revolution to America.

Lowell's health had always been precarious, and he died at the relatively early age of forty-two in Boston on August 10, 1817, without seeing his dream of an industrial empire come to fruition. The Boston Associates showed their respect when, in 1826, they built a new mill town at the Pawtucket Falls in northeast Chelmsford and named it Lowell. (See also **Nathan Appleton**)

James Russell Lowell

James Russell Lowell was a diplomat as well as a poet and author whose literary works give a valuable impression of nineteenth-century American life. Born in Cambridge on February 22, 1819, he was the son of a Congregational minister of little means. His family had only a distant connection to the rich merchant-industrial Lowells. He attended Harvard, where lack of interest in his studies and his taste for pranks led to his suspension, though he finally graduated in 1838. To support himself and his family, he decided to go into the law, graduating from Harvard Law School in 1840.

Unhappy as a lawyer, he began to publish his poems in a variety of periodicals, and received instant acclaim. Popular books of his verse appeared in 1841, 1844, and 1848, with critics promoting his reputation as one of America's leading lyric poets. He also became caught up in the antislavery movement and joined the ranks of the **abolitionists,** writing and lecturing for the cause. His most famous work was the humorous *Bigelow Papers* (1848), a satire on the bureaucratic bumbling that occurred during the Mexican War of 1846. While continuing with his poetry, he wrote literary criticism as well.

In 1855 Harvard University offered him the chair in modern literature once held by **Henry Wadsworth Longfellow.** Lowell went on to become editor of the *Atlantic Monthly* in 1857, a role that put him in a unique position to comment on American literature. In 1864 he became co-editor of the *North American Review,* another prestigious literary journal. Lowell wrote an impressive array of prose and poetry during these years, though none survived to interest future generations. He was an early and ardent supporter of the Republican Party, and in 1877 President Rutherford B. Hayes rewarded him, first with an appointment as minister to Spain, then in 1880 naming him minister to Great Britain, a post he held until 1885. He died in Cambridge on August 12, 1891.

Robert Lowell

A descendant of one of Massachusetts's most prestigious families, Robert Lowell was a well-known poet, noted for his controversial subject matter. Born in Boston on March 1, 1917, the son of a naval engineer, he rebelled against his heritage of privilege, writing vitriolic poems denouncing the Lowell family for using its elite position to exploit the downtrodden. Educated at private schools in Boston, he went on to Harvard but dropped out after two years in 1935. He then rejected New England altogether and set out to find himself elsewhere.

Lowell went south and became a disciple of the poet Allen Tate, who helped the young man channel his talents. Through Tate's influence he met other regional poets—John Crowe Ransom and Randall Jarrell—all the while expanding his poetic talent. He became a student of Ransom's at Kenyon College in Ohio, graduating with honors in 1940. Lowell underwent a religious conversion and became a Catholic. As a conscientious objector in World War II, he spent five months in prison. He privately published his first book of poems in 1944. Public recognition first came in 1946 when his book of verse *Lord Weary's Castle* earned him the Pulitzer Prize. Another book of poems came out in 1951, *The Mills of the Kavanaughs,* but after that he suffered personal problems and a bout of mental illness and stopped publishing.

His battle with manic depression would continue for the rest of his life. Lowell resumed writing in 1959 with *Life Studies,* winner of the National Book Award the following year. Another well-received work was *For the Union Dead* (1964), which contains the famous poem of that name. In the 1960s he became a prominent opponent of the Vietnam War. Other volumes of poetry and prose followed. He died in New York City on September 12, 1977, just after the appearance of his final book of poetry, *Day by Day,* premised on his comparison of the mad King George III with President Richard Nixon. The troubled yet charismatic Lowell retains his reputation as a major contributor to twentieth-century American literature.

Lowell Offering

A women workers' periodical, the *Lowell Offering* first came out in 1840 and continued publication until 1845. Its purpose was to demonstrate that mill work was not degrading, and that workers not only were content but also

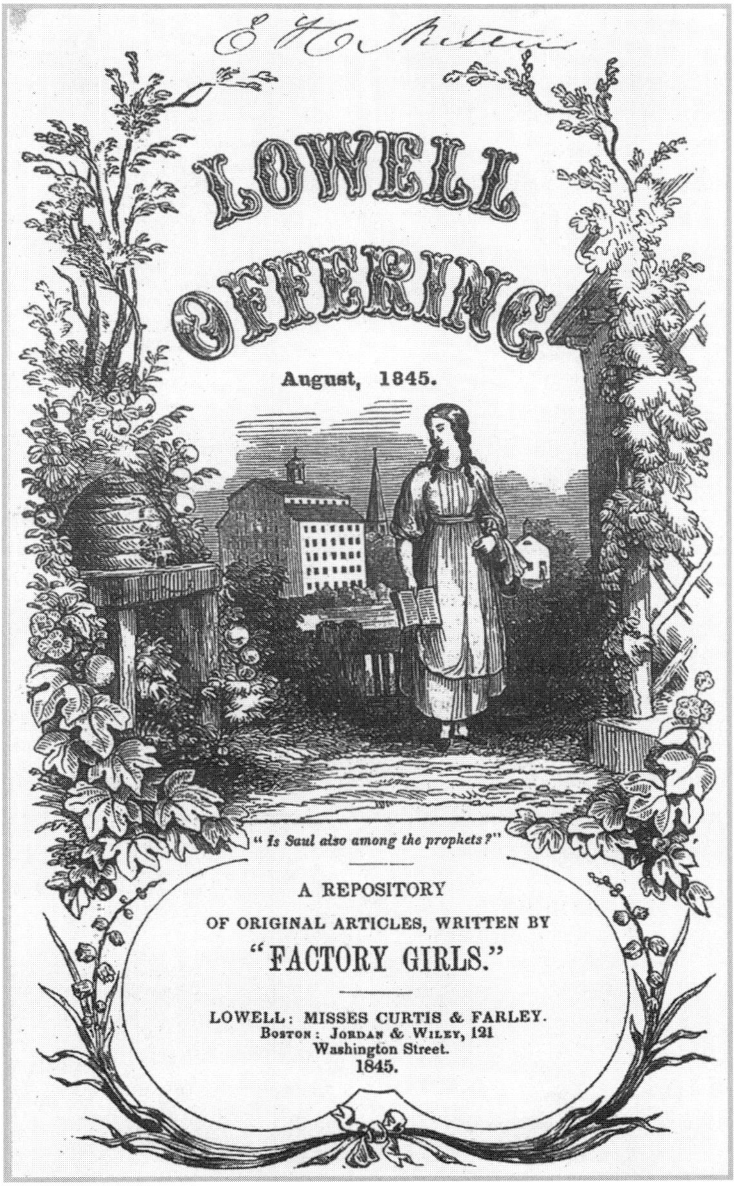

A cover from the *Lowell Offering,* 1845. Courtesy of the University of Massachusetts Lowell Center for Lowell History.

had the leisure to engage in creative activities. Female mill workers produced articles and sketches depicting the good life in the mills of Lowell. The owners supported the publication, which was edited by a carefully selected local minister. Other mill towns followed suit with their own periodicals, but none were as famous as the *Lowell Offering,* which drew attention as far away as England and the Continent.

As a corporation-sponsored journal, the publication avoided articles about controversial issues such as arbitrary pay cuts, production speed-ups, and debilitating and unsafe working conditions, focusing instead on depicting the spiritual and moral uplift gained by the factory workers under the paternal guidance of the owners. A transparent propaganda organ, the journal served to justify the exploitation of workers by conscience-stricken corporations. Even before the demise of the *Lowell Offering,* workers began to publish periodicals that provided more realistic views of factory life in New England. They further demonstrated their discontent by organizing into worker associations, the first unions, such as the 1845 Female Labor Association of Lowell. (See **Sarah Bagley** and **Harriet Hanson Robinson**)

Lynn Shoemakers' Strike of 1860

The nation's largest pre–Civil War strike was the Lynn shoemakers' strike of 1860. Both the introduction of sewing machines and the depression of 1857–59 sorely affected skilled shoe workers, such as binders. Household production was changing over to factory production, and the result was lower wages and the de-skilling of workers. The strike enveloped the Merrimack Valley of Massachusetts and New Hampshire, with more than twenty thousand men and women workers leaving their jobs in protest over reduced wages.

At first the strikers employed parades and demonstrations to win over community support. But the manufacturers would not budge, continuing production with the widespread use of strikebreakers. Finally, when strikers in Lynn spied cases of raw materials being sent by railroad to outworkers, they reacted violently, destroying the shipments and then taking on police who tried to protect the cases. At first the police were overpowered, but reinforcements from other cities and the state militia soon repelled the strikers, who were forced to yield. The financial staying power of the manufacturers and the institutional force of the police and militia finally broke the strike and defeated the shoemakers.

Detail from a portrait of Mary Lyon by Joseph Goodhue Chandler (1813–1884), oil on canvas. Mount Holyoke College Art Museum, South Hadley.

Mary Lyon

Mary Lyon was an educator and the founder of America's first women's college, Mount Holyoke. One of the pioneering woman activists of the nineteenth century, she helped set the stage for twentieth-century advances in the equality of women. Born on February 28, 1797, the daughter of a farm family, she became a teacher in 1814 in rural Shelburne Falls. She continued teaching while at the same time attending various academies to advance her education. She entered a seminary in 1821, became a member of the Congregational Church, and discovered that she could combine her commitment to her faith with her interest in education. She continued teaching, opened her own school for a while, and then worked in several female academies.

Devoted to the notion of training Christian female teachers, Lyon prepared to found her own female educational seminary. She spent years fundraising, finally succeeding in 1837 with the opening of Mount Holyoke Female Seminary in South Hadley. The small school grew steadily and attracted talented and ambitious young women from everywhere in the nation, eventually becoming Mount Holyoke College. After twelve years of leadership, Lyon died on March 5, 1849. Unlike several other of the elite Seven Sisters, Mount Holyoke has resisted the trend toward coeducation and remains a center of excellence in higher education for women, continuing to carry out Mary Lyon's vision.

Contemporary artwork by Matthew Ritchie at MASS MoCA, North Adams.
Courtesy of MASS MoCA.

M

Horace Mann

Horace Mann was an educator and politician generally considered to be the founder of the movement for a mandatory public education for all children. His striving for a free and universal education, backed by government, earned him the apt title of "father of the American public school." Born on May 4, 1796, he was the son of a farming family. Without a formal education, he prepared himself for admission to Brown University in 1816, graduating first in his class three years later. He studied law, then set up a practice in Dedham after passing the bar in 1823. He invested in textile mills, then went into politics and was elected to the Massachusetts House of Representatives in 1827. There he joined the ranks of social reformers espousing penal reform and improved conditions for the mentally ill. He moved to Boston and as a member of the Whig Party won a state Senate seat in 1834. The following year his colleagues voted him Senate president.

He used his position to push for passage of the State Education Act of 1837. The legislation called for the creation of a state board of education presided over by a secretary but lacking a budget and any real power. Nonetheless, Mann, determined that this position would be the catalyst for educational reform, resigned his Senate seat to become the state's new secretary of education. The public school system was in a shambles, lacking financial support from either the state or the towns and cities. Mann believed that access to public education was the key to maintaining a democratic republic. He strove to promote a system that would provide all children with a chance for social mobility, including the growing number of immigrant children entering the state.

Mann gathered information and traveled around the state promoting his reform agenda. He emphasized the need for improved teacher training, and with his own money and charitable donations, matched by the state, he established three normal schools for that purpose. He persuaded the state to provide funding to improve school buildings, to lengthen the term of the school year, to increase teacher salaries, and to open new schools.

In 1848 he resigned as education secretary to begin a new career as a U.S. congressman. He served until 1852, when he ran for governor on the Free Soil Party ticket, but lost. The year 1853 was a turning point in his life, as he accepted an offer to become the president of the nonsectarian, coeducational Antioch College in Yellow Springs, Ohio. There, Mann turned his attention to private higher education, reforming Antioch's curriculum, starting a teacher training program, and introducing a new system of elective courses. He died in office on August 2, 1859.

Rocky Marciano

Rocco Marchegiano, or Rocky Marciano, was the undefeated heavyweight champion of the world. Born in Brockton on September 1, 1923, he was the son of Italian immigrant factory workers. He excelled in athletics but never graduated from high school. During World War II he served in the army, and it was then that he took up boxing. He began as an amateur, then turned professional in 1948, though experts claimed he was too old, too short, and too light to be a winner. While training to become an expert boxer, he worked as a common laborer. Finally, by dint of long preparation, hard work, and a crushing right cross, he started moving up the ladder in his sport.

He became a real contender in 1951 when he knocked out former champ Joe Louis. Marciano earned his first championship shot against Jersey Joe Walcott in 1952, and knocked out the champ after a grueling thirteen rounds. In a rematch in 1953, he knocked Walcott out in the first round. He then went on to beat former champion Ezzard Charles twice, and in his final bout defeated challenger Archie Moore in 1955. He retired a millionaire in 1956. Marciano ended his career with a record of 49 and 0, the only undefeated world heavyweight champion of the twentieth century. This hard-hitting slugger and second-generation Italian American workingman died in a plane crash on August 31, 1969.

Martha's Vineyard (See **Cape Cod and the Islands**)

Massachusetts Bay Colony

In 1630 English **Puritans** established a settlement in Massachusetts that was both a commercial and a religious venture. The Puritans were a Protestant group who believed that the established Church of England was impure and that English society was essentially sinful. They hoped that in the New World they would be free from interference by the English church and state and able to live according to their own religious views. Called Puritans because they claimed that theirs was a purer religion stripped of church ritual and hierarchy, they believed themselves to be predestined for salvation, and they sought to act according to God's will as revealed by the Bible. Religious freedom was not their only reason for emigrating; they were also victimized by the economic hard times that ravaged England in the late 1620s. Thus, by establishing a settlement in New England, they sought to improve their economic condition while creating a more perfect society.

Their vehicle for accomplishing their goal was the creation of an incorporated joint-stock company, the Massachusetts Bay Company, founded on May 4, 1629. Although it was ostensibly a trading company, control was quickly taken over by a small group of Puritans led by **John Winthrop,** elected governor of the corporation in October of that year. The leaders decided to take the royal charter granted their company to the New World and use it as a basis for creating a self-governing Puritan state.

The emigrants embarked on March 22, 1630, and reached Salem on July 12. Displeased with conditions there, they looked further, finally settling on the Charlestown Peninsula, which separated the Charles and Mystic rivers. When disease broke out the settlers dispersed, and by September there were seven different settlements. Winthrop led his followers to the Shawmut Peninsula to a place they named Boston. Within a month the town had over 150 inhabitants with a church and a center of government.

The Massachusetts Bay Colony produced no staple crop in demand in England, and this allowed for decades of noninterference and self-rule by the Puritan settlers. In fact, the area was unsuitable for an agricultural community, being only two miles long and one mile wide, dominated by three hills, with insufficient timber for fuel and building. Although there was plentiful fresh water, the settlers eventually realized that there was not enough land for crops, so they set up farms in adjacent areas while they kept their homes in Boston. The first winter of settlement was a hard one with many deaths. New settlers arrived constantly, however, replenishing the population. From 200 people in 1631, Boston grew to 575 by 1635. But its prime location on Boston Harbor quickly took on the greatest significance, as the town soon became the main port serving all marine traffic in the area. Notions of an agricultural community soon faded with the growing reality of commercial prosperity.

During these early days the Puritans worried about English intervention. They worked diligently to maintain control over all aspects of life in the colony, expelling those with incompatible religious views and keeping a tight rein on government in order to protect their community. They maintained a strict moral code with a long list of penalties for "immorality, debt, trespass, breach of contract, slander, assault, swearing and Blasphemy," as well as adultery and sodomy, drunkenness, and a host of other infractions punishable by fines, whipping, confinement to stocks, banishment, even death.

One of the major contributions of the Puritans was the establishment of a government that was the model in embryo for future democratic government. The Puritans, however, did not believe in democracy as we understand it and had no intention of creating a community ruled by the "consent of the governed." They did believe that the elect, whom they called "saints," should rule the society since they were manifestly following God's will. Originally the company charter gave the stockholders or "freemen" the right to make all company decisions. As church members, they were to make laws for the colony, to be carried out by the governor, the deputy governor, and assistants and deputies elected by the freemen. Governor Winthrop and other officials called the first meeting of the government in Charlestown in 1630.

This assembly, called the Great and General Court, included the entire population of the colony. By a vote of all present, the assistants were transformed from an executive council into a legislative assembly, and all freemen were declared citizens of the colony, with the right to vote and hold office. Citizen freemen would then elect lawmakers, who would elect the governor and deputy governor. A constitution was created, and at the next meeting the General Court admitted 116 people as freemen—a large portion of the adult male population of the colony. Freemen had to be church members; those who did not belong to the church could not vote or hold office. Despite the religious limitation, the constitution granted more political rights than citizens enjoyed in England.

By the 1640s trade had begun to take hold, and the resulting intercourse with the world affected the purity of Puritan beliefs and ideals. As the colony prospered, more and more settlers arrived who were not church members and thus were not entitled to the rights of citizenship. The rise of merchant fortunes led to a growing secularism and a belief that perhaps the elect were not merely those who knew the Bible but also those whose great wealth must have been evidence of God's will. Because of the increasing demands of new arrivals and the fear that their own children might not be among the elect, the Puritans modified their views in 1662 with the **Half-Way Covenant,** which allowed membership in the church for people who could not meet the full requirements, particularly proof of conversion.

After years of indifference, in 1684 the Crown turned its attention to the colony and ended the Puritan polity by revoking the charter. In its place Parliament established a **royal colony** in 1692. Property replaced church membership as the criterion for citizenship. The religious experiment was over, but not before the Puritans had established a legacy that would in later years bear fruit in the concept of individual freedom. (See also **Massachusetts Constitution** and **Pilgrims and Plymouth Colony**)

Massachusetts Bay Transportation Authority (MBTA)

The Massachusetts Bay Transportation Authority, known as the "T," is the major transportation system connecting Boston and its metropolitan area, comprising some seventy-nine cities and towns. There are sixty-four miles of trolley and subway lines as well as over a thousand miles of commuter rail and bus lines. The MBTA has a daily ridership of over 1 million people. The authority derives its power from the state legislature and supports its operations through fares, a state subsidy, and assessments of the communities it serves.

The MBTA originated in the tangled electric trolley system of late-nineteenth-century Boston which congested the downtown. To ease the crowding, the Boston Transportation Corporation opened the nation's first subway, running from Tremont Street to Boylston Street, a distance of six-tenths of a mile, on September 1, 1897. The BTC transferred the responsibility of operating the subway to a private company, the Boston Elevated Railway Company. Years of losses plus steady expansion, and the need for more, led the state legislature to take over the transportation system by creating the Metropolitan Transit Authority (MTA) in 1947. Future expansions of service as a result of suburban growth led to the change of name to Massachusetts Bay Transportation Authority in 1964.

Massachusetts Constitution

John Adams, with the collaboration of **Sam Adams** and James Bowdoin, drafted a state constitution in 1780 at a special convention in Cambridge establishing the Commonwealth of Massachusetts. The document setting up a state government was inspired by the same ideas that had brought about the American Revolution, premised on the notion of rule by consent of the governed. Called a "social compact," it gave evidence of the long history of self-government in Massachusetts and the principle of upholding the common good that originated with the **Mayflower Compact** of the Pilgrims.

Valuing the principle of common action, the document declared that the "Common Wealth" would "be one connected system having but one common interest, and one public will." The centerpiece of the constitution was a bill of rights establishing such freedoms for the individual as "the security of his person and property," free speech, free press, the right of assembly, and the right to bear arms. All power "resided with the people." To embody this power, the constitution established a two-house legislature, a judiciary, and an executive government. The cautious authors, however, fearful of the excesses of democracy, restricted voting to property owners only, and called for public support of Protestant churches. As the years went by, further constitutional conventions broadened suffrage rights and divorced the state from favoring any single religion. The Massachusetts constitution is the oldest state constitution in the nation still in use.

Massachusetts Historical Society

Established in 1799, the Massachusetts Historical Society on Boylston Street in the Fenway in Boston is America's oldest. It houses a large manuscript collection covering centuries of Massachusetts history. After operating at several different locations for a century, it moved to its permanent home in 1899. From its beginnings it has been a place where Boston's elite preserved their papers and artifacts in order to demonstrate their distinguished genealogy and their many achievements. Over three thousand manuscript collections are maintained there now, including those of the Adams family and other Massachusetts notables. Numerous books, maps, newspapers, engravings, and photos constitute a rich assemblage of American historical documents from colonial times to the modern era. In addition, the MHS sponsors publications, conferences, lectures, seminars, and research grants for scholars.

Massasoit

Massasoit was the leader of the Wampanoag tribe, whose peace treaty with the Pilgrims helped promote a permanent English settlement in Massachusetts. Little is known about his life. Probably born in 1600, he died sometime in 1661. In 1621 **Squanto,** a Patuxet friendly to the **Pilgrims and Plymouth Colony,** introduced them to Massasoit, leader of the largest nearby tribe. It was Squanto's diplomacy that resulted in a treaty that pledged peaceful coexistence between the two disparate groups. Massasoit participated in the Pilgrims' first thanksgiving celebration feast in December 1621. Despite the depredations caused by smallpox, Massasoit's people flourished in their relations with the Pilgrims, particularly because of an advantageous trade alliance and a military alliance against warlike neighboring tribes that threatened Wampanoags and Pilgrims alike.

On many occasions Massasoit became an important mediator between hostile tribes and the Pilgrims, helping to defuse many difficult situations. Because of their good relations with the Pilgrims, his tribe was spared the devastation wrought by the **Pequot War** of 1636. Massasoit also established friendly relations with the **Puritans** of the **Massachusetts Bay Colony,** furthering trade and prosperity for his tribe. After his death in 1661, however, one of his sons, Metacom—or King Philip, as he was known—became the archfoe of the English settlers, launching a war against them in 1676 which led to the decimation of the Wampanoag Indians as a significant presence in the colony. (See also **King Philip's War**)

MASS MoCA

The Massachusetts Museum of Contemporary Arts, or MASS MoCA, is located in North Adams in the former mills of the Sprague Company in western Massachusetts. On twenty-eight acres, comprising twenty-seven buildings and over 200,000 square feet of exhibition space, it stands as one of the largest art museums in the world. Hundreds of sculptures representing the best in contemporary art adorn the wide halls. For the first time, large installations and multistory art structures have found a home in this most unusual museum. Opened in 1999, MASS MoCA is also a venue for art in action or performance art, with rehearsal halls and exhibition areas allocated for dance, theater, film, and music. Its directors call it "a work in progress," a place where the public can view cutting-edge art of any medium or dimensions.

Cotton Mather

A Puritan minister who became the conscience of Boston and Massachusetts's elite, Cotton Mather was born in Boston on February 12, 1663, the son of Increase Mather, also a renowned Puritan clergyman. Pious and very serious even as a youth, Cotton Mather early on followed in his father's footsteps. Precocious, he entered Harvard College at the age of twelve, graduating in 1678. After earning his master's degree in 1681, he joined his father as a pastor at the prestigious **Old North Church.** They worked together until the older man's death in 1723, when Cotton Mather took over as chief pastor. He spent his entire career reminding others of the pure faith and principles of the original **Puritans,** castigating any who strayed from their strict precepts.

He also played an active role in the colony's political life, writing a sermon, for example, supporting the Bostonians who imprisoned Governor Edmund Andros in 1689 after the Glorious Revolution in England deposed the Catholic James II and restored a Protestant monarchy. The major publication of his life's work was *Magnalia Christi Americana* of 1702, a blend of history and dogma reiterating the contributions of the first Puritans. He wrote many sermons and articles on religious and scientific subjects and was one of the early proponents of the use of inoculations to prevent smallpox. In 1721, when a particularly severe epidemic broke out, he took a controversial leadership position advocating the inoculation system, even though it was not always successful and could be dangerous. He died on February 13, 1728, having earned a reputation as a serious thinker profoundly concerned with the Puritans' striving for perfection.

Mayflower

The ship known as the *Mayflower* carried the Pilgrims from Southampton, England, on September 16, 1620, to the New World. It was on this ship that the Pilgrims drew up and agreed to a system of governance in a document called the **Mayflower Compact.** Actually, among the ship's 106 passengers only a minority were Pilgrims, or religious dissenters from the Church of England, who had originally fled England for Holland, believing the Anglican Church to be impure because of its adherence to rituals and ceremonies that smacked of Roman Catholicism. Most of the others on board were migrants who sought economic betterment and relief from the chronic poverty and land shortages in England. The **Puritans** called them "the strangers." The *Mayflower* landed first at Provincetown on Cape Cod on November 12, 1620. Finding the area inhospitable, the passengers set sail again, eventually settling at Plymouth on December 16 (or 18, or 22—reports vary), though it is a matter of dispute whether they landed at the place now designated as Plymouth Rock. (See also **Pilgrims and Plymouth Colony**)

Mayflower Compact

The Mayflower Compact was an agreement signed on November 11, 1620, by forty-one adult males aboard the Pilgrim ship ***Mayflower*** off the shore of Cape Cod. The signers contracted to "covenant, and combine ourselves together into a civil body politic, for our better ordering and preservation . . . into which we promise all due submission and obedience." The heads of families, including some of the servants, signed the document. The Mayflower Compact was unique for its time in that it established the principle that all in the colony would be involved in its governance—the notion of rule by consent of the governed that was to become the foundation of the American political system. It was the preservation of this ideal that led colonists a century and a half later to rebel against the oppression of Parliament and successfully launch the American Revolution. (See also **Pilgrims and Plymouth Colony**)

Herman Melville

Herman Melville stands among the greatest literary figures of all time largely on the strength of one novel. The story of Captain Ahab and the great white whale is familiar to many, but it is doubtful that large numbers today have actually read through this densely packed novel with its many concurrent epic themes of good and evil and the primal force of nature. Although Melville's personal connection to Massachusetts is somewhat tenuous, the novel offers a meticulous description of the whaling industry and the seamen of Nantucket and New Bedford, marking it as the quintessential Massachusetts story. Added to this is the fact that Melville wrote the book while living on a farm near Pittsfield in western Massachusetts.

Born in New York City on August 1, 1819, Melville was the son of a businessman who fell on hard times. His father's death left the family in poverty, and Melville received only a spotty education while earning money at a variety of ordinary jobs. He did spend some time working on his uncle's farm in Pittsfield, a connection that remained important to him for years to come. In 1839 he began his travels, signing on as a crewman on a merchant ship, then in 1841 on a whaler that cruised the Pacific. The hard life aboard the whaler was too much for Melville, who deserted in the Marquesas Islands, where he lived among the Typees, a Polynesian tribe. He had further adventures, shipped aboard other whalers, and even joined the U.S. Navy for a Pacific cruise. When he returned to the United States, these adventures became the subject for a host of books about seafarers on tropical isles—*Typee, Omoo, Mardi, Redburn, White-Jacket*—published between 1846 and 1849, which soon earned him a solid reputation as a writer.

In 1850, while vacationing at his uncle's farm, he met **Nathaniel Hawthorne,** who became a close friend. Melville bought a farm next to his uncle's in Pittsfield and began the work that was to make him famous long after his death. Published in London in 1851, *Moby-Dick* appeared to high praise but poor sales. From that time on, despite a considerable literary outpouring, including poetry and short stories, Melville never again achieved the commercial success of *Typee* and *Omoo.* His reputation as a writer disintegrated, and he sold the Berkshire farm in 1863, ending his Massachusetts residence. Only a government sinecure as an inspector of U.S. customs in New York City saved Melville and his family from destitution. On September 28, 1891, with his final novel, *Billy Budd,* still unfinished, Melville died, forlorn and virtually forgotten. In the 1920s his work was rediscovered by literary critics, but not until the 1950s, with the help of Hollywood, did the popular imagination become fully acquainted with his masterpiece, *Moby-Dick.*

Metacom (See **King Philip's War**)

METCO

The Metropolitan Council for Educational Opportunity, known as METCO, is the nation's longest-running voluntary school desegregation plan. It began in 1964 when the town of Brookline invited the Boston School Committee to bus black high school students who chose to participate to its suburban high school. Soon the program grew, and by the end of the twentieth century some three thousand minority high school students were being voluntarily bused from Boston to schools in thirty-six surrounding suburbs. Yearly there are over 12,500 students on waiting lists to enter the program, with some parents putting their children on the waiting list at the age of one.

METCO students get the opportunity to attend better-funded schools that offer enriched facilities, smaller classes, and more opportunities for higher education than in the struggling urban school system. They also learn to participate in the majority world of whites. The drawbacks of the very successful program include the loss to Boston of some of its most highly motivated black students, the psychological difficulties for black students of living in two different worlds, and the effects of racism in the white suburban schools. And of course METCO does nothing to diversify the city schools. Nonetheless, within these limitations this is a desegregation plan that works.

Middlesex Canal

Boston merchants conceived of the Middlesex Canal as a way to open northern trade with the interior of Massachusetts and New Hampshire. The legislature in 1793 approved a charter for the Middlesex Canal Corporation to build a canal from the Mystic River to the Merrimack River. A modification in 1795 allowed for an extension of the canal to the Charles River and Boston. Granted also was the right to collect a toll of 6 ¼ cents per ton-mile. Stockholders included many of Boston's elite, including **John Adams** and **Josiah Quincy.**

Work began in 1794. The absence of machine technology and the requirement that all work be done by hand complicated construction. The completion of the first phase came in 1803, when waters from the canal flowed into the Mill Pond off Charlestown. By 1805 a branch canal connected the main trunk to the Mystic River. Finally, with various extensions, the corporation announced the completion of the entire canal in 1814, all the way from Boston to the Merrimack River, and thence by river to Concord, New Hampshire.

This internal system of transportation allowed for the expansion of the textile industry in New England. By the 1830s, the advent of the railroads, with their greater speed and lower costs, spelled the end of the canal. By 1843 the expenses of running the canal were higher than the earnings brought in by the tolls. The legislature dissolved the Middlesex Canal Corporation in 1860, well after the company had ceased to function.

Minute Men

A resolve of the First Provincial Congress of Massachusetts on October 26, 1774, established the Revolutionary Minute Men of the army, or militia, of Massachusetts "for the defense and safety of the Province" against British occupation. The concept was derived from the old militia system under the British, which included a Minute Man contingent. The "Minute Man" sobriquet meant that this small portion of the militia unit was trained to assemble very quickly—at a minute's notice—to go into combat while the main militia unit was undergoing the assembly process. The instant response capability of a small unit made sense in the dangerous world of colonial America, given the constant warfare against the French and the Indians.

On October 29, 1774, the Provincial Congress sent the militia resolve to all the towns of Massachusetts. The Second Provincial Congress passed a resolve on April 5, 1775, stating the rules, articles, and regulations for a Massachusetts army "that may be raised for the defense and Security of our lives, liberties and estates." It was the Minute Men who responded to the alarm raised on April 19, 1775, warning that the militia's supplies of munitions were to be attacked by the British at **Lexington and Concord.** On that fateful day over 4,000 Minute Men mustered to face 1,500 British regulars in the series of battles that initiated the American Revolution. Four days later the same congress voted unanimously to raise and support a regular Massachusetts army of 30,000 men.

From that time on, rather than send the Minute Men back to join their units, the leaders decided that every militia soldier should become a Minute Man. On June 17, the day of the Battle of Bunker Hill, the Provincial Congress instructed "that all the militia in the colony be ordered to hold themselves in readiness to march at a minute's warning." The idea was so successful that the next day the new Continental Congress at Philadelphia issued edicts establishing that Minute Men units should constitute one-quarter of every militia organized in the colonies to fight the British.

To commemorate the Revolutionary Minute Men, in 1966 a group of interested Massachusetts citizens formed the Council of Minute and Militia Companies to organize parades and historical reenactments. Since they would carry real muskets, the state legislature passed a special act allowing them to bear arms in public. Beginning in 1967, the historical Minute Men have held musket firings at Minute Man National Historic Park in Concord each year on Patriot's Day to celebrate "the shot heard round the world." (See also **Bunker Hill and Monument**)

Mohawk Trail

The Mohawk Trail (Route 2) is a purposely designed sixty-three-mile-long scenic highway that winds its way through fifty thousand acres of woods and state parks. Opened with paved roads in 1914, it was intended to draw tourists to the depressed western part of the state. Originally an Indian trail, it runs south from Greenfield along the Deerfield River through the Connecticut Valley, then west to the **Berkshires** and Williamstown. There are state parks along the trail that offer opportunities for hiking, swimming, boating, and skiing in the winter. The route is lined with motels, bed and breakfasts, camping grounds, souvenir shops, and mock Indian trading posts. Fall foliage season is the busiest time of year, when tourists in large numbers are attracted by the abundance of color. Sights along the way, from east to west, include the Bridge of Flowers at Shelburne Falls, the monument to the Mohawks at Charlemont, the hairpin curve at North Adams, Williams College in Williamstown, and the drive up Mount Greylock, at 3,491 feet the highest point in the state.

The Boston Molasses Flood of January 15, 1919, damaged the Commercial Street Elevated Railway. Photo courtesy of Mark Power.

Molasses Flood

On January 15, 1919, around noon, more than 2 million gallons of raw molasses exploded out of a storage tank at the corner of Foster and Commercial streets in the North End. The tank holding the molasses for processing into industrial alcohol was fifty-eight feet tall and ninety-eight feet wide. The explosion sent 20 million pounds of molasses pouring through the neighborhood. Twenty-one people drowned or suffocated in the flood and 150 were injured. Several buildings were knocked off their foundations by the fifteen-foot-high wave of ooze flowing through the streets. A large section of the elevated structure that carried rapid transit trains crashed to the ground, buildings toppled, and many horses died in the calamity. For weeks afterward the North End smelled foul, as cleanup crews sprayed saltwater from firehoses and used stiff brooms and shovels and sand to scrub the streets.

Museum of Fine Arts

Boston's Museum of Fine Arts (MFA), located in the Fenway section of the city on Huntington Avenue, is one of the leading art museums in the nation. Notable holdings in the permanent collection include nineteenth- and early-twentieth-century American painting and a vast assemblage of European art from the Renaissance through the early twentieth century. Its bountiful Asian and Near Eastern works include decorative arts and artifacts as well as paintings and sculpture. At its beginnings in the 1860s the museum comprised only a single gallery at the Boston Athenaeum. Soon bursting at the seams, it moved to a new building in **Copley Square** in 1876. Constant acquisitions forced trustees to construct a new neoclassical building on Huntington Avenue in 1909. Since then there have been several additions to the original structure.

The North Bridge, site of one of the battles fought at Lexington and Concord, April 19, 1775. Photo by Patricia St. John Tager.

N

Nantucket (See **Cape Cod and the Islands**)

New England Patriots

Patriots football began in 1959 under the aegis of William Sullivan Jr., a former public relations executive for baseball's Boston Braves who was able to secure the final franchise berth available in the American Football League. In 1960 the team, at first known as the Boston Patriots, played its first home game at Harvard Stadium. The Patriots lost. In 1966 the American Football League and the National Football League merged, and the Patriots became an AFC East team within the new NFL.

After playing for a decade at various sites, including Fenway Park, the team moved to Foxboro and Schaefer Stadium, changing its name in March 1971 to the New England Patriots. It was not until 1978 that the team won its first division title, losing in the playoffs to the Houston Oilers. In 1982 Schaefer Stadium became Sullivan Stadium, named after the founder and owner of the team. Three years later the Pats went to the playoffs, defeating three successive teams to win their first AFC championship. They lost Super Bowl XX, however, to an overwhelming Chicago Bears team, 46 to 10.

Sullivan sold the team in 1988, and then it was sold again in 1992, and once again in 1994 to a local owner, Robert Kraft, who restored some stability. In 1996 the Patriots won the AFC title, defeating the Denver Broncos, but went up against the Green Bay Packers in Super Bowl XXXI and lost, 35 to 21. The Patriots won the AFC title once again in 1997. Then at last fans rejoiced when in 2002, with a new stadium about to open, the team won Super Bowl XXXVI, the Patriots' first NFL championship, beating the St. Louis Rams, 20 to 17, in an upset victory under the leadership of a new head coach and a high-spirited young quarterback, Tom Brady.

North Bridge

It was on the North Bridge in Concord that the **Minute Men** returned the fire of the attacking British troops after two of the colonials fell in the early morning of April 19, 1775. The British had advanced on Concord after their clash with patriots at Lexington. The Minute Men, led by Major John Buttrick, held their ground, forcing the redcoats to retreat. The bridge that visitors see today, which is off Monument Street, one-half mile from Concord center, is a replica built in 1956. Near the bridge stands the famous Minute Man statue by sculptor Daniel Chester French (1875). On the base of the statue is engraved the first stanza of the poem "Concord Hymn" by **Ralph Waldo Emerson:**

By the rude bridge that arched the flood
Their flag to April's breeze unfurled
Here once the embattled farmers stood
And fired the shot heard round the world.

(See also **Lexington and Concord**)

Orchard House, in Concord, was the home of the Alcott family and where Louisa May Alcott wrote *Little Women* in 1868. Used by permission of Orchard House/The Louisa May Alcott Memorial Association.

O

Hugh O'Brien

Hugh O'Brien was Boston's first Irish-born mayor. Born in Ireland on August 13, 1827, he arrived in Boston with his parents in 1832, attended public schools, and then at age twelve became an apprentice to the printers of the *Boston Courier,* where he learned the newspaper business. By 1843 he had started his own newspaper, the *Shipping and Commercial List,* and subsequently became a bank president and treasurer of an electric company. Following the pattern of Yankee businessmen, he was involved in various philanthropic activities, standing out in the eyes of Boston's elite as an assimilated and "respectable" gentleman in contrast to most of his Irish compatriots.

Building a base of support among both the Irish and the Yankees, O'Brien won election to the Boston Board of Aldermen in 1875, where he served with distinction for seven years, four as chairman. He scored a concrete victory for laboring men by winning enactment of a two-dollar daily minimum wage for city employees. Because of his successful political record, his reputation for integrity and moderation, and the perception that he had become thoroughly assimilated, the Yankee-controlled Democratic Party nominated him for the mayoralty in 1884. He soundly defeated the Republican incumbent, Augustus P. Martin, to become the first Irish-born Catholic elected to lead this city of over 300,000, more than 60 percent of whom either were foreign-born or had foreign-born parents.

His primary focus as mayor was to bring sound fiscal management procedures to the city bureaucracy, a far cry from the modus operandi of subsequent Irish mayors in the twentieth century. In a hostile response to this Irish upstart, the Yankee-dominated, temperance-influenced state legislature imposed a new city charter on Boston. While several of its measures were moderate and beneficial, the one that clearly struck a blow against the Irish residents of the city was the abolition of the mayor's power to appoint Boston's three police commissioners. It was the commissioners' job to issue liquor licenses, and the legislature feared what would happen once that privilege was in the hands of an Irish mayor. Now the charter stipulated that the governor would appoint the commissioners, clear evidence of the chasm between ethnic Boston and Protestant small-town Massachusetts.

This action revived memories of the anti-Catholic Know-Nothing legislature of 1855, driving the mayor of Boston and his Irish constituents to speak out against prejudice. In the face of growing ethnic divisions, O'Brien remained steady at the helm, winning reelection to one-year terms in 1885, 1886, and 1887. But in 1887 the city's growing anti-Catholic forces gained strength when Bostonians of British ancestry allied themselves with rural Yankees who feared the growing influence of the Irish in politics. In his bid for reelection in 1888, O'Brien was defeated in the wave of anti–Irish Catholic sentiment that swept through the city. He died on August 1, 1895.

O'Brien had accommodated and worked with the Yankee Democratic establishment only to see **anti-Catholicism** again win the day in Boston. His failure changed the political strategy of later Irish American newcomers who followed in his footsteps, such as **John Fitzgerald** and **James Michael Curley.** These two charismatic figures confronted Yankees (Democrats and Republicans alike) in hostile attacks that coalesced ethnic Bostonians and led to their changing the balance of power in that city forever. (See also **Know-Nothings**)

William Henry Cardinal O'Connell

William Henry O'Connell was the Roman Catholic archbishop of Boston through four decades of the twentieth century. He championed Catholicism and the interests of American Catholics during the transformation of Massachusetts from a Yankee culture to a more ethnic and diversified society.

Born in Lowell on December 8, 1859, he was the eleventh son of a factory worker. He went to the Lowell public schools and to Boston College, graduating in 1881, and entered the priesthood. After seminary studies in Rome, he became a Boston parish priest, returning to Rome as the rector of the American College there in 1895.

Close ties with the Vatican brought him appointment as the bishop of Maine in 1901. He rose quickly, becoming coadjutor bishop of Boston in 1906, archbishop in 1907, and in 1911 was elevated to cardinal, the first from Boston and only the third American to be so chosen. Throughout his career he took strong public stands defending the Catholic Church in a state long dominated by Yankee Protestants with a heritage of **anti-Catholicism.** He also took it upon himself to promote Catholic morality and to build up the revenues of the church. He was known for indulging his private tastes and taking many trips, which earned him the sobriquet of "Gangplank Bill." Cardinal O'Connell died in Boston on April 22, 1944.

Old Ironsides (See **U.S.S. *Constitution***)

Old North Church

The fame of the Old North Church lies in its role in the early days of the American Revolution. Rising above the church, on Salem Street in the North End, the steeple could be seen from Charlestown. Following the plan of **Paul Revere,** the church sexton, Robert Newman, on April 18, 1775, hung two lanterns in the belfry to warn the patriots across the river that the British were on their way to **Lexington and Concord** to seize the arms and ammunition of the rebel troops. The lights alerted Revere ("two, if by sea"), who was at that moment being rowed to Charlestown to begin his famous ride immortalized by **Henry Wadsworth Longfellow:**

He said to his friend, "If the British march
By land or sea from the town to-night,
Hang a lantern aloft in the belfry arch
Of the North Church tower, as a signal light,—
One, if by land, and two, if by sea;
And I on the opposite shore will be,
Ready to ride and spread the alarm
Through every Middlesex village and farm,
For the country-folk to be up and to arm."

The Old North Church as it appeared in a 1918 photo. Library of Congress, Prints and Photographs Division.

Old North, built in 1723, was the second Anglican church in Boston and is the city's oldest church building. It was designed in the Georgian style of English architect Christopher Wren. The church also houses the nation's oldest church bells, cast in 1744.

Kenneth Olsen

Kenneth Olsen, a computer scientist, electrical engineer, and entrepreneur, founded the Digital Equipment Corporation (DEC), which became one of the world's leaders in innovative computer technology. Born on February 10, 1926, in Bridgeport, Connecticut, he was the son of a machine tool designer. After a stint in the navy, he entered MIT as a student in electrical engineering in 1947, receiving his bachelor's degree in 1950 and his master's in 1952. He went on to do original research at MIT's Lincoln Laboratory, where he built a computer.

In 1957, with Harlan Anderson, he founded DEC, a computer parts company. Beginning in a rented loft in an old mill in Maynard, by 1959 they had begun building and selling computers. Among his many contributions to computer technology were the personal computer and the matrix system. He devised a way to administer a complex new business that was a research facility, a factory for production, and a marketing entity all in one. DEC became the model for others to follow. Olsen, as its founder, was a pioneer in bridging the gap between science and technology to create a new industry that would become crucial to the economy of the Bay State.

Thomas P. "Tip" O'Neill Jr.

Thomas "Tip" O'Neill was a long-term congressman and Speaker of the U.S. House of Representatives known for the aphorism "All politics is local." Born in Cambridge on December 9, 1912, he was the son of a local politician. The nickname "Tip" came from his love of baseball; it was the name of a former big league player. O'Neill attended parochial schools and Boston College, graduating in 1936. He joined the Democratic Party, campaigned for Al Smith in 1928, lost a bid for Cambridge City Council in 1935, then won his first political race in 1936, when he was elected to the Massachusetts House of Representatives. A champion of the working class and a staunch advocate of liberal causes, he envisioned government as the instrument of social justice.

In 1948, when the Democrats finally became the majority party in the Massachusetts House, the representatives elected O'Neill as the first Democratic speaker in 140 years of House history. In 1952 he won election to the U.S. Congress, taking over the vacated seat of John F. Kennedy, newly elected to the Senate. In Congress he was a strong supporter of the liberal programs of the Kennedy and Johnson administrations. His reputation soared when he joined the antiwar protest over Vietnam. O'Neill became majority leader in 1972 and Speaker in 1976, serving until 1987, when he retired after years of bumping heads with Presidents Johnson, Carter, and Reagan. Representing the old machine school of patronage politics, with its focus on jobs and social programs, O'Neill was a transition figure to a new world of politics based on media consultants and opinion polls. He died in Boston on January 5, 1994, to the last a defender of equal opportunity for all.

Orchard House

Orchard House was the Concord home of the Bronson Alcott family from 1858 to 1877 and the place where **Louisa May Alcott** wrote *Little Women* in 1868. The fourth home for the Alcotts, it consisted of two separate houses joined together on the site. Much of the original furniture and furnishing remains, including paintings by May Alcott. It is located at 399 Lexington Road in Concord and is open to the public.

John Boyle O'Reilly

John Boyle O'Reilly was an author, poet, and editor and co-owner of the Boston Catholic newspaper the *Pilot.* He appealed to his Catholic readers by singing the praises of the Irish, while at the same time preaching an Americanism that helped them assimilate into Yankee Boston.

Born in Ireland on June 28, 1844, he was the son of a teacher. He apprenticed to a newspaper at a young age and learned to be a reporter. In 1863 he joined the British army with the express purpose of persuading Irish soldiers to join the revolution against the English. Three years later the authorities caught him and sentenced him to exile for twenty years in the penal colony of Australia. He escaped and made his way to Boston in 1869.

The *Pilot* hired him and he soon began writing pro-Irish pieces that made Irish Americans proud of their heritage. This positive sentiment was needed in a city that was anti-Catholic and anti-Irish. He also wrote poetry and nature essays. O'Reilly became editor and co-owner in 1876 after he and Boston's Catholic Archbishop John J. Williams purchased the paper. In addition to writing articles and editorials, he continued to publish volumes of poetry, two novels, and essays about sports. Since he believed strongly in assimilation, his work was well received by the Boston Yankee literary community, and O'Reilly received many local honors. He suffered bouts of depression, however, and on August 10, 1890, he died either from an accidental overdose of a powerful medication or by his own hand. (See also **Anti-Catholicism**)

Mary Kenney O'Sullivan

Mary Kenney O'Sullivan was a working-class labor activist who collaborated with upper-class women to promote women's rights in Massachusetts in the early twentieth century. Born January 8, 1864, in Hannibal, Missouri, the daughter of Irish immigrants who worked on the railroads, Mary Kenney knew from personal experience the plight of the working classes. The premature death of her father forced her to leave school in the fourth grade to go to work. In time she took on many industrial jobs, from dressmaker to printer and bookbinder. She began organizing women bookbinders, and at age twenty-eight in 1892 was appointed by Samuel Gompers to continue this work for the American Federation of Labor. She was sent to Boston, where she met and married a labor reporter, John F. O'Sullivan. For a short time she served as deputy factory inspector in Illinois but then returned to Boston, where she and her family lived in the Denison Settlement House.

The settlement house had been established by two upper-class women, Vida Scudder and **Emily Greene Balch.** Part of their goal was to create a female alliance that would bridge the gap between classes. Working with Boston society women who called themselves "the Allies," O'Sullivan organized the National Women's Trade Union League in 1903, in conjunction with New York social worker William English Walling. This was the first national women's trade union. Its purpose was to forge an alliance of women workers and their upper-class friends to promote legislation to protect women's rights in the trades and to enable women to join existing men's labor unions. O'Sullivan went on to help garment and laundry workers to organize and was recognized for her efforts by appointment in 1914 as inspector of industrial safety for Massachusetts. She served in that position until 1934, when she was seventy years old. She died in West Medford on January 18, 1943, having devoted herself to the working women of the state and the nation.

Harrison Gray Otis

A member of Boston's elite merchant class, Harrison Gray Otis was one of the leaders of the Federalist Party. Because of his prominence, he remained an arbiter of the social mores of Boston for many years. Born in Boston on October 8, 1765, he was the son of a rich merchant and a descendant of James Otis of Revolutionary fame. He received a B.A. (1783) and an M.A. (1786) from Harvard, then studied law and opened what became a lucrative law practice. He invested wisely in real estate and became very rich, furthering his fortunes in banking and with investments in the newly developed textile industry, becoming one of the **Boston Associates.** Entering politics, Otis won election to the state legislature as a Federalist in 1796. President Washington appointed him U.S. district attorney that year, but he soon left that position to win election to the U.S. House of Representatives.

A follower of Alexander Hamilton, he advocated the creation of a strong federal government that would espouse the interest of the business community. He joined other Federalists in seeking close ties with Britain, attacking Republicans and their affiliation with France. During the quasi-war with France, he supported the notorious Alien and Sedition Acts of 1798. Fearing the excesses of democracy, Otis was a lifelong supporter of the notion of rule by the elite. Jefferson's victory in 1800 forced the Federalists from power, and Otis spent his remaining years in Boston, involved in state and local politics.

For many years he served in both the Massachusetts House and Senate, always in leadership roles. In 1817 a Federalist-dominated state legislature elected him to the U.S. Senate. He resigned in 1822 to return to Boston. He led the Federalist junto in Boston that turned that town into a city, using the occasion to make a bid to become the city's first mayor. His archenemy **Josiah Quincy,** a maverick Federalist and now leader of the "middling interest," forced the election into a runoff, which neither candidate won. The following year the Federalists of Boston shocked their leader, Otis, when they came out for Quincy in the mayoralty election. Otis ran for the governorship that year but lost. Quincy remained mayor of Boston until 1828, when growing dissatisfaction enabled Otis to defeat him in that year's election. Otis then served as mayor from 1829 to 1831. The eclipse of the Federalist Party finally led him to join the Whigs. He died in Boston on October 28, 1848, a power broker to the end. (See also **John Quincy Adams** and **Essex Junto**)

James Otis (See **Writs of Assistance**)

The Pioneer Valley as viewed from Mount Sugarloaf in Sunderland. Photograph by Richard Wilkie.

P

Elizabeth Palmer Peabody

Elizabeth Peabody was a social reformer, Transcendentalist, and educational innovator. Born in Billerica on May 16, 1804, she was the daughter of professionals. She helped her mother run a school, and at age fifteen took tutoring lessons from **Ralph Waldo Emerson,** who became a lifelong friend. After teaching at various schools, in 1840 she opened a bookstore in Boston and became a publisher. At Emerson's suggestion, in 1841 she took on the post of editor of the Transcendentalists' journal, *The Dial.*

Peabody became a close friend of the educator **Horace Mann,** who interested her in child development. She promoted reforms in school curricula to include the arts. Peabody then became a disciple of the German educational reformer Friedrich Froebel, an innovator in kindergarten training, who inspired her to open the first kindergarten for English-speaking children in Boston in 1861. In 1866 she published her landmark work on early education, *Moral Culture of Infancy and Kindergarten Guide,* which would become the standard work in the field. Peabody next turned her attention to teacher training, publishing a journal for young teachers and writing another seminal book in 1888, *Lectures in Training Schools for Kindergartners.* She died in Boston on January 3, 1894, a renowned pioneer in early childhood education and teacher training. (See also **Transcendentalism**)

Pequot War

The Pequot War of 1637 was a conflict between English settlers and Natives that resulted in the destruction of New England's most powerful tribe and the confiscation of all their lands. The Pequots had been at war for a long time with several other tribes, including the Narragansetts, and with Dutch settlers. During the hostilities, they killed two English sea captains and seven of their crew. The leaders of the **Massachusetts Bay Colony** condemned this attack and demanded retribution. The Pequots, pleading extenuating circumstances, persuaded the English settlers to enter into a peace treaty with them in 1634. As part of the treaty agreement, the Pequots were to pay an indemnity of wampum and furs and would give up the "murderers" for trial in the Bay Colony.

They never carried out their pledges. After another Englishman was killed in 1636, the disgruntled Massachusetts Bay Colony leaders sent a force to attack first a Pequot community on Block Island and then tribal territory in Connecticut to force the Natives to hand over the assassins. The Pequots refused, and a skirmish broke out. They then attacked the English settlement at Saybrook in September 1636.

From that point on the Connecticut Valley faced continuous Indian sorties against the settlements. In April 1637 the Pequots launched a major attack on the undefended Connecticut plantation of Wethersfield, killing nine and carrying off two women. As a result, Massachusetts Bay and Connecticut authorities declared a joint war against the Pequots—the region's first major conflict. Both sides bore responsibility for the hostilities, as both had acted aggressively in order to curb the other's dominion. The Massachusetts Bay colonists had taken the position that it was their responsibility to defend the frontier areas where their compatriots had gone to create new settlements and colonies. Plymouth Colony then joined in an alliance, and two pro-English tribes, the Mohegans and the Narrangansetts, also entered the fray on the colonial side.

A large allied force surprised the Pequots in their fort on the Mystic River in May and slaughtered some four hundred to six hundred men, women, and children, leaving the Pequots in disarray. Some fled to Mohawk territory, as the English went on to capture and kill many others in a mopping-up operation. By mid-July the Pequots had vanished as a functioning tribe, an end symbolized by a peace treaty in 1638 that prevented the few surviving Pequots from ever using that tribal name again. The English victors confiscated the Pequot lands to promote future settlements. As a further result of the war, the balance of power shifted in favor of the English, allowing them to dominate the more populous remaining New England tribes. Not until 1675 was another Indian, Metacom—or King Philip, as he was known—to challenge the hegemony of the English. (See also **King Philip's War** and **Pilgrims and Plymouth Colony**)

Wendell Phillips

Wendell Phillips was an abolitionist and social reformer who supported temperance reform, women's rights, and the eight-hour day for workers. Born in Boston on November 9, 1811, he was the son of a rich politician and philanthropist. He went to Boston Latin, and graduated from Harvard in 1831 and Harvard Law School in 1833. Never really interested in the law, however, and endowed with a large fortune, he turned his full attention to the abolitionist cause. His greatest gift was as an orator, with an eloquence that could leave an audience spellbound and emotionally transfixed by his arguments.

He made a name for himself and for the power of his oratory when, after the death of abolitionist Elijah Lovejoy at the hands of an Illinois proslavery mob, he castigated the state attorney general, James Austin, for defending the attack. From that point on Phillips became the leading public speaker for the antislavery cause. He became close friends with another leader of the **abolitionists, William Lloyd Garrison,** although he supported the use of violence to end slavery and Garrison did not. Phillips also championed the cause of women's rights, which he believed went hand in hand with abolitionism. His zeal and his radical views set him apart from mainstream antislavery groups.

Throughout the 1840s and 1850s he dedicated himself to antislavery activities, lecturing, writing, and working as an active member of Boston's antislavery group, the Vigilance Committee. Along with other radical abolitionists such as **Thomas Wentworth Higginson,** he took the extreme position that since the Constitution condoned slavery, it was an immoral document that should be revoked, even if that meant breaking up the Union. A bloody Civil War redeemed his views. After 1865, when Garrison retired, Phillips stayed on as the president of the American Anti-Slavery Society, now fighting for equality for blacks. The passage of the Fourteenth (1868) and Fifteenth (1870) Amendments seemed to him to fulfill his lifelong dreams. He died on February 3, 1884.

Pilgrims and Plymouth Colony

Americans view the Pilgrims as our first colonists, the people who celebrated Thanksgiving and who initiated democracy with the **Mayflower Compact.** But their story is more complex than suggested by these myths. The Pilgrims were members of a religious sect in England who believed that the established Anglican Church was infected with Catholic rituals and hierarchy and was therefore "corrupt" and degenerate. Unlike their brethren the **Puritans,** who wanted to reform the English church, the Pilgrims rejected it completely. They divorced themselves from it and became separatists. In the late sixteenth and early seventeenth centuries, however, the Crown took the position that all must support the state church, with both their money and their devotion. The state persecuted and harassed all those who disagreed. The Pilgrims suffered grievously under this official intolerance and finally left the country in 1608. They found toleration and acceptance in Holland, where they established a thriving Pilgrim community.

Soon, though, the Pilgrims began to worry about maintaining the rigor of their religious faith and feared that their children might succumb to Dutch influences and assimilate. To keep themselves and their children pure, they decided to build a community in the New World where they could preserve their beliefs and take full control over their destiny. They acquired a patent to settle land within the confines of the Virginia Company Charter. An expedition made ready to set sail from England, but when one of the ships, the *Speedwell,* sprang a leak, the *Mayflower* embarked on its own on September 6, 1620, with 106 passengers.

In November, after a hazardous journey, they reached the eastern shore of Cape Cod near the beach at Race Point, at what later became Provincetown. Because they were nowhere near the boundaries of their patent, they set out again only to encounter more difficult weather. They finally anchored at Plymouth Harbor on December 16 (or 18, or 22), 1620. While on board ship, the forty-one adult males among the settlers agreed to create a government and "to enacte, constitute, and frame such just and equall Laws, Ordinances, Acts, Constitutions, and Offices, from time to time as shall be thought most meete and convenient for the generall Good of the Colonie." This agreement, the Mayflower Compact, was unique in that its basis for governance was the consent of the governed, a principle that would become the matrix of American democracy.

Recognizing that they had neither a charter nor royal permission, the

Pilgrims nonetheless landed at Plymouth and set up a colony on the site of an abandoned Wampanoag village of the Patuxet people, whose inhabitants had died in an epidemic caused by contact with whites in 1617. Their first winter was a difficult one, and many settlers died, reducing the party to fifty. Their encounter with two Indians, Samoset and **Squanto,** who taught them how to cultivate corn, saved them from starvation. Squanto also introduced them to **Massasoit,** chief of the Wampanogs. To serve their mutual needs, the Pilgrims and the Indians entered into a peace treaty that proved beneficial to both. That same year the ship *Fortune* arrived, adding thirty-five new colonists to the Pilgrims' numbers.

With peace assured and a plentiful corn crop, the Pilgrims were able to survive. They celebrated their first harvest in 1621 at a thanksgiving meal with Massasoit and other Natives attending. Although the New England soil was not as rich as that of Virginia, it was sufficient to raise enough crops to keep the settlement going. Disease had abated, but the continual arrival of newcomers overburdened the food supplies and led to conflicts over governance rights. After 1627 families began leaving the enclosed palisade and settled in new towns developed in a process known as "declension." The colony flourished. Although the new **Massachusetts Bay Colony** of the Puritans quickly dwarfed the Plymouth Colony, the Pilgrims benefited from being able to trade foodstuffs and livestock required by the Puritans. In addition, because of their connections among the Native tribes, the Pilgrims were able to establish themselves in the profitable fur trade.

By 1675 the settlement had expanded to reach the boundaries of the colony. Now land could only be purchased from a previous owner. The limited land supply diminished the economic opportunities for the Pilgrims and virtually halted the arrival of newcomers. By 1667, too, the piety of the early Pilgrims was eroding; marking the end of ardent separatism was the arrival of John Cotton, a Puritan from Boston, hired as the new minister of Plymouth Church. The sense of insecurity was exacerbated when disputes with the Wampanoags erupted in **King Philip's War** of 1675–76. Also the Pilgrims constantly feared for the very existence of their community because they lacked a charter and were therefore an illegal entity.

Their precarious position finally caught up with them in 1686, when the new English government under James II revoked the charter of the Massachusetts Bay Colony and in doing so merged the Plymouth Colony with the new Massachusetts entity. But this royal control proved short-lived as James II fell from power during the "Glorious Revolution" and the new monarchy of William of Orange and James's daughter Mary ordered the

New England colonies reorganized in a manner suitable to the colonists. The charter of 1692 consolidated Massachusetts, Plymouth, and Maine into a single colony. The Pilgrims' experiment had ended, but not before their efforts left an indelible mark on the history of America. (See also **William Bradford**)

Pioneer Valley

The Pioneer Valley is the river valley formed by the Connecticut River, which cuts vertically through the western part of Massachusetts. Tourism promoters of the 1940s emphasized the name as a way to attract visitors. From Greenfield in the north, through Northampton and Holyoke, to Springfield in the south, the river valley runs through three counties—Franklin, Hampshire, and Hampden. Two ranges of hills, the Mount Tom and the Mount Holyoke ranges, follow the contours of the valley, providing spectacular views. Fossil evidence showing that the area was once inhabited by small dinosaurs is exhibited at a state park as well as at several museums and commercial "dino tracks" sites.

The valley was home to about twelve thousand Native Americans in 1600 when the first English appeared, primarily the Pocumtuck tribe of the **Algonquins,** who lived in settlements along the riverbanks. By the time **William Pynchon** settled Springfield in 1636, only about two hundred Indians remained, the rest having died of diseases spread by the Europeans.

The Connecticut River was the main route of interior transportation. Towns situated along its banks counted themselves fortunate because they could easily ship their surplus agricultural products downriver. But the towns and cities of the valley grew largely because of the advent of the railroads in the early nineteenth century, making Springfield an important terminus for goods from the west on their way to Boston. Springfield soon became the commercial and cultural center of the valley, and Holyoke and Chicopee became manufacturing centers for textiles and paper. With the decline of the factory system in the late nineteenth and early twentieth centuries, a general economic downturn affected the region, whose prospects have fluctuated throughout the last century.

Specialized communities, like Northampton and Amherst, have prospered, and the carefully preserved New England villages, as well as the natural beauty of the fall foliage season, continue to attract many visitors, thus generating pockets of wealth. Areas of historic preservation include

Deerfield Village and Storrowtown Village in West Springfield. Prestigious private boarding schools such as Deerfield Academy, Northfield–Mount Hermon, and Williston Academy bring students from all over the world. The valley is also the home of the Five Colleges—the University of Massachusetts, Amherst College, and Hampshire College in Amherst, Mount Holyoke College in South Hadley, and Smith College in Northampton.

Sylvia Plath

Only after her untimely death did the poet and novelist Sylvia Plath achieve fame as an artist, a maker of evocative imagery addressing the emotional conflicts inherent in the relationships between men and women. She was born in Boston on October 27, 1932; her father was a Boston University professor and her mother was a schoolteacher. Her father's early death created financial insecurity that plagued the family and affected Plath throughout her life. She attended public schools in Wellesley, and by the time she won a scholarship to Smith College, she was already a published poet.

In 1953, at Smith, she suffered from depression. While at home for treatment, she attempted suicide. After shock treatments and psychotherapy she returned to Smith, graduating in 1955. That same year she won a Fulbright scholarship to study at Cambridge University. In England she met and married the British poet Ted Hughes. Theirs was a tempestuous relationship beset by friction over Hughes's infidelity and their competitiveness as poets. For one year Plath taught at Smith College (1957–58). Then the couple moved to Boston, where they both concentrated on their writing.

Inspired by the work of another young American poet, Anne Sexton, Plath became more and more focused on women's themes. She wrote much autobiographical fiction and poetry, most of which was not published until after her death. The couple moved to England in 1959, where Plath gave birth to two children and created a large body of work. The marriage fell apart, however, and Plath, again suffering from depression, took her own life on February 11, 1963, just two weeks after publishing *The Bell Jar,* her most famous novel. The next decades saw the publication of much more of her fiction and poetry, including a book of collected verse that won the Pulitzer Prize in 1982, by which time she had become an icon of the feminist movement.

Sylvia Plath and Ted Hughes just after their marriage in 1956. By permission of the Estate of Ted Hughes and Faber & Faber Limited.

Plimoth Plantation

Located in Plymouth, Massachusetts, Plimoth Plantation is a recreated Pilgrim village of 1627, established by an independent corporation to serve as a memorial to Massachusetts's first English settlers. The village opened in 1949 and since then has expanded. In its houses and their contents, Plimoth Plantation endeavors to conform as closely as possible to the original settlement, based on historical data. Guides called interpreters dress in the attire of the early Pilgrims, speak in authentic English dialects of the time, and carry out typical daily chores. Not a museum, this is living history, reproducing the day-to-day life of the nation's earliest English colonists. In addition, there are exhibits, a crafts center that sells colonial-style objects produced by artisans, a gift shop, and an extensive array of books on historical subjects. Nearby on the waterfront is anchored a model of a ship that suggests what the original *Mayflower* may have looked like. Next to the ship, enclosed within a vault, is the celebrated Plymouth Rock, supposedly the site where the first Pilgrims landed. (See also **Pilgrims and Plymouth Colony**)

Police Strike Riots of 1919

The riots resulting from a police strike in Boston in 1919 paralyzed the city, horrified the nation, and helped elevate an obscure governor to the presidency of the United States. The year after the First World War ended was a period of turmoil and unrest throughout the country. Among the economic problems engendered by postwar inflation were a number of labor conflicts, with over 396 strikes recorded in Massachusetts alone that year. The Bolshevik Revolution, wartime tensions, and fear of labor radicals, militant suffragists, and immigrants all led to a general hysteria that ballooned into the Red Scare. Inflation seriously devalued the salaries of the Boston police, who attempted to enter into wage negotiations with the police commissioner. Although Boston was a Democratic city, the police commissioner was a Republican appointed by the governor. After fruitless discussions, the police formed a union and declared their intention to affiliate with the American Federation of Labor in order to press their demands. The police commissioner, Edwin U. Curtis, then summarily dismissed the police union leadership.

Angry and frustrated, the rank-and-file policemen, mostly Irish Catholics, went out on strike on September 19, 1919. The lower classes, also mainly Irish Americans and other ethnics, seized the opportunity to engage unimpeded in widespread criminal activities for three full days. At first they assaulted the striking officers in retaliation for past actions. They openly gambled in public in places such as the **Boston Common** and in front of police stations. Then, forming into huge crowds, they broke storefront windows and vandalized and looted shops in the commercial downtown district, in South Boston, and, to a lesser degree, in other neighborhoods. Rioters robbed passersby, stoned non-striking policemen and national guardsmen, and committed various other assaults.

The situation soon became desperate, and the Democratic mayor asked Republican governor **Calvin Coolidge** for help. The police commissioner foolishly told the governor that his assistance was not necessary, and so Coolidge refused to intervene. The distraught mayor then discovered a long-disused ordinance that allowed him to take charge of the police and to bring in local units of the state guard. The Boston guardsmen ended the three-day-long carnival of mayhem by firing point-blank into the crowds, killing nine and wounding twenty-three others. Hundreds suffered wounds and other injuries from the fighting and looting. Damage to property ran into the hundreds of thousands of dollars.

The riot was over and the city was restored to calm. But Governor Coolidge, fearing that the Democrats would gain the credit for stopping the violence, restored the police to the authority of Commissioner Curtis and then mobilized the entire state guard to patrol an already peaceful city, citing the fear that other unions would join in a general strike. The militia remained in Boston for months while Curtis recruited an entirely new police force.

The riot demonstrated the continuing breach between the Yankees and the Boston Irish and other ethnics, and reflected the anti-foreign sentiment pervading the nation in 1919. The authorities used unmitigated force, even executing rioters without benefit of legal procedures. Nevertheless, Coolidge's apparently firm handling of the violence led to his nomination as vice president in 1920. The sudden death of President Warren G. Harding in 1923 catapulted Coolidge into the presidency.

Pope Day

Anti-Catholicism and a taste for the rough sport of recreational rioting were the motives behind the Pope Day festivities that occurred every November 5 in Boston during the pre-Revolutionary eighteenth century. Rabid anti-Catholicism was prevalent in early America, but Boston's populace showed a singular propensity for violence against proponents of this religion. The festival traditionally commemorated the failure of Catholic Guy Fawkes's "Gunpowder Plot" to blow up the Protestant English Parliament on November 5, 1605. Throughout the colonies, Pope Day was largely a lower-class holiday, but nowhere else did it take on the dimensions of violence that characterized Boston's celebrations.

The poor, including servants, sailors, workingmen, apprentices, and slaves, would mount effigies of Satan, as well as the pope and other prominent Catholics, on an open carriage. Followed by young boys playing pipes and drums, costumed revelers would pull the carriage through town. At the intended destination, the crowd burned the effigies, drank and ate to excess, and usually ended the day with some sort of battle royal. At one time a rivalry developed between the lower classes of Boston's North End and South End. As a result, there would be two separate parades meeting at a common destination, where revelers fought it out to decide which group would have the honor of burning its effigy of the pope. The fighting was often quite furious, resulting in many injuries. Vandalism was rampant, as the mobs destroyed and stole property.

The Pope Day riots of 1745 and 1755 were particularly violent, forcing the legislature to pass a riot act in 1755 directly aimed at Boston. Other notably violent Pope Days were those of 1762 and 1764. As in 1755, the legislature passed another riot act in 1769, but to no avail. A major change occurred in 1765, when the violence was redirected from Catholics to a new enemy, the Tories, who had defended the hated **Stamp Act** that year. Pope Day had been enlisted in the cause of Revolution, evolving from a vigorous anti-Catholic mob ritual into a vehicle for Revolutionaries to intimidate British loyalists. The celebration of November 5, 1774, known as the "Union Pope Day," was Boston's last such event.

Praying Indians

After the English settlers of Massachusetts and Connecticut defeated the Indians in the **Pequot War** of 1636–37, the Natives were sold into slavery and dispersed. In spite of the prevailing notion among **Puritans** that the Indians were irredeemable, some clergyman in the colony decided to begin missionary work among the few who remained. The Reverend John Eliot, pastor of the Roxbury church, led the way by first devoting himself to learning various Indian dialects in order to convert the Natives to Christianity as well as to raise their standard of living. To this end he took on the task of translating the Bible into the Algonquian language, thus earning for himself the sobriquet "Apostle to the Indians." By 1646 Eliot had succeeded in mastering the tongue of the **Algonquins** and was able to begin ministering to the Indians, making converts in Neponset, Concord, and scattered other locations.

In 1651 Eliot, with government support, established a community of these "praying Indians" in Natick which thrived for many years. But because of continued hostility toward Natives, the Natick group did not become an official church until 1660. By 1654 Eliot had published a catechism in the Algonquian language, and finally in 1661 Eliot's translation of the Bible came out. Other missionaries joined in Eliot's work and helped set up other towns of praying Indians. In 1657 Indians themselves established another praying town in Ponkapoag. By 1670 ministers and Indians had developed six more praying towns in the colony, mostly among the Massachusetts tribe. Other tribes followed, and by 1674, 1,100 Christian Indians were living in fourteen towns.

At the beginning of **King Philip's War** in 1675, the total number of Indian converts was around 2,500, representing about 20 percent of the remaining Natives of New England. During the war the overwhelming number of praying Indians remained loyal to the English. One group even formed a militia company that fought on the settlers' side. But for the most part, the English did not trust these converts, treated them shabbily, and went so far as to imprison five hundred of them on Deer Island in Boston Harbor for the duration of the war. The final irony was that the death of King Philip came at the hands of a praying Indian marksman.

Because of the ravages of the war which inflamed both sides, the praying Indians suffered bias and discrimination, and their communities declined. By the early 1700s whites had displaced the Natives, and as the praying towns became absorbed into the colony, the Indian population declined precipitously.

Proposition 2½

During the short-term fiscal crisis of 1989–90 many Massachusetts voters were concerned about the spending policies of their communities. To curb rising property taxes, in 1990 voters passed Proposition 2½, a popular tax referendum limiting annual property tax increases to no more than 2½ percent of previous values. Passed over the objections of the state legislature, this referendum has severely curtailed revenues of cities and towns. To increase taxes beyond this level, communities must get voters to pass a local override—legislation specifying the exact dollar amount and the purpose of the one-time tax increase.

Puritans

The Puritans were a minority English Protestant sect of the late sixteenth and early seventeenth centuries who believed that the established English church was corrupt and impure. The Church of England, or Anglican Church, maintained certain practices that were anathema to these dissenters. Many of the ceremonies and paraphernalia of Anglican worship seemed meaningless ritual to those who struggled personally to confront God's will. Dissenters who wished to purify their relationship with God and to ban excess formality of churchly ritual were derisively called Puritans. These religious nonconformists were also critical of England and its sinful society and demanded reform of the people and their institutions. They were not separatists like the Pilgrims, who believed that England was doomed beyond redemption and left to create their own society. Puritans believed that English society could be redeemed by the example of their model behavior and by the efforts of preaching ministers to spread the true word of God.

Their belief stressed the omnipotence of God, the centrality of the Bible as the means to reveal God's will, and the requirement that mankind dedicate their lives to God. The fall of Adam and Eve had left humanity debased and degenerate, they believed, but God had selected a given number to be sanctified, and these would carry out his wishes. Puritans believed that all must work to enact God's will, even those not destined for salvation. Once God had picked an individual for salvation—predestination—he would lead that individual to grace through faith and obedience. Nothing one could do—that is, good works—had any bearing on salvation. The individual was basically evil but could become regenerate if he or she was one of the chosen few. God's will would be discerned by knowledge of the Bible, and those who mastered that book and strictly followed its dictates were considered "visible saints" marked for salvation.

Individuals contracted with God through a series of "covenants"—of works and conversion or grace—so that God might lead them to the salvation already determined. The criteria for admission of new church members were testing of biblical knowledge, examination of conduct, and proof of conversion. Ministers were essential in guiding individuals down the proper path, and their sermons offered vital instruction in the meaning of the Bible and the way to obey God.

By the 1620s England had suffered through a depression in the textile market, farm poverty, high unemployment, and the emergence of a large debtor class. King Charles I, in open conflict with Parliament over taxation, finally dissolved that body in 1629. In matters affecting the church, he favored the notion that one could achieve salvation through one's efforts. This belief was repugnant to Puritans and other post-Calvinists and generated religious controversy throughout the land.

One group of Puritans, led by **John Winthrop,** decided to leave England because of the economic and political turmoil and in order to create a society in which they might carry out God's will while making a decent living. They would create a model for the English of a true earthly paradise, a City upon a Hill, giving truth to God's wishes. Thus, the settlement these Puritans established in Massachusetts in 1630, the **Massachusetts Bay Colony,** was both a religious and a commercial venture. (See also **Covenant and Half-Way Covenant** and **Pilgrims and Plymouth Colony**)

William Pynchon

William Pynchon, the founder of Springfield, Massachusetts, was born in England in 1590 (no precise date is known), the son of a wealthy farmer. He joined the **Puritans** and became one of the founders of the Massachusetts Bay Company. Pynchon and his family sailed on the *Ambrose* in 1630, one of the ships that accompanied the ***Arbella*** to New England. He settled first in Dorchester, then in Roxbury. In addition to being an important government functionary—treasurer of the **Massachusetts Bay Colony**—he became rich in the fur trade.

Because of increasing competition in the trade, he decided to move closer to its source, the Connecticut River Valley. As a site he chose some pasture land across from the Native village of Agawam on the east side of the river. Pynchon and eight others persuaded the Indians to deed them the land for "eighteen fathoms of wampum, eighteen blanket-coats, eighteen hatchets, eighteen hoes, and eighteen knives." He and his partners then set up a town. This was not simply a trading post. They founded a church, hired a minister, and allocated and farmed the land. As the town flourished, Pynchon became the local magistrate. Although the area was originally considered part of Connecticut, Pynchon kept his allegiance to the Massachusetts Bay Colony, and the town seceded in 1638. By 1641 it was known as Springfield.

The town flourished under the beneficent but stern hand of magistrate Pynchon. His religious piety got him into trouble with the Massachusetts

General Court when, in 1650, he wrote a book, *The Meritorious Price of Our Redemption,* in which he disagreed with prevailing interpretations about Christ's bearing sin for mankind and Adam's fall from grace. The General Court had the book burned and demanded Pynchon's presence in Boston. Instead, he signed over his properties to his son John and sailed for England, where he retired in peace. He died October 29, 1662.

The Quabbin Reservoir. Photograph by Richard Wilkie.

Quabbin Reservoir

By the 1920s, rapid growth in the Boston area had made the problem of adequate water supplies a crucial issue. Between 1890 and 1920 the population of Boston increased by 50 percent, and during the same period the population of twenty cities and towns surrounding Boston grew by 60 percent. In response to the burgeoning demand for water, the Metropolitan District Commission and the State Department of Health, in a 1922 joint report to the legislature, advocated building a gigantic reservoir in the Swift River Valley.

By diverting the waters of the Swift and Ware rivers and building an aqueduct connecting the proposed reservoir with the Wachusett Reservoir, creating a safe water supply for the majority of the state's population could become a reality. Construction proved to be a complicated and arduous process. Land acquisition involved a difficult decision affecting the 2,500 inhabitants of the area. Four towns initially settled in the 1730s—Greenwich, Dana, Enfield, and Prescott—and several small villages had to be flooded and their population relocated. Some still mourn the passing of these communities.

Construction of the Quabbin Reservoir began in 1928 and was completed in 1939. In all, builders erected six dams of varied size, with the 2,340–foot-long Winsor Dam the largest. A complex underground aqueduct, horseshoe-shaped and averaging twelve feet in diameter, was bored into bedrock and then lined with cement. This tunnel served to connect the

Quabbin and Wachusett reservoirs. Considered filled by 1946, the Quabbin Reservoir began to deliver water of superb quality in time to meet the heightened demands of the spreading suburbs of eastern Massachusetts. The world's largest man-made domestic water supply, the Quabbin Reservoir, consisting of 39 square miles of water nestled amid 120 square miles of forest reservation, stands today as both a marvel of technology and a beautiful natural setting.

Quartering Act (See **Coercive Acts**)

Josiah Quincy

Dubbed the "Great Mayor," Josiah Quincy was the man who transformed Boston from a small trading town into a prosperous urban center. Born into the merchant aristocracy in 1772, son of the patriot of the same name who died in 1775, Quincy was educated at Harvard. He practiced law until entering politics in 1804, beginning as a Federalist Party state senator, then as a U.S. congressman. His years in Congress were controversial, and he finally had to resign in 1813 when he took a position diametrically opposite to that of his party. From that time forward he was considered a maverick among Federalists, a posture that led to his long-term conflict with one of the party's leaders, **Harrison Gray Otis.**

After mending fences, Quincy was elected to the state Senate, where he served until he once again upset Federalist Party leaders by opposing their plan to sever Maine from Massachusetts. Without Federalist support, he won election to the Massachusetts House of Representatives. After serving as speaker, he resigned in 1821 to become a Boston municipal court judge. As a judge he took several positions that favored the working classes, increasing his popularity but further distressing the Federalists.

To further their own interests, Otis and the Federalist leaders manipulated a change in Boston's charter in 1822, changing the form of government from **town meeting** to a city administration with a mayor and council. Not only did the Federalist elite mistrust the open democracy of town meeting, but also Otis hoped to become the city's first mayor as a steppingstone to the governorship. He was surprised that year to find himself opposed by Josiah Quincy, running as an independent. When neither candidate won a majority, they both withdrew, allowing a compromise candidate, John Phillips, to become the city's first mayor.

The lackluster Phillips satisfied no one. In the next election in 1823, Quincy made use of his increased popularity to attack Otis and the Federalists and won the mayoral election. Beginning with the 1824 election, Quincy garnered the support of both independents and Federalists, to the consternation of Otis. Mayor Quincy strengthened his authority when he began an urban renewal process that was to change the face of Boston. He reformed the volunteer fire corps, hired more police constables, took charge of public health, ordered that streets be swept and paved, introduced a municipal water system, created a House of Industry to separate incarcerated debtors from criminals, and revamped the crowded market district by initiating a project that resulted in the construction of Quincy Market.

Thus the independent Quincy led the transformation of a colonial backwater into a modern city. After five one-year terms (1823–27), however, he had created enemies who now banded together to defeat him for reelection. In 1828 he lost to his old nemesis, Otis. Nonetheless, Quincy went on the next year to an appointment as president of **Harvard University,** serving until his retirement in 1845. He died at age ninety-two in Boston, on July 1, 1864.

The Norman Rockwell Museum at Stockbridge. Photo by Art Evans ©2003 The Norman Rockwell Museum. All rights reserved.

R

Raytheon

Raytheon Corporation, located on Route 2 in Lexington, was one of the pioneering companies in the evolution of the electronics industry. Its concentration on defense technology led to its primacy during World War II and the subsequent cold war. Raytheon continued throughout the latter half of the twentieth century to embody innovative technological developments for both defense and the consumer industry, from missiles to the microwave oven.

The company had its origins when MIT electrical engineering professor **Vannevar Bush,** civil engineer Laurence K. Marshall, and scientist C. G. Smith came together with others in 1920 in a business venture to produce electric thermostats, invented by researcher John L. Spencer. Spencer then invented the S-tube, which allowed radio sets to eliminate batteries and simply plug into a wall socket. This device led Bush, Marshall, and Smith to found Raytheon in 1923 to produce radio tubes. By 1926, sales of radio tubes had reached $1 million.

The depression halted Raytheon's progress, but World War II provided a market for new technologies. During the war, working under a government contract, a Raytheon scientist, Percy Spencer, brother of John Spencer, developed the capability to mass-produce magnetrons for use in radar. The British had invented radar but lacked the skilled machinists and methods to achieve production. Spencer's innovation solved the problem, allowing for full production of one of the most important technologies of the war. It also led to the idea of using radio waves to cook, resulting in the microwave oven and Raytheon's creation of a subsidiary company, Amana Ovens.

Mainly in defense, but in some areas of consumer products as well, Raytheon was to take a leading position from the 1950s through the 1980s by working closely with research laboratories such as those at MIT and Harvard. The company went on to create a wide variety of new products: radar antennas and fire control systems, missiles, electronic naval guns, digital computers for the navy, transistors for aircraft and missiles, guided missile programs, X-ray tubes, radar for air traffic controllers, keyboards and guidance computers for the Apollo lunar spacecraft, guidance systems for Polaris submarine-launched missiles, and power cables, to name only a few of Raytheon's innovations.

By 1982 Raytheon was one of the top five companies receiving Department of Defense contracts, amounting to $1.6 billion. The 1980s and early 1990s saw a fall in defense spending, but by the end of the century federal contracts had resumed. With growing diversification in the area of consumer goods as well, Raytheon continues to be one of the most profitable corporations in the state and the nation.

Paul Revere

Paul Revere was a patriot, silversmith, and industrialist, known for his daring ride to warn colonists about the British march to **Lexington and Concord.** Born in Boston in December 1734 (no precise date is known, but some sources cite December 21), he was the son of an immigrant goldsmith, with whom he apprenticed. He took over the shop after his father's death, maintaining a prosperous business crafting everything from small items to elaborate tea services that are now museum pieces. He also became an adept engraver of illustrations and political cartoons.

During the halcyon days leading up to the Revolution, Revere was an active member of the patriotic society the **Sons of Liberty.** After the **Boston Massacre** of 1770, he published an engraving of the event that served to inflame sentiment against the British and remains today the best-known image of the massacre. He was also one of the ringleaders of the **Boston Tea Party.** Between 1773 and 1775 he was an express rider for several agencies of the Massachusetts colony. On the night of April 18–19, 1775, charged to alert **Sam Adams** and **John Hancock** about the British march on Lexington, Revere rode through the countryside warning of the approach of the

Paul Revere's engraving of the Boston Massacre, printed in 1770. Library of Congress, Prints and Photographs Division.

troops before bringing the news to the two patriot leaders. He set out for Concord with two other riders, but British soldiers stopped them. As soon as he was released, Revere returned to Lexington, where he witnessed the first battle of the Revolution. His ride soon brought him fame, and he became enshrined forever in history by the famous patriotic poem of **Henry Wadsworth Longfellow.**

Unable to go home to Boston because of the British occupation, Revere turned his talents to engraving currency for the new state government. As a member of the militia he fought in a few minor skirmishes. In 1779, after a loss to the British in Maine, fellow officers accused Revere of cowardice and court-martialed him. It took him until 1782 to clear his name.

After the war he returned to Boston and resumed work in his prosperous silver shop. He expanded his interests to metal manufacture, opening a foundry that produced various metals but specialized in copper, bells, and cannon. His skilled work earned him a lofty reputation as well as tidy financial rewards. Over the years he received many honors as a result of his Revolutionary activities. In 1800 he contributed to the rising industrial revolution by opening a copper rolling mill in Canton, which made the dome for the new **State House.** He died in Boston on May 10, 1818, an inventive artisan and mechanic who had been one of the pillars of the American Revolution.

Harriet Hanson Robinson

Harriet Hanson Robinson, author, suffragist, and mill worker, is remembered for her chronicles of early factory life in New England, reporting the experiences of the Yankee farm women who became the region's first industrial workers. Born in Boston on February 8, 1825, she was the daughter of a carpenter. When the death of her father left the family in poverty, her mother moved her four daughters to Lowell, where she earned a living keeping a boarding house for the mill workers. At first young Harriet helped with the housework, but it soon became obvious that the family needed more income. At the age of ten she entered the mills as a "doffer," changing bobbins on spinning frames, working fourteen-hour days in a six-day cycle with only a half hour for her lunch and another half hour for dinner.

But the work was not constant, allowing for many games and good times with the other girls in between changing bobbins. She went to school three months a year while at the mill, spent two years at high school, and then had some private tutoring. While working at the mill she contributed to its famous literary periodical, the *Lowell Offering.* She stayed in the mills for ten years before leaving to marry and bear four children.

Writing years later about her time in the mills, Robinson extolled the new industrial experience as liberating. She recalled it as "a pleasant life," except for "the great hardship" of long hours for children, and praised the fact that work in the mills could save a family from destitution, and could even mean a step up the ladder of success. To work in a factory and earn one's own wages, no longer carrying out the unpaid drudgery of the farm, marked a major transformation in the history of women's liberation. As a result of her factory experience, Robinson became a supporter of women's clubs and a leading suffragist. In addition to her verse, she wrote four books, including *Massachusetts in the Women's Suffrage Movement* (1881) and her most famous work, *Loom and Spindle or Life among the Early Mill Girls* (1898). She died in Malden on December 22, 1911. (See also **Sara Bagley**)

Norman Rockwell

Norman Rockwell was twentieth-century America's most famous illustrator and a beloved artist of everyday life. Born in New York City on February 3, 1894, the son of a well-to-do businessman, he early on set his sights on becoming an illustrator. He studied at several art schools and was a prodigious worker, creating an enormous body of artwork. Rockwell became an instant success, landing his first magazine cover assignment in 1913 at the age of nineteen. From then on he produced countless magazine covers and drawings for hundreds of periodicals. He reached the height of his fame in the 1930s and 1940s with his covers for the nation's most popular magazine, the *Saturday Evening Post,* for which he supplied his first cover illustration at age twenty-two.

Because of his fascination with small-town life, Rockwell moved to rural Vermont in 1939 and then settled in Stockbridge, Massachusetts, in 1953. To Rockwell, his Stockbridge home "was the best of America, the best of New England." It was there that he became famous for his scenes of idealized American family life in all its warmth and humor. He also did a series of paintings depicting Stockbridge and its people, some of which became very popular greeting card illustrations. In the 1960s and 1970s Rockwell became the chief artist for *Look* magazine, treating major themes of the time, including the civil rights movement. While never accepted by the serious art world, Rockwell holds a secure place in the affections of the American public. He died on November 8, 1978, in Stockbridge, now home to the Norman Rockwell Museum, which houses a significant collection of his works. On the grounds is his last painting studio.

Edith Nourse Rogers

Edith Nourse Rogers was the first Massachusetts woman elected to the U.S. Congress, and the first woman to chair a major House committee—the Veterans Affairs Committee. Born in Saco, Maine, on March 19, 1881, she was the daughter of a businessman and politician. She studied with tutors and at private schools but never went to college. After relocating to Lowell, she married and raised a family. Her husband won election to Congress in 1925, and the family took up residence in Washington. When he died in office in 1925, the Republican Party prevailed on her to run for his vacated seat. At age forty-four she ran in a special election on the slogan that it was "time for a woman" and won with 72 percent of the vote.

Rogers served for thirty-five years with little or no opposition, winning office eighteen times. She focused on veterans' affairs, becoming the ranking Republican member of that House committee, and was one of the original sponsors of the GI Bill of 1944. During the cold war she supported Senator Joseph McCarthy and the House Un-American Activities Committee. She retained her popular support in Lowell by devoting her life to protecting the declining textile and leather industries of her district, working tirelessly to improve the lot of her constituents. She died in office on September 10, 1960, in Boston.

Royal Colony

Since their founding, the New England colonies had remained free of English control largely because of other matters more worrisome to the British. But after the restoration of the Stuarts in 1660, attention gradually turned to the New World. In 1685 the Crown revoked the charter of the **Massachusetts Bay Colony,** dissolved the Plymouth and Maine colonies, and created a new entity, the Dominion of New England, comprising New York, Massachusetts, Maine, New Hampshire, Rhode Island, and Connecticut. The plan was to centralize all administration and control all trade out of the prosperous port of Boston.

In 1686 Sir Edmund Andros arrived from England and took charge as the new royal governor. He immediately alienated the colonists by taking drastic steps that eliminated virtually all the practical freedoms that had evolved since 1630. He set aside the General Court, keeping to the executive the right to raise taxes. Next he forbade **town meeting** except once a year to elect officials, and he denied towns the right to collect church tithes used to support the clergy. Finally, he outraged the **Puritans** by taking over a Congregational meetinghouse and turning it into an Anglican church. The people were ready to rebel, having lost all their hard-won freedoms, so they rejoiced when they heard of the Glorious Revolution in England

and the accession to the throne of William and Mary. The colonists banded together and imprisoned Andros, discarding all the new laws of the Dominion.

In 1692 they received a new charter from England creating a Royal Colony. The charter restored the General Court but dropped religious tests for voter eligibility, requiring property instead—a "forty shilling freehold." A royal governor appointed by the king would control the militia, appoint judges, and veto acts of the legislature. A House of Representatives, elected by town meetings, was to choose the members of the Governor's Council, and the legislature would approve the governor's salary. This governing system of a two-house legislature and a separate executive became the model for an independent Massachusetts in 1780 and for the national government laid out by the U.S. Constitution. (See also **Pilgrims and Plymouth Colony**)

The Robert Gould Shaw Memorial, Boston. Sculpted by Augustus Saint-Gaudens, it was built in 1897 to honor the Massachusetts 54th Regiment.

Sacco and Vanzetti

The trial and execution of Nicola Sacco and Bartolomeo Vanzetti remains one of the great legal dramas of Massachusetts and American history because of the apparent injustice to the accused.

An outbreak of robberies in Bridgewater and Braintree in 1919 had resulted in two deaths. The police arrested two Italian immigrants, Sacco, a factory worker, and Vanzetti, a fish peddler, for the high-profile crimes. When arrested, each man was carrying a loaded pistol, and both were known to be active among immigrant anarchists. Vanzetti was convicted for the Bridgewater robbery in 1921, and both men were found guilty of the Braintree robbery and sentenced to death. In both trials there was little evidence connecting the two men to the crimes. The prosecutors presented dubious and tainted evidence, and the presiding judge in the second trial acted so as to prejudice the jury.

Whether the two were actually guilty or not, many observers believed that the state had not proved its case and that Sacco and Vanzetti were victims of ethnic and political bias. For six years the case remained in litigation, as left-wing activists and liberals introduced numerous motions for new trials and succeeded in making the case a national, even an international, cause célèbre. For years the nation was split over the question of the men's guilt or innocence. Then, on August 23, 1927, the Commonwealth of Massachusetts carried out the death sentences on the two men. Their ex-

Bartolomeo Vanzetti (*left*) and Nicola Sacco entering the courthouse at Dedham, 1927. Library of Congress, Prints and Photographs Division.

ecution and the controversy over it exposed the divisions within Massachusetts and American society resulting from the strains that large-scale immigration was placing on the intolerant Yankee host culture.

Salem Witchcraft Trials

The tenuousness of colonial life, exacerbated by the fear of Indian attacks, created the atmosphere of hysteria and insecurity that gave rise to the witchcraft trials in the **Massachusetts Bay Colony.** In late 1691, in the village of Salem in Essex County, several very young women, anxious about what the future might hold for them, began experimenting with fortune-telling. Especially worrisome were their apprehensions about marriage and their status in the community. They created a makeshift crystal ball and attempted to "cast spells." When their visions foretold a dire future, they became hysterical. They suffered fits and strange illnesses. Then they began to denounce other members of the community for practicing witchcraft.

At first the local minister, the Reverend Samuel Parris, father of one of the girls, held prayer meetings in an effort to contain the "deviltry." But as more and more children claimed to have seen devils and witches, more unsuspecting villagers found themselves accused. In February 1692 the girls charged three village women with practicing witchcraft. Two proclaimed their innocence, but the third, a slave named Tituba, confessed to being a witch. By March, local authorities had arrested several more villagers, including a four-year-old. Names familiar to succeeding generations—Sarah Good, Rebecca Nurse, Martha Corey, and then later her husband, Giles Corey—found themselves imprisoned and in chains. By spring the prisons were overflowing with so-called witches, but still no trials took place.

The reason for this inaction was that the colony had no legal government at that time. In 1684 the British had abrogated the governments of the **Massachusetts Bay Colony** as well as Plymouth colony. The government put in their place was itself displaced when the Glorious Revolution of 1689 removed James II from the throne. From 1689 to 1691 the colony had no official charter. Then in 1692 the Crown granted a new charter and sent a royal governor, Sir William Phips, to rule. When Phips arrived in May, he constituted a court to try the witches. That summer the authorities started executing the people held in jail. Among the executed, Giles Corey was pressed to death by heavy stones piled on his body. By September, officials had hanged nineteen people, mostly women, and arrests and accusations continued.

It was the principal ministers of eastern Massachusetts who finally put a stop to the out-of-control proceedings. Led by Increase Mather, one of the colonies' most influential clergymen, the ministers met at a formal gathering in Cambridge on October 3. Mather preached a sermon, "Cases of Conscience Concerning Evil Spirits Personating Men," which directly challenged the spurious charges used by the courts to condemn people as witches. Absolute proof of guilt could not be provided by accusations, he argued; convictions had to be based on evidence from Scripture alone, and this was not being done in the witchcraft trials. The ministers agreed. Mather's strict interpretation of guilt made it impossible to go forward with the trials.

Governor Phips forbade any further imprisonment or trials for witchcraft. By the spring of 1693 he had discharged all remaining prisoners and issued a general pardon. The hysteria was over. But lingering doubts about their future and their relationship with God would engage the **Puritans** in continued discussions about sin and evil, and would lead to a religious revival in the next century known as the **Great Awakening.**

In 1957 the Massachusetts legislature approved a resolution exonerating some of the accused witches, including "Anne Pudeator and certain other persons," and in 2001 descendants of other accused witches pressed acting governor Jane Swift to pardon their ancestors. On Halloween, Swift signed into law a bill exonerating Susannah Martin, Bridget Bishop, Alice Parker, Margaret Scott, and Wilmot Reid as the "certain other persons" of the 1957 resolution.

Saltbox House

The so-called saltbox was the prevailing style of domestic architecture used by the **Puritans** of the **Massachusetts Bay Colony** in the seventeenth century. The design derived from the architecture of East Anglia in England, the region from which the majority had emigrated. At first settlers built two-room houses, containing a hall and a parlor, with a central chimney in between to heat the rooms. As time went by, they added service rooms—kitchen, buttery, dairy—in a lean-to annex covered by a steeply downswept roof, thus creating a structure resembling a saltbox. Danvers (formerly Salem Village) has an excellent example of the style in the 1680 Rebecca Nurse Homestead (149 Pine Street), named for one of the victims claimed by the **Salem witchcraft trials** of 1692.

Leverett Saltonstall

Leverett Saltonstall, governor and U.S. senator, was a descendant of an illustrious Massachusetts family. Born on September 1, 1892, he was the son of a well-to-do Brahmin attorney. He graduated from Harvard in 1914 and Harvard Law School in 1917, saw service in World War I, and then joined the family law practice. He entered politics as a Newton alderman from 1920 to 1922, and held office as assistant district attorney for Middlesex County at the same time. He won election to the Massachusetts House of Representatives in 1922, keeping his seat until 1936, when he ran for lieutenant governor but lost. In 1938 he beat former Boston mayor **James Michael Curley** in a race for the governorship, then won reelection in 1940 and 1942. In 1944 the Republican Party nominated him for U.S. Senate, where he began a long career, being reelected in 1948, 1954, and 1960.

Saltonstall had an indifferent political career, with little noteworthy legislation to his credit. He was diligent, however, and he worked hard for his constituents. He was also one of the few members of the Senate Republican leadership who voted to censure Senator Joseph McCarthy in 1954 for his outrageous Red baiting. Saltonstall's long tenure gave him power over several Senate committees. On most issues his moderate stance, plus his reputation for honesty and integrity, endeared him to Bay State voters. He retired to his Massachusetts farm at the end of his final term in January 1967, where he died on June 17, 1979.

Scrimshaw

While on long sea voyages that could last anywhere from two to five years, whaling crews developed the skill of carving designs on whalebones and walrus tusks. These carved designs depicting sea animals or intricate patterns became much sought after as decorative pieces to be displayed in homes. Nantucket Island is still known today as a center for traditional scrimshaw art, displayed now on the handles and clasps of women's handbags. (See **Cape Cod and the Islands** and **Whaling**)

Robert Gould Shaw

Robert Gould Shaw, who commanded the nation's first all-black regiment in the Civil War, was a Boston native, born October 10, 1837, the son of a rich and influential Brahmin family. His parents were enthusiastic **abolitionists** and members of Boston's fervent antislavery circle. Young Shaw went to preparatory schools in Europe and the United States. After spending time roaming Europe, he entered Harvard College in 1856, but performed there with little distinction or enthusiasm. The outbreak of the Civil War led Shaw to volunteer, ending up in the Second Massachusetts Infantry as a lieutenant. A good soldier, he was wounded at the Battle of Antietam and then rose in rank to captain. Throughout these experiences he showed no interest in the issue of slavery. He considered soldiering his career.

The Emancipation Proclamation of 1863 raised the possibility of forming regiments of black soldiers, something that Massachusetts's abolitionists had long demanded. Massachusetts governor John A. Andrew, an abolitionist and a friend of the elder Shaws, asked them to persuade their son to serve as the colonel of an all-black regiment. Robert Gould Shaw reluctantly agreed and was named commander of the newly formed Fifty-fourth Regiment of Massachusetts Volunteers of African Descent.

With a triumphant parade through Boston on May 28, 1863, the Fifty-fourth took ship and sailed for South Carolina, where, on July 18, Shaw led his troops in battle against the impregnable Fort Wagner. Marching into a fusillade of Confederate fire, Shaw was killed along with sixty-two of his men. A mass grave became the final burial site for the young white officer and his black comrades. One of the soldiers of the Fifty-fourth, Sergeant William Carney, so distinguished himself in the battle that the government awarded him the Congressional Medal of Honor, the first for an African American. The next year, when the regiment saw heavy fighting around Charlestown, South Carolina, Shaw's well-trained troops demonstrated to skeptical whites that black men could be able soldiers, elevating their regiment and their fallen leader as an enduring symbol of individuals sacrificing themselves for the cause of liberty.

A monument sculpted by Augustus Saint-Gaudens and erected in 1897 on **Boston Common** stands as a testament both to the courageous black soldiers and to their commander. The creation of the Fifty-fourth Regiment attests to the idealistic ardor of Massachusetts's abolitionists, who, along with black abolitionists such as **Frederick Douglass** (one of whose sons fought in Shaw's regiment), made an enormous contribution to ending slavery in the United States.

Shays's Rebellion

Between 1786 and 1787, the farmers and small-town residents of western and central Massachusetts were so dissatisfied with the state government that they took up arms in an insurrection. At the time, the Bay State was beset by economic woes epitomized by conflict between the "creditors," the merchant classes and large landowners concentrated in the east, and the "debtors," the farmers and traders living in the interior and the west. Facing a war debt of $14 million, the General Court initiated a series of new property and poll taxes and imposed higher legal fees for those forced into debtors' courts. Disgruntled farmers and rural residents throughout the state met and passed resolutions calling on the legislature to reduce court fees, issue paper money, and reduce taxes. When their pleas went unheeded, farmers in western Massachusetts decided to take action against the state courts, which had been foreclosing against farm properties.

On August 29, 1786, a gang of angry farmers and debtors closed down the court at Northampton. Thus began a series of mob attacks against state courts in Hampshire, Middlesex, Bristol, and Worcester counties. Named after their sometime leader, Daniel Shays of Pelham, the rebellion resulted in forced closures of courthouses in Springfield, Worcester, Great Barrington, and elsewhere. Men from over fifty Massachusetts towns, such as Amherst, Pelham, and Deerfield, formed a military force of "regulators" to protest unfair taxes, harsh credit laws, and farm foreclosures. Many of those involved were, like Shays, former soldiers in the American Revolution who felt they had never received just compensation for their service while merchants in Boston had become profiteers.

After rebel attacks on the Springfield courthouse and armory and another confrontation in Sheffield, the eastern merchants financed a militia, which marched westward. Confronting the rebels with force in a few skirmishes, the militia destroyed the main band at Petersham on February 4, 1787. Shays fled to New York State, where he died in poverty years later. As a result of Shays's Rebellion, legislators in the eastern part of the state agreed to reduce taxation rates considerably. The rebellion also convinced the nation at large that the Articles of Confederation were weak and unwieldy and unable to keep order. This led to the eventual acceptance of a new form of government under the Constitution.

Captain John Smith

John Smith is best known for his adventures in the Virginia Colony, and in particular for the famous story of Pocahontas, the Indian chief's daughter, who saved his life by offering herself in his stead. Smith was a noted explorer, however, who traveled the New England coast in 1614. He wrote a coastal survey and designed a map of the region naming an area Plimoth. A copy of this map was on board the *Mayflower,* and the Pilgrims used it to guide them to a suitable landfall on their arrival in 1620. (See also **Pilgrims and Plymouth Colony**)

Sons of Liberty

The Sons of Liberty of Massachusetts was a loosely organized group of patriots who came together in the mid-eighteenth century to supply the manpower for parades, demonstrations, and even riots to promote the cause of resistance to the British Parliament's attempt to impose its sovereign will over the colonies. Similar groups existed throughout the colonies. In Massachusetts the Sons of Liberty issued a wholesale refusal to accept the **Stamp Act** of 1765, a parliamentary tax on all paper items that was passed without the consent of the colonists. On one occasion the Sons of Liberty organized a demonstration in Boston forcing the designated stamp agent, Andrew Oliver, to agree not to distribute stamps. Later the mob destroyed his office building and then vandalized the home of Lieutenant Governor **Thomas Hutchinson** because of his support of the tax. It was men from the Sons of Liberty, largely artisans, who participated in the **Boston Tea Party.** In these and other protests, they represented the popular backbone of the Revolutionary forces.

Springfield Armory

The siting of the nation's first arsenal in Springfield led to the town's development as the urban center of the **Pioneer Valley** and the third largest city in the state. During the American Revolution, George Washington selected Springfield, because of its safe location on the Connecticut River, to house a national armory to provide guns and munitions for the Continental forces. It remained a government armory well into the twentieth century until its closing. From the Civil War on, the armory was the center of the city's growing prosperity. Over the years it attracted skilled machinists to Springfield as well as peripheral industries that hired trained artisans, thus creating a local agglomeration of technical workers.

It was at the Springfield Armory that Thomas Blanchard invented the gun lathe, which allowed for precision cutting of gunstocks. The presence of the armory encouraged the growth of private gun makers such as Smith and Wesson and Colt of Connecticut. It was armory staff who designed the Springfield rifle used in World War I and John Garrand's semiautomatic rifle, the M-1, which became the army's weapon of choice in World War II.

The Department of Defense closed the armory in 1968 for what appear to have been political rather than economic considerations, though the reason was never entirely clear. Its loss dealt a serious economic blow to the community from which it never fully recovered. The main arsenal, built in 1847, now houses the Springfield Armory Museum, run by the National Park Service Administration. The museum holds one of the oldest and largest collections of small arms, with over eight thousand items on view. Other buildings now are part of Springfield Community College.

Squanto

Squanto (or Tisquantum), the last survivor of the Patuxet tribe, is known to schoolchildren as the Indian who saved the Pilgrims. The truth is more complex. Squanto fell victim to English slavers in 1614, who kidnapped him along with others and brought him to Malaga, Spain, to be sold. Somehow he got to England, where by 1616 he was residing in the home of a wealthy English merchant. After learning English, Squanto returned to New England in order to act as a guide for commercial investors interested in establishing trade relations with the Native tribes. During his absence, in 1616 his Patuxet village had been swept by an epidemic caused by contact with the English traders. Most of the tribe had died, and the few survivors had moved elsewhere. Squanto arrived home in 1619 to find a deserted village, so he too left the area.

In December 1620 the Pilgrims settled in the abandoned Patuxet village, renaming it Plymouth. They suffered badly through the winter, losing half the community to disease and starvation. The survivors were unprepared for the coming planting season. At the end of their rope, they resorted to stealing corn from the surrounding tribes, further inflaming hostility against the English.

It was conflict among the Native tribes that saved the Pilgrims. The Pokanoket tribe, a branch of the Wampanoags, disliked the English, but they hated the more powerful Narragansetts, who forced them to pay tribute. **Massasoit,** the Pokanoket sachem, or chief, thought that an alliance with the English and their firepower might free his people from the yoke of the Narragansetts. He sent two Indians, Samoset and Squanto, to the English at Plymouth to negotiate a peace treaty. Squanto, with his command of English and his acquaintance with English ways, emerged as the major mediator. The result was a peace treaty that lasted fifty years and created a powerful alliance between English settlers and Indians that forced the other surrounding tribes to avoid any thoughts of conflict.

For his services, Squanto became the official guide and diplomat of the Plymouth Colony, thus returning home to Patuxet. In the spring of 1621 he taught the Pilgrims how to plant corn and to use fish as fertilizer, ensuring a continuing food supply for the colony. He had so demonstrated his worth to the Pilgrims that when hostile Indians kidnapped Squanto, the colonists mounted an armed expedition and rescued him. After that, he negotiated further treaties with Native bands from Massachusetts Bay to Cape Cod, thus safeguarding the Pilgrims from attack and ensuring a durable chain of food supplies. In January 1622 the Narragansetts threatened war against the Pilgrims by sending them a snakeskin filled with arrows. On Squanto's advice, the colonists returned the pouch filled with gunpowder and shot. Their firm stand forced the Narragansetts to back down.

Squanto died unexpectedly in 1622 while living among the Pilgrims. Acting as a political mediator, he had served the needs of both Natives and settlers by helping to establish a fifty-year peace that benefited all. The peace finally shattered in 1675 when Massasoit's son Metacom, known as King Philip, initiated a bloody war against the colonists, hoping to drive them from New England. (See also **King Philip's War** and **Pilgrims and Plymouth Colony**)

Stamp Act

The Stamp Act tax was one of many attempts by British government ministers to raise revenue from the colonies which ultimately led to the American Revolution. Parliament argued that it had the sovereign right to levy taxes on the colonies. The stamp tax required a government stamp, purchased from the king's agents, to be affixed to all legal documents, diplomas, newspapers, licenses, pamphlets, almanacs, even playing cards. The tax, which was to go into effect on November 1, 1765, would affect people of all classes.

In June the Massachusetts House of Representatives wrote a circular letter to all the other colonies to call a meeting or congress in New York to discuss the situation. At this Stamp Act Congress, Patrick Henry and his followers presented the Virginia Resolves, which the members approved. Simply stated, the Resolves maintained that Parliament had no right to tax the colonies since the colonists had no representation in that body. Boston responded to the resolution with an outbreak of popular resistance to the tax. Andrew Oliver, the brother-in-law of Chief Justice **Thomas Hutchin-**

son, had been appointed the town's designated stamp agent. On August 14, 1765, a large crowd hanged an effigy of Oliver on an elm tree, at what is now the corner of Washington and Essex streets, and they proceeded to wreck his new office building. That same morning the **Sons of Liberty,** a loosely organized group of patriots, met in front of another large elm tree to demonstrate against the Stamp Act. These "liberty trees" would become symbols of American resistance to British arbitrariness.

The fearful Oliver fled to the sanctuary of Castle William in the harbor, while the crowd marched on his home in the North End and vandalized it. Showing their contempt for the king's men, another crowd formed on August 26 and attacked the home of a customs official and then heavily damaged the mansion of Chief Justice Hutchinson. On September 11, **Sam Adams** and the Sons of Liberty met at the elm tree from which the crowd had hung the effigy of Oliver and consecrated the tree as the "Liberty Tree." On December 17, Adams and the Sons of Liberty forced Oliver to go to the Liberty Tree, swear never to distribute the hated stamps, and resign as stamp agent.

Following Boston's lead, colonists in the major cities rioted and demonstrated against the Stamp Act, making its enforcement impossible. Bowing to the inevitable, Parliament in 1766 revoked the act. But it was too late; the seeds of liberty had been planted. The colonists contended that Parliament had no right to levy taxation without representation. This notion of rule by consent of the governed would soon become the driving force behind the American Revolution.

Myles Standish

Captain Myles Standish was the leader of the small military contingent among the Pilgrim settlers who came to Massachusetts in 1620. When the *Mayflower* first landed on Cape Cod, on November 15 Standish led a group of men to search for a suitable place to settle, but they were unsuccessful. In the process, however, he aroused the Natives' hostility by pillaging Indian graves, grain stores, and villages. Standish and his men returned to the ship and set sail again in search of an appropriate landfall. On December 12 he led a small expedition to what is now Plymouth, and on December 16 the *Mayflower* arrived there safely in the harbor. Standish's crude military policies created tension with the local Indian tribes that took years to overcome.

Some two hundred years later, **Henry Wadsworth Longfellow** made

Captain Standish famous along with John and Priscilla Alden in his poem *The Courtship of Miles Standish.* As the story goes, the gruff soldier Standish was too shy to ask Priscilla Mullins to be his bride, so he enlisted John Alden to act as an intermediary for him. The seventeen-year-old Priscilla interrupted Alden to ask, "Why don't you speak for yourself, John?" Whether the story is true or not, the couple married in 1623. They had ten children. (See also **Pilgrims and Plymouth Colony**)

State House

The State House in Boston is the home of the Massachusetts legislature, or General Court, and contains the office of the governor and other executive branches of government. By 1795 the Old State House, or Town House as it had been called since its construction in 1711, was no longer capable of housing the state's growing government, so the state paid **John Hancock**'s heirs £4,000 for a cow pasture on a slope of **Beacon Hill** as the site for the new state capitol. Designed by architect **Charles Bulfinch,** the new State House opened in January 1798.

Imposing at 172 feet across, 65 feet deep, and 155 feet high, with its famous golden dome, the structure looks down from the heights of Beacon Street over the **Boston Common** and downtown. In 1802 artisan **Paul Revere** redesigned the dome, replacing the original wood with copper. In 1874 the legislature sponsored a design in gold leaf to be overlaid on the dome, giving the State House its current splendid appearance. Officials authorized additions to the building throughout the nineteenth and early twentieth centuries. The House and Senate chambers are on the third floor, and the governor's office occupies the southwest corner of the second floor. Throughout the building are statuary and paintings depicting the state's important leaders and events from its past.

Lucy Stone

An abolitionist, social reformer, suffragist, and feminist, Lucy Stone was a leading exponent of vital social reforms that eventually became reality owing to her pioneering efforts. Born on August 13, 1818, in West Brookfield, she was the daughter of farmers. She went to local schools and attended Mount Holyoke Seminary for one term in 1839, then enrolled at

Oberlin College in Ohio in 1843. Stone graduated in 1847, becoming the first Bay State woman to receive a bachelor's degree. **William Lloyd Garrison,** a leader of the **abolitionists,** then hired her as an agent for his Massachusetts Anti-Slavery Society. She spoke at public gatherings on antislavery and women's rights issues, which was unusual for the day as women were not supposed to speak in public. She helped organize the first national convention for women's rights in Worcester in 1850.

When she married fellow abolitionist Henry B. Blackwell in 1855, he agreed that she should keep her own name. Protesting the disfranchisement of women, in 1858 Stone and her husband refused to pay taxes, a stance that resulted in the confiscation of the family's household goods. She also worked for equal rights for African Americans after the Civil War and was a founder of the American Equal Rights Association. She and others established the American Woman Suffrage Association in 1869, which was a rival of Susan B. Anthony and Elizabeth Cady Stanton's National Woman's Suffrage Association. In 1879, when women earned the right to vote in Boston School Committee elections, Stone was turned away because she refused to register under her husband's name.

Stone and Blackwell had settled in Dorchester in 1867 and started their own periodical, the *Woman's Journal.* She continued her suffrage and reform activities, but focused her attention on editing the journal. She died in Dorchester on October 18, 1893, leaving her daughter **Alice Stone Blackwell** to carry on her work.

Sturbridge Village

Built on the site of an early-nineteenth-century farm, located near the junctions of Routes I-90 and I-84 in central Massachusetts, Old Sturbridge is the recreation of a model rural village of between 1790 and 1840. It comprises forty buildings set on two hundred acres, the largest outdoor historic restoration in the Northeast. Authentic furnishings and demonstrations of crafts and rural trades by guides wearing period costumes bring an early American farm town to life. Interpreters busily spin, weave, cook, and do farm chores, just as villagers would have long ago. Many fascinating collections of artifacts are on display, and there is a book and gift shop. A tavern offers food based on 1830s recipes, cooked over an open hearth.

The village was the work of the Wells family, owners of the American Optical Company of Sturbridge. They became absorbed in collecting antiques and Americana in the 1920s and 1930s and decided to make these available to the public. The family provided the money and their collections to recreate an ideal New England village. Opened in 1946, Sturbridge now welcomes over half a million visitors a year to this "living" village of the past.

Suffolk Resolves

After the **Boston Tea Party** uprising, the British government responded in the spring of 1774 with the **Coercive Acts,** which closed the port of Boston, and other laws that abrogated local control over governance of the colonies. Rallying against this arrogant display of imperial power, representatives from the towns of Suffolk County drafted a series of nineteen resolutions lambasting the British actions. These resolves condemned the Coercive Acts as illegal and "arbitrary," "the attempts of a wicked administration to enslave America." They called on all citizens to refrain from paying taxes, demanded a boycott of British goods, and hinted at preparations for armed resistance. The resolves were forwarded to the Continental Congress that was meeting in Philadelphia, where they received a warm and enthusiastic response. The Continental Congress passed a resolution approving the sentiments and urging Massachusetts to persevere and hold firm.

John L. Sullivan

Known as the "Boston Strong Boy," John L. Sullivan was a championship boxer of the late nineteenth century who became an exemplar of Boston Irish social mobility. Sullivan helped transform boxing from an underground activity into a popular sport. Born on October 12, 1858, in Boston's South End, the son of poor Irish immigrants, he attended public schools (he may also have attended Boston College for a while) and worked at various blue-collar jobs. Sullivan always excelled at sports. He began fighting in 1878 and quickly became noted for his aggressiveness and stamina. At that time prizefighting was illegal and unregulated. It is noteworthy that Sullivan was one of the first boxers to make his living by this illicit sport. He fought all over the country, winning decisively each time. An informal

John L. Sullivan, champion pugilist of the world, c. 1883. Library of Congress, Prints and Photographs Division.

heavyweight championship bout took place between Sullivan and Paddy Ryan in Mississippi in 1882, with the Boston Strong Boy an easy winner.

Using the title of world heavyweight champ, Sullivan continued his boxing career. His fame widened, making him perhaps the most popular sports figure in the nation in the 1880s. His Boston Irish fans exulted as Sullivan's star brightened. A growing dependence on alcohol and desultory training soon took a toll on his fitness, however, and imprudent spending brought him near to bankruptcy. To recoup his fortunes, on September 7, 1892, he fought the up-and-coming young boxer James J. Corbett for the championship. The younger and faster Corbett won, ending the boxing career of Sullivan. He subsequently went into show business, owned various saloons, and finally retired to a farm in West Abington, where he died on February 2, 1918, still idolized by the immigrant working poor as a champ who always remained proud of his humble Boston origins.

Charles Sumner

A U.S. senator, abolitionist, and social reformer, Charles Sumner labored in the Senate for twenty-three years in the cause of racial equality to help move the nation from slavery to freedom. He was born the son of a lawyer in a middle-class Boston family on January 6, 1811. He entered Harvard in 1826, graduating four years later, and then went on to Harvard Law School, though he did not earn a degree. He practiced law in Boston from 1835 to 1837, but became increasingly involved in the antislavery movement. His relationships with reformers such as **Samuel Gridley Howe** and William Ellery Channing enhanced his social reform beliefs.

Sumner began to give public lectures which brought him notoriety, speaking on subjects such as the impropriety of the Mexican War and the evil of slavery and its connection to the Constitution. As a member of the "conscience" Whigs (those opposed to the expansion of slavery into the territories), he joined the Free Soil Party and attacked the "cotton" Whigs (those who wanted to maintain good relations with the South because of their textile interests) and Whig moderates such as **Daniel Webster.** In 1849 he argued a case against the Boston School Committee for blacks who hoped to end public school segregation. Although he failed to convince the court, he laid the groundwork for success, and the Massachusetts legislature ended public school segregation in 1855.

When Massachusetts Democratic **abolitionists** joined with Free Soilers in 1851 to capture control over the state legislature, the antislavery legislature appointed Sumner as the new U.S. senator from Massachusetts. In the Senate he kept up a constant and vitriolic attack on the slave South and its disproportionate influence over Congress. Sumner worked to repeal the 1850 Fugitive Slave Act, and was in the forefront of those fearful of the consequences of the 1854 Kansas-Nebraska Act, which opened the territories to the possibility of slavery should the people vote for it under the "popular sovereignty" principle. One of the founders of the Republican Party, in 1856 he gave a speech in the Senate on "the Crime against Kansas," in which he viciously attacked other senators, particularly compromiser Stephen A. Douglass of Illinois, for opening the territories to slavery. His speech so angered the South that one southern congressman, Preston Brooks of South Carolina, entered the Senate chamber and beat Senator Sumner into unconsciousness with a stick.

It took Sumner over three years to recover and return to the Senate. The incident made clear the substantial chasm that existed between the North and the South on the issue of slavery. Sumner welcomed the outbreak of the Civil War and worked on the reluctant Abraham Lincoln to free the slaves. After the death of Lincoln and the end of the war, the lenient reconstruction policies of President Andrew Johnson infuriated Sumner. He led the fight for Johnson's impeachment, and was one of the authors of the radical reconstruction program that began in 1867. Into the early 1870s he worked to provide full legal equality for blacks, playing an important role in the passage of the Fourteenth and Fifteenth Amendments. He died in Washington on March 11, 1874. (See also **Fugitive Slaves**)

Symphony Hall

The Huntington Avenue home of the famed Boston Symphony Orchestra and the Boston Pops, Symphony Hall was the work of one dedicated man, the Boston banker Henry Lee Higginson. A lifelong lover of music, Higginson believed that every great city should have a symphony and a grand hall to house it, and that became his goal for Boston. Single-handedly, he provided the funds for founding the BSO. Its first home in 1881 was at the Music Hall in downtown Boston. Bringing together like-minded supporters, Higginson created a corporation that engaged the famed architectural firm of McKim, Mead, and White to build an auditorium for the orchestra that would offer the finest acoustics of the day. To make sure that the hall would provide the best possible sound, Higginson hired Harvard physics professor Wallace C. Sabine, who invented the science of acoustics by calculating the mathematical relationships between the volume and shape of the auditorium. Construction began in June 1899, and Symphony Hall opened on October 15, 1900, with a celebratory concert for 2,600 patrons. Over the years Symphony Hall has drawn both Boston Brahmins and those of more modest means and pedigree, who have donated their money and given their support to keep this musical gem in full operation.

A summer concert at the Koussevitzky Shed, Tanglewood. Photograph by Stu Rossner.

T

Tanglewood

Tanglewood is the summer home of the Boston Symphony Orchestra, located in Lenox in the **Berkshires** in western Massachusetts. Here the BSO provides a wide range of summer concerts for visitors to enjoy either in the Shed auditorium or on the surrounding lawns, where picnickers relax while listening to great music. The Tanglewood Music Center opened in 1940 under the leadership of former BSO conductor Serge Koussevitzky as a place for the education of musicians. Thus Tanglewood is both an academy for musical training and a performance center. It is the world's only musical academy associated with a major symphony orchestra. Each year over 1,500 students apply, but only 100 are selected, all for full scholarships. At the school BSO musicians mentor the budding instrumentalists and singers in the midst of a summer-long music festival. Illustrious graduates of the school include Leonard Bernstein, Leontyne Price, Zubin Mehta, and longtime BSO conductor Seiji Ozawa. Tanglewood serves as the premier cultural center of summer life in the Berkshires, attracting visitors from throughout the Northeast and beyond.

Thanksgiving (See **Pilgrims and Plymouth Colony**)

Henry David Thoreau

Born in Concord on July 12, 1817, Henry David Thoreau was a famous Transcendentalist and author of *Walden,* among other widely read works.

Fascinated by nature, he spent much time walking through the fields and woods of Concord, observing and studying. He went to Harvard and, after graduating in 1837, returned to Concord to teach school, working also as a carpenter and gardener. At that time he became heavily influenced by the work of **Ralph Waldo Emerson,** who had moved to Concord. Both men believed strongly in the healing powers of nature and the Transcendentalist notion of overcoming societal materialism by devoting oneself to more nature-oriented interests. Thoreau lived in Emerson's house at one point, each comforting the other in their losses after the deaths of Thoreau's brother and Emerson's first son.

Eager to become a writer, and seeking solitude, at age twenty-eight Thoreau went to live near **Walden Pond** on land owned by Emerson. Here he built his famous cottage with materials costing twenty-eight dollars and twelve and a half cents, moving in on July 4, 1845. Thoreau wrote of his decision, "I went to the woods because I wished to live deliberately, to front only the essential facts of life, and see if I could not learn what it had to teach, and not, when I came to die, discover that I had not lived." He spent his time intensely studying nature, putting his thoughts and observations on paper, and writing his first book, *A Week on the Concord and Merrimack Rivers,* the journal of a trip taken with his brother in 1839.

While at Walden, Thoreau walked often to Concord village, visiting Emerson and others, and working as a surveyor. He left the house on the pond in 1847 to live permanently in Concord. In 1849 he published his famous essay "On Civil Disobedience" after spending a night in jail for refusing to pay his taxes during the Mexican War. He worked for seven years on what was to become *Walden,* published in 1854. Thoreau also worked part-time and spent his remaining hours reading, writing, lecturing, and studying nature on his constant walks. With Emerson he became an avid advocate of abolitionism, particularly after the unsavory events surrounding the return of fugitive slave Anthony Burns in 1854. He died at age forty-four on May 6, 1862, after contracting tuberculosis. Along with Emerson, **Nathaniel Hawthorne,** and other writers, he is buried on Author's Ridge in Sleepy Hollow Cemetery in Concord. (See also **Abolitionists** and **Transcendentalism**)

Town Meeting

Long considered a major component of American democracy, the idea of town meeting was brought from England by the **Puritans** as a community meeting restricted to the elect only. It became the means by which the inhabitants of the **Massachusetts Bay Colony** dealt with the requirements of local governance. As defined by the General Court in 1636, town meeting initially had low levels of participation, except when controversial matters arose. Issues such as the choice of a new minister or the location of the meetinghouse often inspired full attendance. The members of town meeting would tax themselves to pay for the community's needs. The intent was not to pursue democratic practices but to rule through consensus.

Town meeting set community needs above individual freedom. For example, when the town of Eastham was overrun by birds, town meeting decreed that no man could marry until he killed six blackbirds or three crows. Thus, personal liberty was tied to the notion of the general welfare, for the **Puritans** believed that true liberty was not the right to do as one pleased but a moral imperative to subject oneself to the authority of the community of saints. With the revocation of the Massachusetts Bay Charter in favor of the **Royal Colony** in 1692, town meeting continued to be a vehicle for local government. Now, however, membership was predicated on the basis of taxable goods or ownership of land, not on religion. Eventually the legislature ended all financial requirements for inclusion in town meeting. Town meeting continues today as a viable form of local government for many communities in the state.

Transcendentalism

Transcendentalism was a naturalistic philosophy that emanated from New England in the 1840s but had roots in both Unitarianism and the work of the German philosopher Immanuel Kant. Its main spokesman was **Ralph Waldo Emerson.** The philosophy promoted a way of life predicated on the intuitive appreciation of nature as a force of liberation from the growing materialism of the day. It stressed the spiritual rather than the corporeal side of humanity, emphasizing the ability to "transcend" into the orbit of God or nature through personal revelation and intuition. Truth was a product of innate spirituality, not cognitive learning.

The Transcendentalist movement got its start in Boston in 1840 when a small group led by Emerson founded a periodical, *The Dial.* At first it was edited by **Margaret Fuller,** but eventually Emerson, supported by **Henry David Thoreau,** took over the reins. The movement became centered in Concord, where both Emerson and Thoreau lived. Other writers associated with Transcendentalism were William Ellery Channing and Bronson Alcott, who spread the gospel both in their writings and on the lecture circuit, thus making Transcendentalism nationally known. Transcendentalists were also involved in many of the social reform movements of the day, from antislavery and penal reform to temperance and women's suffrage. By the end of the Civil War, however, the movement had dissipated. (See also **Brook Farm**)

Triangular Trade

By the end of the eighteenth century it was obvious that Massachusetts would never prosper as an agricultural entity. Unable to grow a marketable staple crop, a small group of resourceful men turned their eyes to the sea. The new focus on seafaring and trading, however, also brought the colony into direct conflict with British mercantilist policies. The move to maritime commerce meant that the proscriptive Navigation Acts, with their prohibitions on markets and their duties on trade with other countries, were by necessity to be circumvented. Smuggling occurred on a grand scale. The move seaward forged a new outlook, one that was more worldly and secular, resulting in the gradual transition from Puritan to Yankee, from theocracy to merchant-civic polity.

Close proximity to the rich Grand Banks fishing area, with its cod, mackerel, and herring, and an enviable coastal location with good harbors catapulted Massachusetts into its new status as the world's primary commercial fishing community. Ever larger vessels were outfitted from Nantucket, Marblehead, and New Bedford to scour the oceans for whales and their precious oil. By 1740 over 150 whaling ships from Nantucket alone plied the North and South Atlantic and Arctic oceans. Other products for trade, such as timber, foodstuffs, horses, furs, and rum, came directly from the forests and farms of Massachusetts. Industrious merchants and seamen ignored most prohibitions on products and markets. The world was their trading ground. It was re-exporting, the "triangular trades," that was to create a new class of merchant princes.

The West Indies, particularly the non-English islands that were legally off-limits, became the primary target for Massachusetts's traders. Three triangular trade routes took shape: the first carried rum from Massachusetts to the west coast of Africa to trade for slaves, who were carried to the West Indies and exchanged for sugar and molasses, which went back to the colony to be made into more rum: the second brought fish, foodstuffs, timber, and horses to the West Indies in exchange for sugar, which was taken to England to be traded for manufactured goods to be sold in Massachusetts and other colonial markets; the third sent fish, foodstuffs, timber, and fur to southern Europe to be exchanged for wine, silk, spices, and fruit, which were brought to England and again traded for manufactured goods bound for the colonies. The merchants of the coastal towns grew rich from their ability to exploit the booming maritime trade of the eighteenth century. By the coming of the Revolution, Boston and other seaport towns had in place a well-to-do merchant elite who would lead the movement to cast off the rule of Great Britain, which had imposed economic restraints on them.

William Monroe Trotter

William Monroe Trotter was a fighter for black civil rights and a crusading journalist. The African American Trotter used his newspaper the *Boston Guardian,* like **William Lloyd Garrison**'s *Liberator* in Boston, as a powerful voice in the quest for equal rights. Born in Ohio on April 7, 1872, he was the son of a Democratic politician, but he grew up in Boston. He received a B.A. in 1895 from Harvard and later an M.A. as well, then set up a real estate business in Boston in 1899. Displeased with the rising segregation movement dubbed "Jim Crow," Trotter opened a newspaper in 1901, the *Boston Guardian,* to promote legal equality for blacks.

He used the growing popularity of his newspaper to attack the accommodation policies of the black leader Booker T. Washington. When Washington came to Boston to speak in 1903, Trotter and his followers first heckled him, then disrupted the meeting, declaring that they wanted equality now, not at some future time. Trotter's insistence on immediate equality found him in tune with another black leader, **W. E. B. Du Bois,** and the two men began working together. They both participated in the founding of the National Association for the Advancement of Colored People (NAACP) in 1909. But Trotter broke with Du Bois, rejecting any white participation in that organization.

His growing radicalism left him on the fringes of the black movement for equality. He further distanced himself from moderates when, in a meeting at the White House, he argued strenuously with Woodrow Wilson over the president's failure to support civil rights for blacks, embarrassing the other delegates. He became one of the first black leaders to organize protest marches, and he used the pages of the *Guardian* to harangue apathetic whites and moderate blacks alike. The Great Depression caused the demise of his newspaper, and he died in a fall from a building in a probable suicide on his sixty-second birthday, April 7, 1934.

The ruins of the Ursuline Convent in Charlestown, burned down and vandalized by Yankee rioters on August 11, 1834. From Justin Winsor, *The Memorial History of Boston,* vol. 3 (1881).

U

University of Massachusetts

The state's center of public higher education is the five-campus University of Massachusetts system. Its early origins as an agricultural school in a state rich in private colleges and universities made for difficulties in achieving growth and prosperity. Funded under the Morrill Land Grant Act of 1862, the Massachusetts Agricultural College at Amherst came into being one year later, endowed with the specific purpose of improving farming and rural life in the state. Its first class of fifty-six entered in 1867, just as the state was flowering as an industrialized and urbanized community. This emphasis on a dying enterprise, agriculture, retarded the school's progress.

It was not until 1931 that the legislature recognized the need to provide alternatives to private higher education. The goal of a low-cost education for state residents was realized with a change of name to Massachusetts State College, which offered a B.S. degree in addition to agricultural training. After World War II a large number of returning veterans, with support from the G.I. Bill, created significant pressure to expand the size and mission of public higher education. The legislature established the University of Massachusetts in 1947 to cope with the rising need.

Nevertheless, in comparison to the Midwest and other regions, Massachusetts ranked last in the amount of per capita spending on public higher education. Intensive demand forced grudging legislators to support increased budgets, especially in the 1960s. Impressive growth occurred even with weak backing from the legislature and direct opposition of the state's many private schools. The Amherst campus grew from 6,300 students in 1960 to 17,800 in 1970. During this time the legislature became more attuned to the demands of its citizenry for access to higher education. The legislators created a network of community colleges and revamped the state's teachers' colleges into full-fledged liberal arts institutions. Bridgewater, Fitchburg, Framingham, North Adams (now the College of Liberal Arts), Salem, and Westfield become home to state colleges, while over fifteen community colleges sprang up all across the state. Although opportunities had opened up for many, the flagship university now faced increased competition for state funds.

Nonetheless, the university expanded, opening a medical school in Worcester in 1962, and then incorporating Boston State College in 1965 as UMass Boston. Campuses at Lowell and Dartmouth became part of a newly organized five-campus system in 1991, with a centralized president's office in Boston, and UMass Boston moved to a new campus near the harbor. Though never funded as richly as other state universities, UMass flourished and attracted a superb research faculty who raised its reputation nationwide. The inflation of the 1970s caused a setback in university funding, preventing further expansion and ending plans for a law school. Despite increased state funding in the prosperous 1980s and 1990s, the university never fully recovered from the shortfalls of the 1970s. It has remained only modestly supported, unable to expand its student body or fully realize its plans for new ventures.

Ursuline Convent Riot

On the evening of August 11, 1834, a large crowd of Yankee Protestant workingmen vandalized and burned down the Roman Catholic Ursuline Convent in Charlestown. The convent, a finishing school for a small number of Catholic girls and for the daughters of Boston's upper-class Unitarians and Episcopalians, was a convenient target for working-class fundamentalist Protestants who were rabidly anti-Catholic.

The period was one of Protestant evangelical fervor heightened by the schism that occurred when Boston's upper classes turned to Unitarianism and away from the stricter Calvinist ideas of their Puritan ancestors. By the 1820s, the rising tide of Catholic immigration from Ireland revived intolerance among the majority Protestant population of Boston. The newcomers personified a long-hated religion that seemed to endanger prevailing beliefs, causing a virulent Yankee response. In addition, the immigrants had begun to compete directly with Yankee workers for the scarce unskilled labor jobs of commercial Boston.

False rumors persisted over the years of scandalous sexual activities, murder, and kidnapping in convents and monasteries. In August 1834 rumors spread of a nun being forcibly held in the Ursuline Convent after attempting to leave. A large crowd of workers from Charlestown and Boston gathered outside the convent on the evening of August 11. Thousands of bystanders applauded as a group of some fifty to one hundred roughnecks, disguised as Indians or wearing masks or petticoats, assaulted the convent buildings. These men—truck men, brick makers, sailors, firemen, apprentices, and assorted juveniles—represented the Protestant working poor of the community. The nuns and the children fled as the mob ransacked the buildings and then set them ablaze.

Boston's leaders met at Faneuil Hall and condemned the action of the crowd. The authorities arrested several of the rioters and brought them to trial, but a Yankee jury of workingmen acquitted all but one of the accused. The defense statement to the jury was simple: all the witnesses against the defendants were Catholics and thus suspect. The jury was asked to reject Catholic "imported testimony" in favor of "domestic testimony." This manifestation of anti–Irish Catholic sentiment did not abate, as additional riots occurred. It was not until the twentieth century that the Irish came to feel welcome in Boston. (See also **Anti-Catholicism, Broad Street Riot,** and **Pope Day**)

U.S.S. *Constitution*

The U.S.S. *Constitution,* also known as "Old Ironsides" for having survived many sea battles thanks to its durable hull, is a naval battleship that served principally in the War of 1812. Launched in 1797, and built of oak and pine, this sailing ship is the world's oldest such vessel still in existence. It is docked at the Charlestown Navy Yard, part of Boston's National Historical Park, and is one of the stops on the **Freedom Trail.** The ship is open to the public, and U.S. Navy personnel give guided tours. Once a year on July 4, the ship is towed out into Boston Harbor and turned to change sides when docked again.

The Volleyball Hall of Fame, Holyoke. (*Inset*) William G. Morgan, the inventor of volleyball, 1895. Courtesy of the Volleyball Hall of Fame.

V

The Vault

The Vault was the nickname given the group of prominent Boston businessmen in 1959 who created an organization called the Coordinating Committee in order to reverse the city's declining prosperity. Meeting in the boardroom of the Boston Safe Deposit and Trust Company, located next to the vault, these men mobilized their money and expertise to sponsor studies and support politicians who promised to safeguard and enhance their investments in the city. They avoided publicity, kept no minutes, and generally worked behind the scenes, backing Mayor John Collins and Boston Redevelopment Authority head Edward Logue in their efforts to bring urban renewal to Boston. They gave crucial financial support to Collins in his 1959 mayoralty win, and to **Kevin H. White** in his victory over **Louise Day Hicks** in 1967.

Originally fourteen corporate leaders, Vault members numbered thirty-two by 1988, including directors or chairmen of Boston's most prestigious firms, such as Blakely, Maddox Investment; the Bank of Boston; Cabot, Cabot, and Forbes; Liberty Mutual Insurance, Teradyne Incorporated; Bank of New England; State Street Bank and Trust; Stop and Shop Company; Shawmut Bank; Hale and Dorr; Boston Gas; Houghton Mifflin; New England Telephone; Filenes; and Boston Edison. The Vault disbanded in 1997, when many of Boston's individual corporations had been merged into national and multinational concerns with little interest in local affairs.

Volleyball Hall of Fame

Located within Holyoke's Heritage State Park in western Massachusetts, the Volleyball Hall of Fame is the official home of that worldwide sport. It houses a collection of memorabilia that commemorates volleyball's growth as a sport, and holds special events and volleyball tournaments.

William C. Morgan invented volleyball at the Holyoke YMCA in 1895 in order to create a sport that could be played indoors by relatively few participants. Originally called "mintonette," the game changed its name to volleyball in 1896. The appeal of the sport quickly spread, and by 1910 people were playing volleyball all over the world, from Cuba to Japan, China, and the Philippines. During the early 1970s private organizations began raising funds for a building in downtown Holyoke, and the Volleyball Hall of Fame opened on June 6, 1987.

WALDEN;

OR,

LIFE IN THE WOODS.

BY HENRY D. THOREAU,

AUTHOR OF "A WEEK ON THE CONCORD AND MERRIMACK RIVERS."

I do not propose to write an ode to dejection, but to brag as lustily as chanticleer in the morning, standing on his roost, if only to wake my neighbors up. — Page 92.

BOSTON:

TICKNOR AND FIELDS.

M DCCC LIV.

Title page from the first edition of *Walden,* 1854, showing Thoreau's cabin at Walden Pond, Concord. Library of Congress, Prints and Photographs Division.

W

Walden Pond

In 1845 **Henry David Thoreau** built a cabin in Concord on the shore of Walden, a kettle pond left by the retreat of a glacier. There he stayed in relative solitude for two years, reveling in nature. In 1854 he published his thoughts and perceptions in a journal, *Walden.* While living at Walden, Thoreau made the first accurate survey of the pond. When he left, he deeded the house to his friend **Ralph Waldo Emerson,** who later sold it. Eventually, it was dismantled.

In 1922 the Emerson, Forbes, and Heywood families gave the eighty acres surrounding the pond to the state for the creation of a park. In 1965 Walden Pond became a National Historic Landmark, Walden Pond State Reservation, a protected space of 411 acres, open to the public for recreation, fishing, boating, and swimming. Today, the state Department of Environmental Management supervises the reservation, which greets over six hundred thousand visitors annually, who come to enjoy the woods and wildlife that so enriched Thoreau's thinking. A replica of Thoreau's cabin sits near the visitors' entrance, and a stone marks the original site on the pond's north side.

David I. Walsh

David Ignatius Walsh was the Bay State's first Irish American governor in the twentieth century and the first Irish American in Massachusetts history to be elected to the U.S. Senate. He was born on November 11, 1872, in Leominster, the son of Irish immigrants. His father, James, died in 1885, leaving his widow with ten children. Overcoming the adversity of poverty, Walsh worked his way through Holy Cross College and Boston University Law School. In 1897 he passed the bar and set up a practice in Fitchburg. The following year he entered politics as a Democrat, and in 1899 won election as a state representative.

His chance for major office came in 1912, when Theodore Roosevelt's Progressive Party campaign split the Republican Party, allowing Walsh to win the job of lieutenant governor. Championing progressive reform and appealing to Irish Catholic voters, Walsh went on to gain the governorship in 1913 and again in 1914. As governor he was able to achieve improvements in the state's labor codes, and he established a state-supported system of university extension courses for workers. He lost his bid for reelection in 1915, after the Republicans had healed their party breach.

Walsh's growing popularity with ethnic voters, however, resulted in his election to the U.S. Senate in 1918 against a Republican, William Weeks. He lost in 1924 to another Republican, Frederick Gillett, largely because he had rejected Wilson's League of Nations for failing to provide independence for Ireland. Walsh ran again in 1926 to fill the two-year vacancy left by the death of Republican senator **Henry Cabot Lodge Sr.** He was the one Democrat who could attract working-class Yankees and upper-class reformers as well as the newer immigrants. Walsh's success was to signal the beginning of the realignment of political power from the Republican to the Democratic Party in Massachusetts.

From 1928 on, Walsh was unbeatable for many years. During the 1930s he was the leading advocate of workers' causes. The approach of World War II, however, led to his undoing. He took a pro-Irish, anti-British, and isolationist position in opposition to President Franklin D. Roosevelt. This foreign policy stance became untenable after Pearl Harbor, and Republican **Henry Cabot Lodge Jr.** defeated him in 1946. He died soon after leaving office on June 11, 1947.

Waltham-Lowell Labor System

Early in the nineteenth century, Boston financiers organized as the **Boston Associates** undertook the task of establishing a textile industry in New England. To ensure control over the workforce and to avoid labor discontent, the factory owners developed a system of paternalistic labor relations known as the Waltham-Lowell system, used in the creation of two Massachusetts factory towns, Waltham in 1813 and Lowell in 1823. This system of labor became the standard for the textile industry until the 1850s, displacing the old village communities of New England.

The introduction of industrialization required the transformation of farm workers into an industrial labor force, often necessitating their resettlement in urban areas. In order to ensure a reliable supply of workers and avoid what capitalist **Nathan Appleton** described as the "degradation" of the English factory operatives, the Boston Associates began to recruit unmarried young women and youth from the farms of New England. Thousands of young Yankee farm women and children streamed to work in the mills and to live in factory-owned boardinghouses.

While the Boston Associates claimed that their purpose was to "rescue" the women workers from the "idleness" of farm life, in reality they were setting up a system that would give them full control over their workers, thus avoiding costly labor disputes and work stoppages. The women lived in supervised boardinghouses under rules and regulations that controlled their behavior and social interactions, ensuring that they would get to work on time and not be distracted by other pursuits. The textile mill corporation owned and regulated the boardinghouses, requiring church attendance, standards of dress, and curfews. After a twelve- to fourteen-hour day, the young operatives were supposed to spend their spare time in sewing or Bible classes. The owners deducted the charge for room and board directly from the pay of the workers. Supervisors and foremen were all men, who were paid a considerably higher wage than the mill women, which caused resentment among the workers. Disorderly or "independent" workers would lose both their jobs and their homes if they displeased the mill owners.

It was not long before the female workers in the factory towns began to express outrage at both the strict paternalism and the unequal wage policies of the factory owners. Increased competition in the textile industry led mill owners to cut wages as the quickest way to lower their costs. These cuts alarmed the working women, who depended on fixed wages. Moreover, the mill owners never reduced the costs of room and board. The mill women began to organize against the long hours in poorly ventilated and dangerous factories, the speed-ups, the oppressive regulations, the constant wage cuts, and the attacks on their independence. One of the nation's first factory strikes took place in Lowell in 1836.

Rising costs in the 1850s brought an end to the costly paternalistic labor system. Mill owners gave up the boardinghouses and began to employ Irish immigrants from overseas, who had to find their own housing. New factory towns such as New Bedford and Fall River avoided the Waltham-Lowell system, setting the stage for the fierce cutthroat competition that would characterize the future industrialization of the United States.

An Wang

An Wang was a computer innovator and entrepreneur, a technical genius who helped promote a new industry. Born in Shanghai on February 7, 1920, to a father who taught English, he studied electrical engineering in China and came to the United States as a student in 1945, obtaining a master of science degree from Harvard a year later and a Ph.D. in 1948 in nonlinear mechanics. After becoming a U.S. citizen in 1955, Wang worked at the Harvard Computation Laboratory in the field of computers. He established his own firm, Wang Laboratories, in 1951. His major focus was on the principle of storing information electronically, and in 1955 he received a patent for a device that would serve this purpose.

By 1964 Wang had developed a number of smaller digital computers which became extremely popular, and his company prospered over the years, expanding into word processors. Sales reached $1 billion by 1981. His wealth allowed him to support philanthropic causes, many of them in Boston, including the renovation of the old Music Hall theater downtown, renamed the Wang Center for the Performing Arts in his honor. But as his firm expanded, he lacked the management skills to keep it going effectively. The invention of the multipurpose computer and the personal computer soon diminished the market for the Wang word processor. After his son took over the company, it went into further decline. Losses mounted, and the company went bankrupt in 1994, four years after Wang's death on March 24, 1990.

Warning Out

Warning out was a system whereby **Puritans** kept out of the community anyone who was considered undesirable. This was a means of maintaining control in the face of threats to their communal beliefs. Potential paupers who might become dependent on the town for charity were one group that townspeople warned out. The Puritans also used this method to banish those who followed religious beliefs that offended the townspeople. For example, in 1649 Boston town leaders expelled the town's first Jewish settler, Solomon Franco, who was warned out because of his "differing faith."

Daniel Webster

The famous senator from Massachusetts whose multifaceted career made him one of the most prominent figures of the pre–Civil War era, Daniel Webster was a legendary orator. His main passion was his staunch defense of the Bay State's business interests, and he toiled to preserve the Union in the face of threats from both the slave South and **abolitionists.** Born to farming parents in New Hampshire on January 18, 1782, Webster went to Dartmouth College, taught school, and then became a lawyer. He moved to Boston in 1816, where he became the legal adviser to the **Boston Associates,** a powerful group of businessmen who financed the textile industry in New England.

Webster gained a national reputation as a defender of conservatism in several cases that he won before the Supreme Court. In the *Dartmouth College* case of 1819, the Republican state legislature of New Hampshire had revised the college's charter, changing it from a private to a public institution. Defending his alma mater, Webster argued successfully that the grant setting up the college was a contract and therefore could be voided only by mutual consent, not by state decree. In *McCulloch v. Maryland,* in which the state government of Maryland had attempted to tax a Baltimore branch of the Federal Bank of the United States, he defended federal power over state power by arguing that state taxation would destroy the federal bank and thus part of the federal government. Brought fame by his skill as an attorney, Webster won election to Congress from Boston in 1823, serving till 1827, when he became a U.S. senator. First as a Federalist, then as a Whig, Webster defended the dominant entrepreneurial interests of his region and the prerogatives of the national government over state's rights.

Such was the case in the famous Webster-Hayne debates in the Senate in January 1830. Senator Robert Hayne of South Carolina raised the issue of the misuse of federal power, as demonstrated by the tariff of 1828, which southerners called the "Tariff of Abomination." Hayne referred to the legal concept of "interposition," a southern doctrine which maintained that a state could interfere against or block measures of the federal government when it deemed federal policy unlawful or unconstitutional. Webster responded with a learned and powerful argument that interposition meant nullification of federal law and thus was unconstitutional. In his arguments Webster laid out the justification for preserving the Union which was later to become so crucial to the nation's survival. The Union, he said, derived from powers given it by the people through the Constitution and was not answerable to the states. It was in these debates that Webster uttered the famous line, "Liberty and Union, now and forever, one and inseparable." This concept of federal sovereignty over the states became his greatest contribution to the nation.

In 1836 he was one of the Whig Party's nominees for the presidency, but lost badly to Democrat Martin Van Buren. The Whig William Henry Harrison, who succeeded Van Buren, appointed Webster secretary of state, and he stayed on in the John Tyler administration. By 1845 he was back in the Senate. His support of the Fugitive Slave Law and the Compromise of 1850 made him anathema to the growing antislavery forces in Massachusetts. When the Whig Party split over this issue, Webster was left without a party and with few supporters. In 1850 Millard Fillmore appointed him secretary of state. He died in Marshfield, Massachusetts, at the age of seventy on October 24, 1852, after a long career during a period of turmoil over slavery, trade, and territorial expansion. Although he compromised on many issues, he always stood firm as a defender of the Constitution.

Whaling

The practice of hunting the great whales for food began with the Native Americans and continued with the English settlers. Offshore whaling to acquire the great mammal's oil as a source of fuel for lighting began in earnest in the fifty years before the American Revolution. Whalers from **Cape Cod and the Islands** took the lead, fitting out special ships that allowed them to harpoon the giants and tow the carcasses ashore for boiling down the blubber to oil. Later the ships included works on board for the boiling process, allowing for long voyages all over the world. Whaling declined precipitously during the Revolution because of British control of the seas, but by 1789 the whalers had come back. They sought out the right whale in northern waters and the more valuable sperm whale off the coast of Brazil, then moved on into the far Pacific in their now global search for the great whale.

By 1810 Nantucket had become the center of the industry, producing and marketing oil on the island for use in candles. The heyday of the whalers was from 1815 to 1860, as New Bedford, with its superb harbor, superseded Nantucket as the main whaling port. New Bedford also offered readily available railroad connections that made for easy transport of whale oil all over the nation. Many small seaports on the Massachusetts coast outfitted whalers, but New Bedford surpassed them all to become the fifth-largest port in the nation, all as a result of whaling. By 1840, whaling and whaling products constituted the third-largest industry in the Bay State, after textiles and shoes.

Life on the long sea voyages was harsh, as owners and skippers were notorious for their parsimony and cruelty toward their crews. In lieu of wages, whaling crews received shares of the profits based on their specialties on board the ship. Crewmen often deserted, and ships constantly had to reman at every port. The difficult life of the whaling mariner became the subject of novels by **Herman Melville,** including *Typee* and *Moby-Dick.* The emergence of oil fields in Ohio and Pennsylvania after the Civil War and the development of cheap kerosene for fuel and lighting put an end to the colorful era of whaling, although nations such as Japan and Norway carry on the industry even today, as a source of food, despite the protests of conservationists.

Phillis Wheatley

Phillis Wheatley was a notable American poet of the late eighteenth century. Her circumstances were most unusual for authors of her day, for she was an African American slave woman—the first African American author of significance. In time, **abolitionists** and others opposed to slavery pointed to her as proof that blacks deserved more humane treatment.

She was born in West Africa sometime around the early 1750s. When she was only a child, slavers kidnapped her and took her to the West Indies to be sold. A Boston tailor named John Wheatley bought her in 1761, installing her in his home. Recognizing her abilities, the Wheatley family tutored their young slave. Phillis wrote letters to public officials and then tried her hand at poetry.

She first gained recognition in the colonies with a poem published in 1770 on the death of the famed preacher George Whitefield. She traveled to England with the Wheatleys in 1773, where they succeeded in getting a book of her verse printed, *Poems on Various Subjects, Religious and Moral,*

Phillis Wheatley, from an engraving published in 1773. Library of Congress, Prints and Photographs Division.

probably the first published book by an African American. Since the publisher feared that no one would believe that "Phillis, a young Negro Girl, who but a few Years since, [was] brought an uncultivated Barbarian from Africa," could be the author of these poems, he included remarks from several prominent Bostonians, including Governor **Thomas Hutchinson,** Lieutenant Governor Andrew Oliver, **John Hancock,** and sixteen others, attesting to its authorship.

After they returned to Boston that year, the Wheatleys freed Phillis, but she continued to live with them. After John Wheatley's death in 1778, Phillis Wheatley left the household and married a poor African American, John Peters. She worked as a seamstress and continued writing poetry. Her verse found difficult acceptance in a nation of slaveholders, however. That racial equality was on her mind is evident in these lines from one of her poems:

Some view our sable race with scornful eye,
"Their colour is a diabolic die."
Remember, Christians, Negroes, black as Cain,
May be refin'd and join th' angelic train.

She died impoverished in 1784 at the age of thirty-one.

Kevin H. White

Kevin Hagan White was mayor of Boston for a record four consecutive four-year terms, from 1968 to 1983. During his sixteen years in office he faced several crises, including the school busing controversy and a momentary economic decline. Born on September 25, 1929, he was the son of former city council president Joseph White and grandson of Henry Hagan, also a former city council president. His wife, Kathryn H. Galvin, was the daughter of William Galvin, another former city council president. As a result, White's early years were suffused with the politics of Irish Boston, and early on he harbored political ambitions.

He graduated from Williams College in 1952 and Boston College Law School in 1955. In 1958 he won appointment as an assistant district attorney for Suffolk County. The election of **John F. Kennedy** to the presidency in 1960 left **Edward M. Kennedy** in search of a political job from which he could run for his elder brother's vacant senatorial seat in 1962. The Kennedy family fixed on the district attorney's office and forced young White out of his job so that Ted Kennedy could get some political experience. Undaunted, White ran for Massachusetts secretary of state and won. By 1967, ready for bigger things, he jumped into the high-profile Boston mayoral race against **Louise Day Hicks** and several other contenders. This time with Senator Kennedy's support and the financial backing of the business community, who feared Hicks's populism, White won a very close race.

As mayor he attempted to bring together the discontented ethnic neighborhoods and the more affluent business interests. White gave local communities a voice and a means to air grievances through his "little city halls" initiative; and he worked to deflect racial tensions with his "Summerthing" neighborhood programs. Between 1968 and 1975, the White administration spent over $500 million on neighborhood capital improvements. At the same time he championed the pro-growth agenda of the business community, nevertheless making sure that housing units would not be lost in the process of raising skyscrapers.

During the school desegregation crisis of the mid-1970s and the accompanying **busing riots,** White promised to promote community safety, but he waffled on the issue and failed to take a forthright stand on ending segregation for fear that doing so would jeopardize his political career. There was also little he could do to temper the national recession of the late 1970s which was adversely affecting Boston. He won the mayoralty four times—in 1967, 1971, 1975, and 1979—but by 1983 was under attack from the *Boston Globe* for alleged improprieties during his administration, and as a result he decided not to run for reelection. The intervening years have burnished his reputation as a skillful politician who oversaw the rebirth of Boston after decades of provincialism and decline.

John Greenleaf Whittier

John Greenleaf Whittier, the poet, social reformer, and abolitionist, was born on December 17, 1807, in Haverhill, the son of Quaker farmers. Largely self-taught, he began writing poetry on rural themes at an early age. Editor **William Lloyd Garrison** published Whittier's first poems in his Newburyport weekly beginning in 1826. More poems followed in 1829, many of them on antislavery themes. Garrison also helped Whittier find a job as editor of a political weekly in Boston.

In addition to supporting the **abolitionists,** Whittier became devoted to several other reform causes, including temperance, an end to debtor's prison, and the promotion of Quakerism. He edited several newspapers, and by 1831 had published his first collection of poems, *Legends of New England.* In 1833 he printed his first antislavery pamphlet and helped establish the American Anti-Slavery Society. After being elected to a term in the Massachusetts House of Representatives in 1835, he continued publishing his poems and collections of his poetry while promoting social reform.

Whittier eventually broke with Garrison, who demanded immediate emancipation, while Whittier opted for the gradual abolition of slavery through legislative means. He gained prominence as a poet and in 1857 became one of the founders of the *Atlantic Monthly.* His most famous poem, the patriotic "Barbara Frietchie," appeared in a collection of his verse in 1863. With the abolition of slavery he turned from his political focus to writing about New England locales and family life, publishing ten books of verse between 1866 and 1890. He died on September 7, 1892, in Hampton Falls, New Hampshire.

Roger Williams

Roger Williams's fame rests on the fact that he was banished from the **Massachusetts Bay Colony** because he dared to disagree with the **Puritans.** Born sometime in 1603 in London, he became a religious separatist, believing that the Church of England was corrupt and unredeemable. He arrived in Massachusetts in that difficult first winter of 1631 along with others who wished to leave forever what they considered the sinful English church. Once in Massachusetts, however, he grew unhappy with his Puritan brethren because they still maintained connections with England and were thus, he believed, in collusion with corruption. Puritans, such as **John Winthrop,** governor of the colony, felt that "weak" Christians should be converted, not cast aside as separatists demanded. While insisting that the Boston church was not pure enough for him, Williams further antagonized the Puritans when he declared that civil authorities had no right to rule over religious matters. In doing so, of course, he struck at the heart of the Puritan Commonwealth, the belief that the state was the proper instrument to uphold religiosity and must use its power against the ungodly to force compliance.

In 1635 Williams became minister to the church in Salem, whose members were more amenable to separatist ideas. He preached sermons condemning the Puritans for taking away Indian lands. Charging that the Crown had no authority to grant such lands to the Puritans in the colony's charter, he called the king a liar and a hypocrite. He stirred up a hornet's nest with such views, and by declaring that the English church was anti-Christian as well. In the face of such radical claims that threatened the vision of the Puritans, the General Court called him for a hearing on the charge of heresy. As a minister to the Salem congregation, Williams denied that the General Court had authority over him. The General Court banished him with the idea of sending him back to England in chains. Williams fled with a few followers to Narragansett Bay, Rhode Island, in January 1636.

Rhode Island had become a home for fugitives from strict religious communities who wished to satisfy their personal beliefs. The colony, unlike Massachusetts or Connecticut, had no common church, and it did not even have a government until 1647. Once resettled, Williams stressed his belief in the separation of church and state and in freedom of conscience. It was not the right of toleration he claimed but recognition of the "absolute equality" of all religions. In 1644 he journeyed to England and received a patent from the Long Parliament incorporating Rhode Island as a colony in 1647. In 1663 the Restoration government recognized the legality of the patent by making it a royal charter.

It was Williams's separatist views that created the spark for the eventual acceptance of the separation of church and state and for a tolerance of diversity that was repudiated by Winthrop's Massachusetts. He died in Providence sometime in 1683. In an interesting footnote, Thomas O'Connor's *Boston A to Z* (2000) points out that in 1936 the Massachusetts legislature granted Williams a pardon, thus rescinding the banishment order. (See also **Royal Colony**)

Ted Williams

Ranked along with Babe Ruth and Joe DiMaggio as one of the greatest baseball players of all time, Ted Williams played his entire career with the **Boston Red Sox.** Born August 30, 1918, to an impoverished California family, he spent his youth devoted to baseball, pitching for his San Diego high school team. In 1936 he started his professional career by joining the San Diego Padres of the Pacific League. Word of his hitting prowess soon got out, and the Red Sox signed him in 1938, sending him to the minors. There he batted .366 with 41 homers, but displayed poor fielding skills that would plague him for years.

Promoted to Boston in 1939, in his first astounding year he batted .327 with 31 home runs and 145 runs batted in (RBI). He also committed 19 errors in the outfield. Management criticized him for "loafing," but Yankee great Babe Ruth termed him "rookie of the year." His second season, 1940, was another banner year for Williams, but he had trouble with the fans, becoming oversensitive to remarks from the stands and losing his temper. That year he called Boston a "lousy" sports town and asked to be traded. Management sensibly refused to let him go, though Williams typically responded to fans' catcalls with obscene gestures and spitting and was surly toward reporters. The next year became one for the record books when Williams hit .406, a batting average never since equaled. In 1942 he won the triple crown of baseball with the highest batting average (.356), the most homers (36), and the lead in RBI (137).

Williams's career was interrupted when he enlisted in the U.S. Marines and served as an aviator for the duration of the Second World War. Returning to the Red Sox after the war, from 1946 to 1949 he hit in the .300s,

Ted Williams (*right*) with Jimmie Fox in 1941, the year in which Williams became the last major leaguer to hit .400. National Baseball Library, Cooperstown, N.Y.

winning another triple crown in 1947. Then in 1952, during the Korean War, he went back into service, flying thirty-nine combat missions, on one occasion landing his fighter in flames on the deck of an aircraft carrier. After being discharged from the marines in July 1953, he returned once again to the Red Sox. Plagued by injuries, he retired from baseball in 1954 only to change his mind and come back to the Sox in 1955.

He continued his glorious career, including several spitting and bat throwing incidents. The team had little success during Williams's tenure. He finally announced his retirement at the end of the 1960 season. Phenomenally, in his last at bat on September 28, he hit a home run, emerging from the dugout to acknowledge his cheering fans, something he had steadfastly refused to do throughout his career. In retirement Williams remained an avid sportsman—particularly enjoying fishing and hunting.

For all the problems he had had with the fans, his lofty reputation reached a new high point when, during his induction into the Baseball Hall of Fame on July 25, 1966, he called for a similar honor to be given to two superb Negro League athletes, Satchel Paige and Josh Gibson, who had long been denied a place in the Major Leagues because of their race. The Hall of Fame finally admitted Paige in 1971 and Gibson in 1972.

Nicknamed "the Thumper," and "the Splendid Splinter" in his playing days, Williams seemed to mellow a bit with age and enjoyed the role of baseball's elder statesman. He made a memorable guest appearance at the 1999 All-Star Game in Fenway Park. In honor of his elevated place in local sports lore, in 1995 the newly constructed tunnel between Boston and Logan Airport was named the Ted Williams Tunnel. After years of declining health, Williams died in Florida on July 5, 2002.

John Winthrop

John Winthrop (born 1588) was the founder and leader of the **Massachusetts Bay Colony** and a major contributor to the success of the settlement in its first nineteen years. A lawyer and lord of the manor of Groton in the county of Suffolk, he was a leading figure among the English Puritans. His strength of purpose and his almost fanatical zeal for promoting Puritan ideals helped hold together a growing community that faced many difficult challenges in its early days.

The economic depression of the late 1620s and differences over church practices between Anglicans and religious purists—the Puritans—led

Winthrop and some of his followers to decide to leave England. The New World beckoned as a place where a godly society could be established, where men would contract with God in a covenant of grace to provide a model for all good Protestants to follow. Winthrop helped found the Massachusetts Bay Company, a joint-stock trading company granted a royal charter to set up a colony, a commercial venture in New England. The stockholders elected him the colony's first governor in 1629, and he was put in charge of preparations for the expedition.

During the voyage aboard the *Arbella* in 1630, he delivered a sermon titled "A Model of Christian Charity," in which he declared that in the new colony "wee shall be as a City on a Hill," a place for all the world to emulate. When the Puritans arrived in June 1630, Winthrop was instrumental in establishing the colony first in Charlestown, and then on the Shawmut Peninsula at a place the Puritans called Boston. His presence during those precarious years served to keep the new settlement together until it could prosper. Along the way there were many challenges to his hopes for a covenanted community, particularly from forceful radicals such as **Roger Williams** and **Anne Hutchinson.** By his resolute will and his willingness to banish or punish those who disagreed, he protected his vision of a society of "saints."

Perhaps his major contribution was his role in setting up the government of the new colony. He persuaded the stockholders of the company to transfer power to an assembly of freemen, or members of the church, who would elect a governor and deputy governor and assistants who would make the laws. By including almost all the male members of the early colony in the process of governance, he got them to agree to uphold law and order. Winthrop was not a proponent of democracy—for only church members could be freemen—but he recognized that the more people were included in upholding the covenant, the less likelihood there was of rebellion on the one hand or the emergence of an aristocracy on the other. Winthrop stressed time and again that the people should always submit to authority and never question the decisions of the leaders whom God had put in charge of them. His vision of government was thus based on a notion of harmony and obedience.

He served as governor from 1629 to 1634, again from 1636 to 1640, from 1642 to 1643, and from 1646 to 1649. When not acting as governor, he was either deputy governor or one of the assistants. He died March 26, 1649, leaving behind a legacy of stability and prosperity in the Massachusetts Bay Colony.

Woods Hole

Here in a small town on the southwestern tip of Cape Cod, just below Falmouth, is a community of scientific endeavor famous the world over for the study of the sea and its creatures. Surrounded on three sides by water—Buzzards Bay, Vineyard Sound, and Nantucket Sound—Woods Hole is a place perfectly situated for the scientific investigation of marine life. It is the home of several independent research agencies working toward similar ends.

The Woods Hole Oceanographic Institute (WHOI), a private corporation endowed with federal funds, is the nation's largest independent marine engineering laboratory. Teams of scientists, scholars, engineers, and students work on a vast array of scientific projects related to the sea, including the use of two oceangoing research vessels. The Marine Biological Laboratory, established in 1888, studies marine organisms. It is now the oldest private marine science laboratory in the United States. The National Marine Fisheries Service runs the nation's oldest aquarium, where fish are kept for study in research projects. Also located here are the U.S. Geologic Survey's Coastal Geology Program and the Sea Education Association. Most of these organizations have visitors' centers open to the public. (See also **Cape Cod and the Islands**)

Writs of Assistance

The Writs of Assistance were legal documents that allowed customs officials in the colonies to search ships or any premises for smuggled goods. Smuggling was widespread among Boston merchants in the late seventeenth and eighteenth centuries as a way of avoiding import duties assessed by the British Navigation Acts. Until 1760 smuggling was difficult to prevent, and many customs officers were influenced by bribes. When George II died in 1760, all writs in his name had to be reissued in the name of his successor, George III. Since the royal provincial government of the colony received one-third of all smuggled goods found, Governor Francis Bernard was eager to have a new writ of assistance proclaimed.

In 1761 a collector in Salem officially asked the colony's superior court to provide a new writ. Chief Justice **Thomas Hutchinson,** a Crown appointee who took a dim view of smuggling, was to preside over the hearing. The Boston merchants hired the irascible but brilliant lawyer James Otis to argue against issuance of new writs. His peroration to the court raised for the first time the issue of imperial despotism and colonial rights. He denounced writs as a form of arbitrary power that destroyed liberty, introducing into legal discourse the principle that mankind had natural rights and liberties that superseded even the powers of the British Parliament. **John Adams** was to say later that in this courtroom "the child independence was born." Otis lost the case, but the writs inspired many Boston merchants to ally themselves with the growing number of radicals led by **Sam Adams,** who were determined to free themselves from British rule.

The National Yiddish Book Center, Amherst. Photo by Ned Gray, used by permission of the National Yiddish Book Center.

XYZ

Yiddish Book Center

Housed on the campus of Hampshire College in Amherst, the Yiddish Book Center is the repository for a treasure trove of previously lost literature written in Yiddish. A German language written in Hebrew characters, Yiddish was the language developed by eastern European Jews to express the culture of their village life. With the death and dispersal of millions of European Jews in the Holocaust, the language became virtually extinct, and many Yiddish publications were lost. To preserve what remained of this heritage, the National Yiddish Book Center was founded in 1980 to house books shipped from all over the world. The center, itself a replica of an eastern European village, holds over one million books and offers reading areas, an auditorium, a dining area, and a visitors' center. Rediscovered manuscripts and books continue to arrive at this unique site in the **Pioneer Valley,** where Yiddish language and culture are preserved rather than forgotten.

Zoar

Zoar, the only geographic place in Massachusetts to have a name beginning with *Z,* is a section of unincorporated land in the northwestern portion of the state. Details of its origin are unknown, but it was named after the city in the Bible where Lot and his family took refuge during the destruction of

Sodom and Gomorrah. On April 2, 1838, authorities gave permission for the land of Zoar to be divided and annexed to the towns of Charlemont and Rowe in Franklin County. Although it is listed on the state map, no markers exist to apprise the traveler of where Zoar actually is located. It is an area of about one square mile, called by locals "the Zoar Gap," with eight scattered houses on land where Charlemont blends into Rowe on the Zoar Road.

Year by Year to 2000

1. Native Peoples and European Contacts

10,000–9000 B.C. Approximate first appearance of Paleo-Indians (users of fluted stem projectile) in New England.

8000–6000 B.C. Estimated date of Early Archaic settlement.

6000–4000 B.C. Middle Archaic settlements established.

4000–1500 B.C. Late Archaic (narrow stem projectile and stone bowl pottery) settlements established.

1000 B.C. Estimated start of the Early Woodland culture (pointed base bowl).

A.D. 1 Middle Woodland culture recognized for use of decorated pottery.

A.D. 500 Late Woodland culture (ceramic pottery).

A.D. 1000 Approximate beginnings of agriculture by Natives.

1497–98 Italian explorer Giovanni Caboto (John Cabot), working for the English, voyages along the New England coast.

1524 Giovanni Verrazano explores New England coast and encounters Natives several times. European deep-sea fishermen come to the New England coast to dry their catches along the shorelines, engaging in casual trade with Indians.

1602–3 Beginnings of trade contacts as captains Bartholomew Gosnold and Martin Pring initiate trading with Indians.

1605 Explorer Samuel de Champlain stops at Plymouth harbor, which he later designates Port St. Louis on his map.

1608 Captain Edward Harlow captures several Natives along the coast and on Martha's Vineyard and brings them to England.

1609 Henry Hudson explores Massachusetts Bay.

1614 John Smith of Virginia explores and maps the New England coast, renaming a Wampanoag village Plimouth. Captain Thomas Hunt captures the Patuxet brave Squanto and sells him into slavery in Spain.

1616–1620s Virulent epidemics caused by contact with Europeans decimate large numbers of Natives, causing vast economic and social repercussions.

2. Seventeenth Century: English Settlement

1620 Pilgrims land at Plymouth, using the Mayflower Compact to govern their new colony.

1621 Chief Massasoit of the Wampanoags establishes treaty relations with Plymouth Colony. Squanto, returned from Europe, teaches the Pilgrims to plant corn, enabling them to survive. Pilgrims celebrate the nation's first Thanksgiving.

1623 Governor William Bradford of Plymouth Colony ends communal holdings and establishes family plots.

1625 Violent clashes between French fur traders and Indians of Massachusetts Bay ends with defeat of the French.

1629 Royal Charter of Incorporation granted to the Massachusetts Bay Company granting full power to legislate and organize a government for the new colony. Puritan emigration begins.

1630 Puritans led by John Winthrop resettle at Boston on the Shawmut Peninsula. In a "Great and General Court" on October 19, Winthrop elected governor of the colony and Thomas Dudley deputy governor.

1632 Puritans vote for their first tax. Boston becomes official capital of Massachusetts Bay Colony. Representation of towns granted in the General Court. William Pynchon purchases land from an Agawam village which becomes Springfield.

1633 Smallpox epidemics kill many more Indians. First town meeting in America held in Dorchester.

1634 Representative government system established. First bridge erected—over the Neponset River. Boston Common designated as common pasture.

1635 Boston town meeting establishes nation's first public tax-supported school, Boston Latin School.

1636 Roger Williams expelled from Massachusetts Bay Colony for religious dissent; founds Rhode Island. Harvard College, first in the colonies, founded.

1637 Massachusetts colonists join Connecticut colonists to attack and destroy the Pequot Indians. Anne Hutchison banished for heresy. First slave arrives in Boston.

1638 America's first printing press set up in Cambridge by Stephen Daye.

1639 Bostonians open America's first post office.

1640 Boston printers publish the first full-sized book in North America, the *Bay Psalm Book.*

1641 Legislature enacts Body of Liberties to protect citizens against unlawful violations of "natural liberties."

1643 First counties created: Suffolk, Middlesex, Essex, and Norfolk.

1644 Legislature split into two branches, an assembly and a council. Iron works furnaces open in Braintree, Lynn, Quincy, and Saugus.

1646 First tool-making patent granted to Joseph Jenkes of Saugus.

1647 Partial funding provided by towns for education.

1648 General Court recognizes the first labor organization, "the shoemakers of Boston."

1649 Boston town leaders "warn out" the town's first Jewish settler, Solomon Franco.

1651 Parliament passes the first Navigation Act, taxing colonial imports.

1652 Bostonian John Hull sets up the first mint in America.

1660 Bostonians hang Quaker Mary Dyer because of her religion.

1662 Legislature adopts the Half-Way Covenant. Boston passes America's first copyright law and establishes the first almshouse in the colonies, a dwelling place for the homeless poor and the "debauched."

1675–76 In King Philip's War English colonists kill Chief Metacom and virtually eliminate the Wampanoags, ending the meaningful presence of Indians in Massachusetts.

1676 Colony enacts the first legislation concerning the mentally ill, entrusting their care to the selectmen of each town. (The state takes over this responsibility in 1864.)

1677 Massachusetts Bay Colony purchases title to Maine.

1684 British authorities rescind charter of the Massachusetts Bay Company, revoking the colony's system of governance that began in 1630.

1685 Boston authorities attach a "workhouse" to a newly built almshouse so the poor can be made to work on public projects for their support.

1686 Sir Edmund Andros assumes the governorship of New England. He closes the General Court, ends town meeting except for election of officials, and issues taxes as an executive privilege.

1689 News of the overthrow of King James II in England leads to armed insurrection by Bostonians, who imprison Governor Andros.

1690 First newspaper published in America on September 25, the *Boston Publick Occurrances, Both Foreign and Domestic.* Governor Simon Bradstreet suppresses the paper four days later for being "distasteful" in discussing government difficulties with the Indians, Boston's smallpox epidemic, and a foreign sex scandal.

1691 Parliament grants Massachusetts a new royal charter restoring the legislature, with the royal governor as executive. Property ownership becomes the new criterion for voting. Plymouth Colony and Maine officially become part of Massachusetts.

1692 Witchcraft trials held in Salem.

3. Eighteenth Century: English Colony to Yankee State

1701 A customs riot occurs in Boston.

1702 Queen Anne's War (1702–13) begins.

1703 Brookline separates from Boston.

1704 New England military expeditions fail in two attempts to capture Port Royal in French Acadia. Indians loyal to the French destroy Deerfield (February

28–29). The *Boston News-Letter* becomes the nation's first regularly published newspaper.

1705 Legislature passes a law forbidding interracial marriage.

1710 A New England military expedition captures Port Royal in Nova Scotia. Grain riot in Boston.

1711 Fire destroys the center of Boston; crowds loot a grain warehouse and shops.

1713 Bread riot in Boston.

1714 First schooner built and launched in Gloucester.

1716 First lighthouse built in Boston Harbor.

1721 Dr. Zabdiel Boylston begins smallpox inoculations in Boston.

1730 With a population of 13,000, Boston becomes the largest urban center in the colonies (until 1755, when it is surpassed by Philadelphia).

1737 Bostonians riot and destroy three public markets.

1739 Chelsea becomes part of Boston.

1740 English Methodist preacher George Whitefield brings the "Great Awakening" to Massachusetts.

1742 Faneuil Hall opens to the public.

1744 King George's War (1744–48 in the colonies) begins.

1745 Massachusetts governor William Shirley mounts a successful expedition to capture the French fort at Louisburg (given back to French in treaty of Aix-la-Chapelle of 1748 in exchange for British control over Madras, India).

1747 In the Knowles Riot, Boston citizens take naval officers and seamen hostage to force the return of those illegally impressed into the British navy.

1755 The Massachusetts militia forcibly removes the last of the French settlers from Nova Scotia (Acadia) and resettles them in Louisiana.

1756 The French and Indian War, or Seven Years' War, begins.

1759 Massachusetts troops participate in the British victory over the French at Quebec.

1761 James Otis attacks Parliament's Writs of Assistance, signaling the beginning of revolutionary sentiment.

1764 Sugar Act passed by Parliament to raise revenues from the colonies. Smallpox epidemic causes many to flee Boston.

1765 Parliament enacts a stamp tax and Stamp Act riots ravage Boston. Sons of Liberty groups and Committees of Correspondence organized.

1766 Violence and boycotts result in repeal of Stamp Act. Parliament passes the Declaratory Act asserting its authority over the colonies.

1767 Townshend Acts passed by Parliament to raise revenue in the colonies, leading to more commercial boycotts. Poet Phillis Wheatley publishes her first work.

1768 General Court sends a circular letter throughout the colonies condemning British actions. British troops land in Boston to quell continued unrest.

1770 Hostile interaction between troops and citizens results in the Boston Massacre. The British officer in charge is acquitted in a murder trial owing to the vigorous defense of John Adams. Townshend Acts repealed except for the duty on tea.

1773 Tea Act passed by Parliament culminates in Boston Tea Party.

1774 England closes Boston's port and imposes other "Coercive Acts" in response to Boston Tea Party, including a Quartering Act requiring colonists to house British troops. Colonists authorize election of representatives to meet as a provincial congress and pass the Suffolk Resolves, condemning the Coercive Acts and calling for nonpayment of taxes and strengthening of militias.

1775 In April, British troops march out of Boston to seek out colonial arms caches. Warned by Paul Revere, colonists take a stand on April 19 at Lexington and Concord, the first battle of the American Revolution. In July the British attack a colonial force camped in Charlestown, resulting in the Battle of Bunker Hill. In Cambridge, George Washington assumes command of the Continental Army. Colonists revive the General Court.

1776 Surrounded by Washington's troops, the British evacuate Boston on March 17. On July 4 the Continental Congress in Philadelphia votes for independence from Britain. France recognizes the new government of the United States.

1780 On June 7 state revolutionary leaders ratify a state constitution under the Articles of Confederation. A judicial interpretation of the constitution finds slavery to be unlawful.

1781 John Hancock becomes the first governor of Massachusetts.

1783 The Supreme Judicial Court pronounces all slaves free in Massachusetts. The legislature bans the slave trade.

1786–87 Farmers and debtors from western Massachusetts take up arms against the "arbitrary" power of the legislature in Shays's Rebellion. Militia from Boston put down the rebels and arrest their leaders.

1788 State legislature ratifies the U.S. Constitution by a vote of 187 to 168, the sixth state to do so.

1790 Boston's *Columbia Rediviva* becomes the nation's first ship to circumnavigate the globe.

1793–94 The first U.S. canal built—two miles long in South Hadley Falls.

1794 Congress authorizes construction of U.S. Armory in Springfield. First survey of Boston, 783 acres, completed.

1796 John Adams elected president.

1798 Legislature moves into the newly constructed State House, designed by Charles Bulfinch.

4. Nineteenth Century: Industry and Immigration

1803 Middlesex Canal opens, connecting Boston to the Merrimack Valley via the Charles and Merrimack rivers. As a fire safety measure, legislature requires that all buildings over ten feet in height be made of stone or brick.

1804 Massachusetts breaks with the Federalist Party and votes for Democratic Republican Thomas Jefferson for president. Boston annexes South Boston from Dorchester. Beacon Hill partially leveled to fill in Mill Cove and South Cove.

1806 The African American Meeting House opens its doors in Boston.

1807–9 Boston shipping totals over 310,000 tons, more than one-third of the nation's total mercantile trade. Jefferson's embargo adversely affects the region's economy.

1810 Salem ranks as sixth-largest commercial town in the nation. Nantucket Island becomes fourth in the state for wealth and population, with whaling predominating.

1811 State legislature incorporates Massachusetts General Hospital in Boston, to be supported by private subscriptions. (The hospital opens its doors in 1821.)

1812 General Court initiates "gerrymandering." Size of legislature peaks at 749 members.

1813 Francis Cabot Lowell and associates establish Waltham, the first planned factory town, with a water-powered loom in the textile mill.

1814 Massachusetts delegates at the Hartford Convention threaten secession owing to the deleterious effects of the War of 1812 on trade. The convention rejects their views. Stage service begins between Boston and New York.

1817 Legislature issues the first charter in the nation to a savings bank, the Boston Provident Institution.

1820 A Constitutional Convention reworks the state constitution, with Maine becoming a state and the General Court given the right to charter cities. Boston opens a House of Correction for vagrants and other "undesirables."

1822 The Boston Associates establish Lowell as a planned factory town. Boston incorporated as a city, with a mayor, aldermen, and councilors replacing town meeting.

1823 Boston builds a new House of Industry to put debtors and those receiving charity to work on public projects. The first state psychiatric hospital opens in Worcester.

1824 U.S. House of Representatives elects John Quincy Adams president after no candidate receives a majority of electoral votes. The nation's first high school for girls opens in Worcester.

1825 In April six hundred Boston house carpenters go on strike in one of the largest labor actions in the nation to demand higher wages and a ten-hour day.

1826 Workers in Quincy finish construction of the first American horse-drawn railroad, built to deliver granite to the proposed Bunker Hill Memorial.

1827 Legislature permits localities to tax residents for support of public schools.

1828 John Quincy Adams loses to Andrew Jackson in the presidential election. The Blackstone Canal opens, connecting Worcester and Providence.

1831 Abolitionist William Lloyd Garrison founds the *Liberator* newspaper in Boston.

1832 Massachusetts votes for Henry Clay for president, but he is defeated by Andrew Jackson.

1833 Political support of religion is ended by an amendment to the state constitution (Article 11) disestablishing the Congregational Church.

1834 Anti-Catholic mob in Charlestown burns down the Ursuline Convent. For the first time, the name "Whig" is used as a party label. The first strike in the textile industry occurs in Lowell when eight hundred women oppose wage reductions. Legislature requires each county to set up and administer a house of correction for "undesirables."

1835 In Boston anti-abolitionist crowds attack William Lloyd Garrison, causing a riot. The Boston and Worcester Railroad opens, connecting those two cities. The Boston and Lowell Railroad opens, connecting Boston and Providence.

1836 The state votes for Daniel Webster for president, but Martin Van Buren defeats him. Women textile workers form the Factory Girls Association, an early union organization.

1837 Investors set up ten textile mills in Fall River. Fifteen thousand Yankee Bostonians, incited by volunteer firemen, participate in the anti-Irish Broad Street Riot. Mary Lyon founds Mount Holyoke Seminary in South Hadley, the nation's first women's college. Ralph Waldo Emerson delivers the Phi Beta Kappa address, "The American Scholar," at Harvard University.

1838 Temperance-minded legislators pass the "15 gallon law," prohibiting the sale of alcohol in small quantities. (After much strife the legislature repeals it in 1840.)

1839 The nation's first state-supported normal school for women opens in Lexington. Boston teamster William Herndon founds the nation's first express company, carrying goods from ships and railroad terminals to destinations all over the city.

1841 The Western Railroad opens, connecting Worcester, and thus Boston, with Albany. Transcendentalists establish a commune at Brook Farm.

1843 Legislature repeals the 1705 law prohibiting interracial marriage. On July 2 a fire started by exuberant holiday makers destroys the Pocasset Mills and most of the town of Fall River.

1844 Textile worker Sarah Bagley organizes a statewide women's labor union, the Lowell Female Reform Association.

1846 Massive Irish immigration begins. John B. Fitzpatrick ordained Boston's first Irish Catholic bishop. Concord officials jail Henry David Thoreau for non-payment of the poll tax. Elias Howe of Spencer receives a patent for the sewing machine. At Massachusetts General Hospital, William Barton uses ether as an anesthetic for the first time.

1848 Boston Associates found Lawrence as a new company town. Boston Public Library established, the first publicly funded free municipal library of substantial size.

1849 In *Roberts v. City of Boston,* Supreme Judicial Court rules that Boston School Committee may establish separate schools for black and white children, the first such case in the nation, thus establishing the segregationist doctrine of "separate but equal." Henry David Thoreau publishes his essay "Civil Disobedience."

1850 First National Women's Rights Convention held in Worcester. Irish immigrants now account for 25 percent of Boston's population.

1851 Legislature mandates compulsory public education for children ages eight to fourteen for a minimum of twelve weeks per year. Herman Melville publishes *Moby-Dick.* The first state school for the retarded, the Walter E. Fernald School, opens.

1852 Legislature passes a temperance law prohibiting the sale of alcohol, which proves difficult to enforce and is widely ignored. (Repealed in 1875.) The state votes for Whig Winfield Scott against victor, Democrat Franklin Pierce, in the presidential election.

1854 Abolitionists attack a Boston courthouse in an unsuccessful attempt to free fugitive slave Anthony Burns. Boston creates a professional police force. A major cholera epidemic hits the Northeast, inflaming anti-Catholic sentiment. Henry David Thoreau publishes *Walden; or Life in the Woods.*

1855 Know-Nothing Party captures the governorship and General Court. Blacks boycott Boston's schools to protest segregation. A sympathetic General Court responds by desegregating all public schools. Boston annexes Washington Village from Dorchester. Fill-in of the Back Bay commences. The state's first industrial school for girls opens.

1856 State votes for Republican John C. Fremont for president over victor James Buchanan in the presidential election.

1857 Size of state House of Representatives fixed at 240, Senate at 40.

1859 A constitutional amendment aimed at the Irish prohibits people of foreign birth from voting for two years after naturalization. (Annulled in 1863.)

1860 The nation's first major industrial strike occurs in Lynn, where 20,000 shoe workers protest wage reductions. The state votes for Abraham Lincoln, who wins the presidential election. In Lawrence the walls of the Pemberton Mills collapse on January 10, killing and injuring many. Elizabeth Peabody opens the first English-speaking kindergarten in the nation.

1861 Rebel sympathizers in Baltimore attack four Massachusetts regiments on their way to protect Washington, D.C. Clara Barton arrives to assist the troops. Massachusetts Institute of Technology (MIT) moves from Boston and is incorporated in Cambridge.

1862 Massachusetts raises a black regiment (the Fifty-fourth) commanded by Robert Gould Shaw. General Benjamin Butler of Massachusetts and his army occupy the city of New Orleans. A land swap agreed to by Rhode Island and Massachusetts gives the former Rehoboth and the latter Fall River.

1863 Rebelling against a national conscription law, the Boston Irish of the North End riot. Shaw and many others of his command die in a frontal assault on a Confederate fort. President Lincoln appoints General Joseph Hooker of Massachusetts commander of the Army of the Potomac. After the Union defeat at Chancellorsville, Hooker resigns.

1864 Legislature sets up a Board of Charities to take responsibility from the towns for the mentally ill.

1865 State law passed forbidding discrimination in public accommodation. Boston becomes the nation's fourth-largest manufacturing city, specializing in the garment trade. Large-scale immigration of French Canadians commences statewide. Legislature authorizes the creation of State Constabulary, the nation's first law enforcement agency to be given statewide powers.

1866 Factory Inspection Act passed by the legislature, first in the nation; child labor law prohibits children under ten from factory work. Fort Hill leveled to provide Back Bay fill.

1867 The state's first factory inspector appointed. Mary Baker Eddy founds the Christian Science Church.

1868 New England Woman Suffrage Association formed with Julia Ward Howe as president. Roxbury annexed to Boston. Legislature passes the state's first tenement house law regulating multiple dwellings.

1869 Patrick Collins becomes the first Boston Irish Catholic elected to the Massachusetts Senate. Lucy Stone organizes the Boston American Women's Suffrage Association. Duxbury becomes the terminus for the new Atlantic cable. Women workers in Lynn found the Daughters of Saint Crispin, the first national women's trade union. Massachusetts becomes the first state to establish a Bureau of Labor Statistics. An act of the General Court establishes the first state board of health in the nation.

1870 Twenty-five percent of the state's population is now foreign-born. Sixty million pairs of shoes are produced annually. Dorchester annexed, and parts of Brighton ceded to Boston. Boston incorporates the Museum of Fine Arts.

1870s Influx of English and Irish workers from textile factories begins in Fall River.

1872 Great Fire of Boston destroys the central business district, killing fourteen and causing the destruction of 776 buildings at a cost of $75 million. Dr. Marie Zakrzewska opens the nation's first nursing school at New England Hospital for Women and Children in Roxbury. First issue of the *Boston Globe* published on March 4.

1873 Brookline votes to reject annexation with Boston. A storm knocks down the old elm known as the Liberty Tree on Boston Common.

1874 Legislature passes a ten-hour workday limit and renews the prohibition on employing children under ten. Charlestown, Brighton, and West Roxbury annexed to Boston. MIT sets up the nation's first Sanitary Chemistry Laboratory to carry out water analyses for the State Board of Health.

1875 Prohibition repealed. For the first time, over 50 percent of the population live in urban areas, making Massachusetts the most densely populated state in the nation. The state now has 235,000 Irish-born residents. Work completed on the Hoosac Tunnel, connecting Boston with the Erie Canal. Smith and Wellesley colleges for women opened. Louis Prang of Boston prints the nation's first Christmas card.

1876 Alexander Graham Bell makes the world's first telephone call in Boston.

1877 Legislation passed requiring protective barriers on factory machinery to prevent injuries to workers—the first in the nation.

1878 Boston Girls' Latin School founded.

1879 School Suffrage Law secures the right of women to vote for and hold office on their local school committees. Harvard Annex for Women (later Radcliffe) established. Hugh O'Brien becomes first Irish-born Catholic elected chairman of the Boston Board of Aldermen.

1880 Boston land area now 23,085 acres. Irish-born immigrants make up 18 percent of Boston's population in a total foreign-born population of 32 percent. Lynn becomes the leading shoe manufacturing city in the nation, with a population of 38,000 largely native-born workers and 170 factories.

1881 State law allows married women to own their own clothing. John Breen becomes the first Irish-born Catholic mayor of a large city (Lawrence). Of 1,783,085 state residents, 439,341 have at least one foreign-born parent. The textile industry employs 93,000 workers. Massachusetts becomes first in the nation in proportion of the population engaged in manufacturing (40 percent) and non-agricultural pursuits (90 percent), with 75 percent of the laboring force listed as working class.

1882 Brookline opens the nation's first country club for golf.

1883 Legislature passes the state's first civil service law.

1884 Hugh O'Brien becomes the first Irish-born Catholic elected mayor of Boston. Despite the Mugwump revolt in the Republican Party, Massachusetts votes for Republican James G. Blaine for the presidency over Democratic victor Grover Cleveland. Telephone service initiated between Boston and New York.

1885 Boston charter changed by the state to reduce the power of the mayor because of Yankee fear of the Irish.

1887 Labor Day declared a state holiday. Ventilation legislation for the workplace passed—first in the nation—and legislature passes the first toilet facility requirement in factories.

1888 Secret Ballot Act enacted, first in the nation.

1889 Boston's first electric trolley system established. Metropolitan Sewage Commission set up, serving thirty-three towns of Greater Boston. Legislature passes a compulsory education requirement of at least twenty weeks a year for children aged eight to fourteen. MIT establishes the nation's first program in Sanitary Engineering.

1890s Large-scale immigration of eastern Europeans and Italians commences.

1891 Legislature abolishes the poll tax for voting. The first basketball game is played in Springfield.

1892 Vida Scudder and Emily Green Balch establish the Denison Settlement House in the South Cove section of Boston. Andover Settlement House set up by Robert Woods in the South End of Boston. In Fall River, Lizzie Borden is acquitted of the murder of her parents. In Springfield, Frank and Charles Duryea produce the first automobile in the nation powered by a gasoline engine.

1893 Legislature establishes the Metropolitan Park Commission, first in the nation. Non-support of women becomes a criminal offense. The state elects its first foreign-born governor, Frederick T. Greenhalge (England).

1894 Immigration Restriction League founded in Boston.

1895 A riot breaks out in Boston on July 4 between Irish Catholics and Irish Protestant members of the American Protective Association. Legislature establishes the Metropolitan Water District Commission, serving twenty-two towns and cities of Greater Boston area. The nation's first volleyball game played in Holyoke. Boston Public Library moves to its permanent site at Copley Square.

1896 French Canadians reach 42 percent of Fall River's population, with the Irish dropping to 16 percent.

1897 First Boston Marathon held on April 19.

1898 First subway in U.S. opens in Boston, connecting Park and Boylston streets. The state's first year-round bathhouse (Dover Street Bath) opens in Boston.

5. Twentieth Century: Decline and Rebirth

1900 Seventy-six percent of the state's population now lives in urban areas. Foreign-born or second generation make up 75 percent of the workforce. In Boston, 40 to 50 percent of families are classified as middle class, one-third of the population considered poor. Seventy-seven percent of Boston's black men and 46 percent of Irish males work in menial labor jobs. Fall River has the highest percentage of child laborers (25 percent) in the state.

1901 The state Water District and Sewer District merge into the Metropolitan Water and Sewer Board. Patrick Collins becomes second Irish-born Catholic to be elected mayor of Boston. A smallpox epidemic hits Boston; 400,000 are vaccinated.

1903 Women's Trade Union League founded in Boston. Alderman James Michael Curley sent to prison for taking a civil service exam "for a friend"; while in jail Curley is reelected to the Boston Board of Aldermen. Yankee elites form the Boston Good Government Association to combat the threat of Irish political takeover. Isabella Stewart Gardner opens her home in the Fenway as an art museum. Boston Red Sox win the first World Series. On January 18 inventor Guglielmo Marconi sends the first transatlantic wireless radio broadcast from Wellfleet on Cape Cod.

1905 Irish ward boss John F. Fitzgerald elected mayor of Boston.

1906 The nation's first radio program broadcast from Brant Rock in Marshfield.

1907 Yankee Republican George Hibbard defeats John F. Fitzgerald for mayoralty of Boston. William O'Connell becomes archbishop of Boston.

1908 Fire destroys the city of Chelsea. Legislature purchases and floods land in Clinton, Boylston, and West Boylston to create the Wachusett Reservoir to supply Boston with water.

1909 To curtail Irish political power in Boston, legislature changes the Boston city charter, establishing nonpartisan citywide elections: Board of Aldermen and Common Council abolished in favor of a nine-member city council elected at large; mayor serves a four-year term, with budgetary power and veto over city council actions; permanent Finance Commission established as state watchdog agency.

1910 State's foreign-born population reaches a record 31.5 percent. John Fitzgerald narrowly defeats Yankee James Jackson Storrow for mayoralty of Boston.

1911 Statewide primary system adopted for nominating candidates for office. William O'Connell becomes the first Boston archbishop to be named a cardinal.

1912 For the first time since 1820, Massachusetts votes Democratic for the presidency: 35.5 percent for Woodrow Wilson, the winner. Bread and Roses Strike of textile workers occurs in Lawrence. Hyde Park annexed to Boston. The Boston Red Sox open play at Fenway Park. Legislature enacts a minimum wage for women and children and organizes the nation's first retirement system for state employees.

1913 Democrat David I. Walsh of Fitchburg elected governor—first second-generation Irish Catholic elected to statewide office. First state primary held to nominate candidates for office.

1914 Irish American James Michael Curley wins the first of four terms as mayor of Boston. Cape Cod Canal opens.

1916 State returns to the Republican fold, voting for Charles Evans Hughes for president against Democratic victor Woodrow Wilson. Incumbent Henry Cabot Lodge Sr. becomes the state's first popularly elected U.S. senator, defeating John F. Fitzgerald.

1917–19 A Constitutional Convention amends the state constitution: governor to be elected for a two-year term beginning 1920. Initiative and referendum passed.

1918 David Walsh elected U.S. senator, first Democrat since well before the Civil War, and first Catholic. John F. Fitzgerald wins a congressional election against incumbent Peter Tague but is unseated three months later on charges of illegal voter registration and ballot box stuffing. Republican congressman F. H. Gillett elected Speaker of the U.S. House of Representatives. Six cities besides Boston reach populations over 100,000 (Worcester, Fall River, New Bedford, Cambridge, Lowell, and Springfield). Worldwide influenza epidemic hits Boston. The Boston Red Sox win the World Series, defeating the Chicago Cubs.

1919 Boston police strike leads to three days of violence and is finally put down by force. A strike by Boston telephone operators disrupts service in New England. General Court votes to ratify the Nineteenth Amendment (women's suffrage), the eighth state to do so. Legislature creates Department of Public Welfare. Metropolitan District Commission established, combining water, sewage, and parks. On January 15, a large molasses storage tank explodes, flooding the North End and killing twenty-one people.

1920 Women win the right to vote. Legislative terms increased from one year to two. Former governor Calvin Coolidge elected vice president. Babe Ruth sold to New York Yankees. East Brookfield incorporated—the last such incorporation in the twentieth century.

1921 Nicola Sacco and Bartolomeo Vanzetti, anarchists, found guilty of murder and robbery, sparking a decade of protest. Boston police force changes its rules, allowing women to join the force. First AM radio station begins broadcasting in New Bedford.

1922 The first two women are elected state representatives, Republican M. Sylvia Donaldson of Brockton and Democrat Susan W. FitzGerald of Boston. The Republican legislature amends the Boston city charter to prevent Mayor Curley from succeeding himself.

1923 Former Massachusetts governor Calvin Coolidge becomes president on the death of President Harding.

1924 Coolidge elected president. By successful home rule petition, the Boston city charter reverts to ward representation on a twenty-two-member city council.

1925 Edith Nourse Rodgers becomes the first Massachusetts woman elected to Congress.

1926 State Representative M. Sylvia Donaldson presides over the Massachusetts House for one day—the first woman to do so. Robert H. Goddard achieves the first liquid-propelled rocket flight. The state opens the nation's first cancer hospital in Pondville.

1927 Sacco and Vanzetti executed August 23.

1928 The state votes for Alfred E. Smith for the presidency, the first Democratic majority in Massachusetts, though he loses to Herbert Hoover. Construction of the Quabbin Reservoir begins as four towns (Greenwich, Dana, Enfield, and Prescott) and several villages are scheduled to be flooded. Vannevar Bush of MIT develops the first non-electronic computer. The first automatic digital computer developed by Howard Aiken of Harvard.

1929 In a worsening economy shoe production declines to 23 percent of nation's output and textile industry loses 158,000 jobs.

1930 Boston census shows a population of 781,188, 29 percent foreign-born and 42 percent with at least one foreign-born parent. First- and second-generation Irish account for 20 percent of population, Italians 12 percent, Jews about 11 percent, English-speaking first- and second-generation Canadians 11 percent, and French Canadians about 1 percent. The Boston metropolitan area is defined as covering 1,021 square miles, with a population of 2.3 million in nineteen cities and sixty-one towns in six different counties—in area 13 percent of the state, in population 54 percent. The Boston Bruins win their first Stanley Cup. Two women enlist in the state police, the first in the nation. Legislature organizes the nation's first compulsory motor vehicle inspection program.

1932 Democrats win the state auditor's office and keep it (with one lapse in 1939–40) thereafter. The state votes Democratic in the presidential election (and continues to do so until 1952).

1934 James Michael Curley elected governor. Democrat Edward Bacigalupo of Boston first Italian American elected state representative.

1935 With conditions worsening, the number of jobs in the shoe industry declines a further 25 percent (from 69,397 in 1925 to 44,371). Under the auspices of the federal government, the Boston City Council creates the Boston Housing Authority to sponsor public housing in the city for the deserving poor.

1936 Henry Cabot Lodge Jr. defeats former governor James Michael Curley for the U.S. Senate. Republican Sybil Holmes of Brookline first woman elected to the state Senate.

1938 Legislature creates the Department of Mental Health.

1941 The state again amends the Boston city charter to allow the mayor to succeed himself, allowing incumbent Democrat Maurice Tobin to ward off the challenge of James Michael Curley.

1942 A tragic fire in Boston at the Cocoanut Grove nightclub leaves 492 dead.

1943 Boston Irish toughs, blaming Jews for the war, mount anti-Semitic attacks on Jewish schoolchildren.

1945 Congressman James Michael Curley, while under federal indictment for mail fraud, elected mayor of Boston and serves eight months in jail until pardoned by President Harry S. Truman. Cynthia Belgrave becomes the first black woman hired as a retail clerk in a Boston department store. Harvard University medical school decides to admit women as students.

1946 Henry Cabot Lodge Jr. defeats longtime incumbent Democrat David Walsh for the U.S. Senate. John F. Kennedy elected to Congress from Boston's Eleventh District. Emily G. Balch of Boston wins the Nobel Peace Prize. Jury service for women approved by public referendum but rejected by the legislature. The first publicly owned venture capital investment firm, American Research and Development, established. The Quabbin Reservoir reaches full capacity of 412 billion gallons of water.

1947 Republican congressman Joseph W. Martin Jr. elected Speaker of the U.S. House of Representatives. The state's average industrial wage begins a decade-long decline below the national average. The Commonwealth purchases the Boston Elevated Railway and creates the Metropolitan Transit Authority (MTA).

1948 Democrats take permanent control of the state House of Representatives (with one lapse, 1953–54). State votes for Democrat Harry Truman in the presidential election and Republican Leverett Saltonstall (versus John Fitzgerald) in the senatorial election. Dr. Erich Lindemann establishes the first community mental health center in the nation, the Human Relations Service, Inc., in Wellesley.

1949 Thomas P. "Tip" O'Neill Jr. becomes first Democrat elected speaker of the Massachusetts House. Democrats take over the offices of state treasurer and secretary of state. The first black, Republican Lawrence Banks, elected to the Boston City Council, but the election is contested in the courts and he is never seated. Republican Leslie B. Cutler of Needham, ten-year veteran of the House, becomes the second woman elected to the state Senate. Twenty-six percent of labor force unemployed in Lawrence, 18 percent in New Bedford, with a state total of 5.8 percent. Boston city charter again changed: district council abolished for nine-member at-large council; mayor to be chosen first by preliminary election and then run-off between top two candidates; mayor to appoint police commissioner.

1950 Legislature passes law allowing women to serve on juries but permits them to excuse themselves based on gender. (This exemption abolished in 1979.) Minimum wage law enacted for women and minors. Boston's population reaches a peak of 801,444. Black migration to Boston up from 23,679 in 1940 to 40,457. The Open Kettle in Quincy is renamed Dunkin' Donuts.

1951 Notorious Brink's payroll robbery in Boston.

1952 John F. Kennedy defeats Henry Cabot Lodge Jr. for the U.S. Senate, but state votes for Republican presidential winner, Dwight D. Eisenhower. George Fingold, Republican of Concord, elected attorney general—first Jew to hold statewide office. Foster Furcolo, Democrat of Longmeadow, elected state treasurer—first Italian American elected to statewide office. Massachusetts Turnpike Authority established.

1954 The number of industrial workers in the state declines to 42.98 percent while service workers rise to 54.89 percent, marking the transformation of the state to a service and high-tech economy. Surgeons at Boston's Peter Bent Brigham Hospital perform the world's first human organ transplant. Columbia Point, the state's largest public housing project (5,000 units), opens on an isolated peninsula in Dorchester. The legislature establishes the nation's first permanent Commission on Aging.

1956 Foster Furcolo becomes first Italian American elected governor. The state votes again for Eisenhower.

1957 Boston Redevelopment Authority created. Lincoln G. Pope of Boston's South End becomes the first black elected representative to the General Court in the twentieth century.

1958 For the first time Democrats take over the majority in the state's U.S. congressional delegation, as well as the state Senate. Boston's West End is slated for urban renewal—thirty-eight square blocks, forty-one acres, and over nine thousand residents to be affected.

1959 Men included in the state minimum wage law. A group of predominantly Yankee banking and corporate leaders form the Coordinating Committee (the "Vault") to stimulate urban revival in Boston.

1960 John F. Kennedy elected president. Benjamin Smith II appointed for two-year remainder of Kennedy's U.S. senate seat. Republican John Volpe elected governor. Boston mayor John Collins appoints Edward Logue director of the Boston Redevelopment Authority to initiate major urban renewal program. Black population of Boston increases from 5 percent in 1950 to 9.1 percent (63,165).

1961 Democratic congressman John W. McCormack becomes Speaker of U.S. House of Representatives.

1962 Edward M. Kennedy defeats George Cabot Lodge for U.S. Senate. Republican Edward Brooke of Newton elected attorney general—first black elected to statewide office.

1963 President John F. Kennedy assassinated. Louise Day Hicks of South Boston elected to the Boston School Committee. Katherine Craven first woman elected to Boston City Council.

1964 Boston's blacks boycott schools to protest segregation. Metropolitan Council for Educational Opportunity (METCO) is organized to allow some black students from Boston to attend public schools in Brookline. Legislature dissolves the MTA and sets up the Massachusetts Bay Transportation Authority (MBTA), extending the boundaries of the system.

1965 Legislature passes the Racial Imbalance Act for public schools, stipulating remedies for schools with over 50 percent minority student body.

1966 Edward Brooke becomes first black elected to U.S. Senate from Massachusetts. Margaret Heckler, Republican of Wellesley, is second woman from the state elected to U.S. Congress. Governor's term increased from two to four years. State sales tax enacted. METCO receives federal funds for busing of 220 black children to seven suburban towns.

1967 Violence escalates into rioting in Boston's black neighborhoods during the summer, mirroring unrest throughout urban America. Kevin White defeats Louise Day Hicks for the mayoralty. Thomas Atkins becomes first African American to be seated on Boston City Council in the twentieth century. Supreme Judicial Court outlaws criminal sanctions for "vagrants." Edward Logue leaves the Boston Redevelopment Authority with legacy of $200 million in urban renewal funds invested in Boston: 3,223 acres of city land involved; 9,718 low-rent housing units erased, with 3,504 units constructed, only 982 of them low-rent units.

1968 The state votes for Democrat Hubert Humphrey against victor Richard M. Nixon for the presidency. Riots break out in Boston after assassination of Martin Luther King Jr. on April 4. Robert F. Kennedy assassinated June 5. Mayor John Collins becomes the first Boston mayor to receive an honorary doctorate of laws from Harvard University. U.S. Defense Department closes the Springfield Armory.

1969 Students for a Democratic Society (SDS) protest the Vietnam War by seizing control of Harvard's University Hall.

1970 The Reverend Robert Drinan, Democrat of Newton, first Catholic priest from Massachusetts elected to Congress. Monsignor Mimie B. Pitaro, Democrat of East Boston, first priest elected to the Massachusetts House of Representatives. Black population of Boston increases to 16.3 percent (104,596). Sociologists Karl and Alma Tauber cite Boston as 91.4 percent segregated.

1971 Thomas Atkins becomes the first African American to run (unsuccessfully) for mayor of Boston. Five blacks elected to state legislature: Doris Bunte, Bill Owens, Royal Bolling Sr., Royal Bolling Jr., and Mel King. State lottery established.

1972 Massachusetts earns notoriety as the only state in the nation to vote for the loser in the presidential election, Democrat George McGovern. Boston NAACP sues the Boston School Committee for fostering racial segregation in the public schools.

1974 Federal judge W. Arthur Garrity finds the Boston School Committee guilty of willfully segregating the public schools and orders busing as a remedy under Phase I plan. Anti-busing resistance leads to receivership of the public school system. Michael Dukakis elected governor—first Greek American to hold that office.

1975 Community resistance to Phase II plan busing results in the calling in of federal marshals; South Boston High placed under personal control of Judge Garrity.

1977 John O'Bryant becomes the first black elected to Boston School Committee since 1895. Democratic congressman Thomas P. O'Neill elected Speaker of the U.S. House of Representatives.

1978 Massachusetts House reduced in size from 240 to 160. Boston Police Department organizes a special unit to deal with racial crimes—first in the nation. Receivership of South Boston High lifted. A February blizzard wreaks havoc in the state. A court decision mandating that the state devise a comprehensive community mental health system leads to the closing of the state's psychiatric hospitals.

1979 Kevin White becomes the first mayor of Boston elected to four consecutive four-year terms. In response to suits by public housing tenants, Massachusetts Superior Court judge Paul G. Garrity imposes receivership on the Boston Housing Authority, especially for mismanaging the Columbia Point housing project. John F. Kennedy Presidential Library dedicated at Columbia Point. Legislature abolishes all special exemptions for women jurors.

1980 Proposition 2½ becomes law, limiting property tax increases by local communities. The state completes transition to service/high-tech economy. Senator Edward Kennedy wins the state Democratic primary for the presidency but loses nomination in the national convention to President Jimmy Carter. Robert Drinan required by Catholic Church to resign his seat in Congress. From a peak of 801,444 in 1950, Boston's population drops to 562,000. The city's black population up from 16.3 percent in 1970 to 22 percent (122,000). Sixty percent of all jobs in the city are held by commuting suburbanites, with only 20 percent of city dwellers working in suburbs. Boston's white-collar work force reaches 51,977, up from 33,476 in 1960, while blue-collar jobs fall from 52,175 in 1960 to 17,320.

1982 Boston's apartment dwellers pay the highest rents in the nation, with a vacancy rate of only 3.5 percent. Over three thousand black Boston students are bused by METCO to thirty-four suburban towns.

1983 Legislature passes a statute requiring refunds for beverage containers—the Bottle Bill. Mel King becomes the second African American to run for mayor of Boston but loses to Ray Flynn. Boston city charter revised to allow city council to include four members elected at large and nine by district (same for school committee).

1984 Mayor Flynn given back control over Boston Housing Authority when Superior Court relinquishes receivership. Private developers take over remains of Columbia Point housing project. Legislature creates Massachusetts Water Resources Authority to combat pollution in Boston Harbor and to avert a court-ordered takeover of the MDC sewer division. Local and state agencies report widespread discrimination in housing against blacks and Hispanics in Boston, Cambridge, Somerville, and suburban areas.

1985 Federal judge W. Arthur Garrity returns the public schools to the control of Boston School Committee. Boston home prices are third most expensive in the nation. Asian American population of Boston jumps from 8,443 (1.3 percent) in 1980 to 19,330 (3.2 percent). Haverhill-Lawrence metropolitan area has fastest-growing population in Massachusetts, up 5 percent from 1980. Lowell metropolitan area is second with a 3 percent jump since 1980.

1986 Evelyn Murphy elected lieutenant governor—first woman elected to statewide office. Construction begins on new Harbor Point mixed-income housing development to replace Columbia Point.

1987 Bruce Bolling becomes first black elected president of Boston City Council. National Oceanic and Atmospheric Administration cites Boston Harbor as the most polluted harbor in the country. Massachusetts prisons are the most overcrowded in the nation per capita.

1988 Governor Michael Dukakis loses presidential election to George H. W. Bush but takes Massachusetts, 54 to 46 percent. Nelson Merced of Dorchester becomes the first Latino elected to the legislature.

1990 Republican William Weld narrowly defeats Democrat John Silber for the governorship, 52 to 48 percent. Thieves steal priceless paintings from the Isabella Stewart Gardner Museum in the Fenway. Harbor Point housing development completed.

1992 Massachusetts votes for Democrat Bill Clinton over incumbent George H.W. Bush for the presidency, 1,311,845 to 802,479. Legislature sets up the first mental health insurance system in the nation under Medicaid.

1993 Supreme Judicial Court rules in *McDuffy v. The Executive Office of Education* that financing schools through property taxes alone results in unequal education, violating the state constitution, thus leading to state funding for education to supplement property taxes. Thomas Menino elected first Italian American mayor of Boston.

1994 Governor William Weld reelected.

1995 First stage of Big Dig completed with the Ted Williams Tunnel under Boston Harbor. Rosaria Salerno elected first woman city clerk of Boston.

1996 Republican governor William Weld challenges Democratic senator John Kerry for his seat. Kerry wins. Weld resigns from the governorship and Lieutenant Governor Paul Celucci becomes acting governor. In the presidential election Massachusetts supports the victor, President Bill Clinton, against Republican challenger Robert Dole. Representative Thomas Finneran of Mattapan (first elected to the Massachusetts House in 1976) wins the Speaker's post and begins a long reign of power.

1998 Acting governor Paul Celucci defeats Democrat Scott Harshbarger for the governorship.

2000 Massachusetts votes for Al Gore in his unsuccessful bid for the presidency against George W. Bush. State population increases to 6,349,097, with whites at 81.9 percent (down from 87.7 percent), Latinos at 6.8 percent, blacks at 5 percent, and Asians at 3.7 percent. Boston population increases to 589,141, with whites down from 59 percent to 49 percent. Blacks are the largest minority at 23.8 percent (down from 1990). Latino population rises to 14.4 percent and Asian to 7.5 percent. Women compose 26 percent of the General Court.

Statistical Appendix

Statistics on Massachusetts Towns and Cities

City/Town	County	Year Settled	Year Incorporated	Size (sq. mi.)	Population 1790	1820	1860	1900	1920	1940	1960	1980	2000
Abington	Plymouth	1668	1712	9.97	1,453	1,920	8,527	4,489	5,787	5,708	10,607	13,517	14,605
Acton	Middlesex	1680	1735	20.06	853	1,047	1,726	2,120	2,162	2,701	7,238	17,544	20,331
Acushnet	Bristol	1659	1860	18.00	—	—	1,387	1,221	3,075	4,145	5,755	8,704	10,161
Adams	Berkshire	1762	1778	23.01	2,040	1,836	6,924	11,134	12,967	12,608	12,391	10,381	8,809
Agawam	Hampden	1635	1855	23.35	—	—	1,698	2,536	5,026	7,842	15,708	26,271	28,144
Alford	Berkshire	1740	1773	11.57	577	570	542	272	248	201	256	394	399
Amesbury	Essex	1654	1666	12.65	1,801	1,956	3,877	9,473	10,036	10,862	10,787	13,971	16,450
Amherst	Hampshire	1703	1775	27.70	1,233	1,917	3,206	5,028	5,550	6,410	13,718	33,229	34,874
Andover	Essex	1642	1694	31.10	2,863	3,889	4,765	6,823	8,268	11,122	15,878	26,370	31,247
Aquinnah	Dukes	1669	1870	6.02	—	—	—	173	144	127	103	220	344
Arlington	Middlesex	1630	1807	5.18	—	1,064	2,681	8,603	18,665	40,013	49,953	48,219	42,389
Ashburnham	Worcester	1736	1765	39.15	951	1,230	2,108	1,882	2,012	2,255	2,758	4,075	5,546
Ashby	Middlesex	1676	1767	23.66	751	1,188	1,091	876	834	1,026	1,883	2,311	2,845
Ashfield	Franklin	1743	1765	40.28	1,459	1,748	1,302	955	869	872	1,131	1,458	1,800
Ashland	Middlesex	1750	1846	12.41	—	—	1,554	1,525	2,287	2,479	7,779	9,165	14,674
Athol	Worcester	1735	1762	32.34	848	1,211	2,604	7,061	9,792	11,180	11,637	10,634	11,299
ATTLEBORO	Bristol	1634	1694	27.51	2,166	3,055	6,066	11,335	19,731	22,071	27,118	34,196	42,068

Auburn	Worcester	1714	1778	15.70	473	608	914	1,621	3,891	6,629	14,047	14,485	15,901
Avon	Norfolk	1700	1888	4.35	—	—	—	1,741	2,176	2,335	4,301	5,026	4,443
Ayer	Middlesex	1668	1871	8.82	—	—	—	2,446	3,052	3,572	4,927	6,993	7,287
Barnstable	Barnstable	1637	1638	60.17	2,160	3,824	5,129	4,364	4,836	8,333	13,465	30,898	47,821
Barre	Worcester	1720	1774	44.30	1,613	2,077	2,973	2,059	3,357	3,528	3,479	4,102	5,113
Becket	Berkshire	1740	1765	46.92	751	984	1,578	994	674	689	770	1,339	1,755
Bedford	Middlesex	1640	1729	13.73	523	648	843	1,208	1,362	3,807	10,969	13,067	12,595
Belchertown	Hampshire	1731	1761	52.52	1,485	2,426	2,709	2,292	2,058	3,503	5,186	8,339	12,968
Bellingham	Norfolk	1713	1719	18.55	738	1,034	1,313	1,682	2,102	2,979	6,774	14,300	15,314
Belmont	Middlesex	1636	1859	4.59	—	—	1,198	3,929	10,749	26,867	28,715	26,100	24,194
Berkley	Bristol	1638	1735	15.56	850	1,060	825	949	935	1,130	1,609	2,731	5,749
Berlin	Worcester	1665	1784	13.01	512	625	1,106	1,003	868	1,057	1,742	2,215	2,380
Bernardston	Franklin	1738	1762	23.46	912	968	792	769	954	1,370	1,750	1,790	2,155
BEVERLY	Essex	1626	1668	15.14	3,290	4,283	6,154	13,884	22,561	25,537	36,108	37,655	39,862
Billerica	Middlesex	1637	1655	25.46	1,191	1,380	1,776	2,775	3,646	7,933	17,867	36,727	38,981
Blackstone	Worcester	1662	1845	10.97	—	—	5,453	5,721	4,299	4,566	5,130	6,570	8,804
Blandford	Hampden	1735	1741	52.70	1,515	1,256	836	479	479	636	1,038	1,210	1,214
Bolton	Worcester	1682	1738	19.93	1,229	1,348	770	708	775	1,264	2,530	3,020	4,148
BOSTON	Suffolk	1625	1630	43.18	18,320	43,298	177,840	560,892	748,060	770,816	697,197	562,994	589,141

Statistics on Massachusetts Towns and Cities (*continued*)

City/Town	County	Year Settled	Year Incorporated	Size (sq. mi.)	Population 1790	1820	1860	1900	1920	1940	1960	1980	2000
Bourne	Barnstable	1640	1884	41.02	—	—	—	1,657	2,530	3,315	14,011	13,874	18,721
Boxborough	Middlesex	1680	1835	10.39	424	403	316	298	376	744	3,126	3,240	4,868
Boxford	Essex	1645	1698	23.80	925	906	1,020	704	588	778	2,010	5,374	7,921
Boylston	Worcester	1705	1786	15.84	839	902	929	1,364	794	1,388	2,367	3,470	4,008
Braintree	Norfolk	1634	1640	13.70	2,771	1,466	3,468	5,981	10,580	16,378	31,069	36,337	33,828
Brewster	Barnstable	1656	1803	22.55	—	1,285	1,489	829	688	827	1,236	5,226	10,094
Bridgewater	Plymouth	1650	1656	27.29	4,975	1,700	3,761	5,806	8,438	8,902	10,276	17,202	25,185
Brimfield	Hampden	1706	1731	35.37	1,211	1,612	1,363	941	778	1,012	1,414	2,318	3,339
BROCKTON	Plymouth	1700	1821	21.37	—	1,480	6,584	40,063	66,254	62,343	72,813	95,172	94,304
Brookfield	Worcester	1664	1718	15.68	3,100	2,292	2,276	3,062	2,216	1,393	1,751	2,397	3,051
Brookline	Norfolk	1638	1705	6.62	484	900	5,164	19,935	37,748	49,786	54,044	55,062	57,107
Buckland	Franklin	1779	1779	19.86	718	1,037	1,702	1,446	1,433	1,527	1,664	1,864	1,991
Burlington	Middlesex	1641	1799	11.84	—	508	606	593	885	2,275	12,852	23,486	22,876
CAMBRIDGE	Middlesex	1630	1636	6.25	2,115	3,295	26,060	91,886	109,694	110,879	107,716	95,322	101,355
Canton	Norfolk	1630	1797	19.01	—	1,268	3,242	4,584	5,945	6,381	12,771	18,182	20,775
Carlisle	Middlesex	1650	1780	15.37	555	681	480	463	747	1,488	3,306	4,200	4,717
Carver	Plymouth	1660	1790	38.41	847	839	1,186	1,104	891	1,469	1,949	6,988	11,163

Charlemont	Franklin	1742	1765	26.05	665	1,081	1,075	1,094	808	789	897	1,149	1,358
Charlton	Worcester	1735	1775	42.86	1,965	2,134	2,047	1,860	1,995	2,557	3,685	6,719	11,263
Chatham	Barnstable	1665	1712	15.88	1,140	1,630	2,710	1,749	1,737	2,136	3,273	6,071	6,625
Chelmsford	Middlesex	1633	1655	22.54	1,144	1,535	2,291	3,984	5,682	8,077	15,130	31,174	33,858
CHELSEA	Suffolk	1624	1739	1.86	472	642	13,395	34,072	43,184	41,259	33,749	25,431	35,080
Cheshire	Berkshire	1766	1793	27.06	—	1,202	1,533	1,221	1,476	1,708	2,472	3,124	3,401
Chester	Hampden	1760	1765	36.76	1,119	1,526	1,314	1,450	1,302	1,284	1,155	1,123	1,308
Chesterfield	Hampshire	1760	1762	31.01	1,183	1,447	897	611	441	422	556	1,000	1,201
CHICOPEE	Hampden	1652	1848	22.91	—	—	7,261	19,167	36,214	41,664	61,553	55,112	54,653
Chilmark	Dukes	1671	1714	20.58	771	695	654	324	240	226	238	489	843
Clarksburg	Berkshire	1764	1798	12.70	—	274	420	943	1,136	1,317	1,741	1,871	1,686
Clinton	Worcester	1654	1850	5.36	—	—	3,859	13,667	12,979	12,440	12,848	12,771	13,435
Cohasset	Norfolk	1647	1775	9.86	817	1,099	1,953	2,759	2,639	3,111	5,840	7,174	7,261
Colrain	Franklin	1735	1761	43.21	1,417	1,961	1,798	1,749	1,607	1,497	1,426	1,552	1,813
Concord	Middlesex	1635	1635	24.96	1,590	1,788	2,246	5,652	646	7,972	12,517	16,293	16,993
Conway	Franklin	1762	1775	37.81	2,092	1,705	1,689	1,458	961	944	875	1,213	1,809
Cummington	Hampshire	1762	1779	23.01	873	1,060	1,085	748	489	608	550	657	978
Dalton	Berkshire	1755	1784	21.79	554	817	1,243	3,014	3,752	4,206	6,436	6,797	6,892
Danvers	Essex	1636	1752	13.64	2,425	3,646	5,110	8,542	11,108	14,179	21,926	24,100	25,212

Statistics on Massachusetts Towns and Cities (*continued*)

City/Town	*County*	*Year Settled*	*Year Incorporated*	*Size (sq. mi.)*	*Population 1790*	*1820*	*1860*	*1900*	*1920*	*1940*	*1960*	*1980*	*2000*
Dartmouth	Bristol	1650	1664	60.91	2,499	3,636	3,883	3,669	6,493	9,011	14,607	23,966	30,666
Dedham	Norfolk	1635	1636	10.50	1,659	2,493	6,330	7,457	10,792	15,508	23,869	25,298	23,464
Deerfield	Franklin	1673	1677	32.57	1,330	1,868	3,073	1,969	2,803	2,684	3,338	4,517	4,750
Dennis	Barnstable	1639	1793	20.66	—	1,997	3,662	2,333	1,536	2,015	3,727	12,360	15,973
Dighton	Bristol	1678	1712	21.81	1,793	1,607	1,733	1,802	2,574	2,983	3,769	5,352	6,175
Douglas	Worcester	1721	1725	36.93	1,079	1,375	2,442	2,113	2,181	2,617	2,559	3,730	7,045
Dover	Norfolk	1635	1836	15.16	485	548	679	656	867	1,374	2,846	4,703	5,558
Dracut	Middlesex	1664	1702	20.84	1,217	1,407	1,881	3,253	5,280	7,339	13,674	21,249	28,562
Dudley	Worcester	1714	1732	21.07	1,114	1,615	1,736	3,553	3,701	4,616	6,510	8,717	10,036
Dunstable	Middlesex	1656	1673	17.02	380	584	487	353	447	824	1,671	2,180	2,829
Duxbury	Plymouth	1624	1637	24.32	1,454	2,403	2,597	2,075	1,553	2,359	4,727	11,807	14,248
East Bridgewater	Plymouth	1649	1823	17.29	—	1,435	3,207	3,025	3,486	3,832	6,139	9,945	12,974
East Brookfield	Worcester	1664	1920	9.89	—	—	—	—	—	1,016	1,533	1,955	2,097
East Longmeadow	Hampden	1740	1894	13.03	—	—	—	1,187	2,352	3,403	10,294	12,905	14,100
Eastham	Barnstable	1644	1646	14.25	1,834	766	779	502	430	582	1,200	3,472	5,453

Easthampton	Hampshire	1664	1809	13.29	457	712	1,916	5,603	11,261	10,316	12,326	15,580	15,994
Easton	Bristol	1694	1725	29.04	1,466	1,803	3,067	4,837	5,041	5,135	9,078	16,623	22,299
Edgartown	Dukes	1642	1671	26.79	1,352	1,374	2,118	1,209	1,190	1,370	1,474	2,204	3,779
Egremont	Berkshire	1730	1775	18.77	759	865	1,079	758	441	463	895	1,311	1,345
Erving	Franklin	1801	1838	14.04	—	331	527	973	1,295	1,328	1,272	1,326	1,467
Essex	Essex	1634	1819	14.18	—	1,107	1,701	1,663	1,478	1,384	2,238	2,998	3,267
EVERETT	Middlesex	1649	1870	3.36	—	—	—	24,336	40,120	46,784	43,544	37,195	38,037
Fairhaven	Bristol	1670	1812	12.15	2,733	3,118	3,567	7,291	10,938	14,339	15,759	16,159	
FALL RIVER	Bristol	1656	1803	32.89	—	1,594	14,026	104,863	120,485	115,428	99,942	92,574	91,938
Falmouth	Barnstable	1660	1694	44.52	1,637	2,370	2,456	3,500	3,500	6,878	13,037	23,640	32,660
FITCHBURG	Worcester	1730	1764	27.47	1,151	1,736	7,805	31,531	41,029	41,824	43,021	39,580	39,102
Florida	Berkshire	1783	1805	24.55	—	431	645	390	298	421	569	730	676
Foxborough	Norfolk	1704	1778	19.77	674	1,004	2,879	3,266	4,136	6,303	10,136	14,148	16,246
Framingham	Middlesex	1650	1700	23.92	1,598	2,037	4,227	11,302	17,033	23,214	44,526	65,113	66,910
Franklin	Norfolk	1660	1778	26.80	1,101	1,630	2,172	5,017	6,497	7,303	10,530	18,217	29,560
Freetown	Bristol	1675	1683	34.57	2,202	1,863	1,521	1,394	1,532	1,584	3,039	7,058	8,472
GARDNER	Worcester	1764	1785	22.02	531	911	2,646	10,813	16,971	20,206	19,038	17,900	20,770
Georgetown	Essex	1639	1838	13.10	—	—	2,075	1,900	2,004	1,803	3,755	5,687	7,377
Gill	Franklin	1776	1793	13.84	—	800	683	1,015	879	931	1,203	1,259	1,363

Statistics on Massachusetts Towns and Cities (*continued*)

City/Town	County	Year Settled	Year Incorporated	Size (sq. mi.)	Population 1790	1820	1860	1900	1920	1940	1960	1980	2000
GLOUCESTER	Essex	1623	1642	26.18	5,317	6,384	10,904	26,121	22,947	24,046	25,789	27,768	30,273
Goshen	Hampshire	1761	1781	17.31	681	632	439	316	224	237	385	651	921
Gosnold	Dukes	1641	1864	12.65	—	—	—	164	131	136	66	63	86
Grafton	Worcester	1718	1735	22.83	872	1,154	4,317	4,869	6,887	7,457	10,627	11,238	14,894
Granby	Hampshire	1727	1768	28.01	596	1,066	907	761	779	1,085	4,221	5,380	6,132
Granville	Hampden	1736	1775	43.20	1,979	1,643	1,385	1,050	655	668	874	1,204	1,521
Great Barrington	Berkshire	1726	1761	45.45	1,373	1,908	3,871	5,854	6,315	5,824	6,624	7,405	7,527
Greenfield	Franklin	1686	1775	21.47	1,498	1,361	3,198	7,927	15,462	15,672	17,690	18,436	18,168
Groton	Middlesex	1655	1655	32.54	1,840	1,897	3,193	2,052	2,185	2,550	3,904	6,154	9,547
Groveland	Essex	1639	1850	8.90	—	—	1,448	2,376	2,650	2,122	3,297	5,040	6,038
Hadley	Hampshire	1659	1661	23.16	882	1,461	2,105	1,789	2,784	2,576	3,099	4,125	4,793
Halifax	Plymouth	1670	1734	16.15	664	749	766	522	563	867	1,599	5,513	7,500
Hamilton	Essex	1638	1793	14.66	—	802	789	1,614	1,631	2,037	5,488	6,960	8,315
Hampden	Hampden	1741	1878	19.66	—	—	—	782	624	1,023	2,345	4,745	5,171
Hancock	Berkshire	1767	1776	35.55	1,211	1,165	816	451	464	332	455	643	721
Hanover	Plymouth	1649	1727	15.46	1,084	1,211	1,565	2,152	2,575	2,875	5,923	11,358	13,164

Hanson	Plymouth	1632	1820	15.17	—	917	1,245	1,455	1,910	2,570	4,370	8,617	9,495
Hardwick	Worcester	1737	1739	38.40	1,725	1,836	1,521	3,203	3,085	2,154	2,340	2,272	2,622
Harvard	Worcester	1704	1732	26.35	1,387	1,597	1,507	1,139	2,546	1,790	2,563	12,170	5,981
Harwich	Barnstable	1670	1694	20.93	2,392	1,980	3,423	2,334	1,846	2,535	3,740	8,971	12,386
Hatfield	Hampshire	1661	1670	16.21	703	823	1,337	1,500	2,651	2,216	2,350	3,045	3,249
HAVERHILL	Essex	1640	1641	33.11	2,408	3,070	9,995	37,175	53,884	46,752	46,346	46,865	58,969
Hawley	Franklin	1760	1792	30.99	539	1,089	671	429	390	257	251	280	336
Heath	Franklin	1765	1785	24.95	379	1,122	661	441	325	359	304	482	805
Hingham	Plymouth	1633	1635	22.46	2,085	2,857	4,351	5,059	5,604	8,003	15,378	20,339	19,882
Hinsdale	Berkshire	1763	1804	21.16	—	822	1,511	1,485	1,065	1,235	1,414	1,707	1,872
Holbrook	Norfolk	1710	1872	7.30	—	—	—	2,229	3,161	3,330	10,104	11,140	10,785
Holden	Worcester	1723	1741	35.50	1,077	1,402	1,945	2,464	2,970	3,924	10,117	13,336	15,621
Holland	Hampden	1725	1835	12.35	428	453	419	169	153	247	561	1,589	2,407
Holliston	Middlesex	1659	1724	18.90	875	1,042	3,339	2,598	2,707	3,000	6,222	12,622	13,801
HOLYOKE	Hampden	1745	1850	21.16	—	—	4,997	45,712	60,203	53,750	52,689	44,678	39,838
Hopedale	Worcester	1660	1886	5.12	—	—	—	2,087	2,777	3,113	3,987	3,905	5,907
Hopkinton	Middlesex	1715	1715	26.40	1,317	1,655	4,340	2,623	2,289	2,697	4,932	7,114	13,346
Hubbardston	Worcester	1734	1775	40.34	933	1,367	1,621	1,227	1,045	1,022	1,217	1,797	3,909
Hudson	Middlesex	1699	1866	11.66	—	—	—	5,454	7,607	8,042	9,666	16,408	18,113

Statistics on Massachusetts Towns and Cities (*continued*)

City/Town	*County*	*Year Settled*	*Year Incorporated*	*Size (sq. mi.)*	*Population* 1790	1820	1860	1900	1920	1940	1960	1980	2000
Hull	Plymouth	1624	1644	2.43	120	172	285	1,703	1,771	2,167	7,055	9,714	11,050
Huntington	Hampshire	1769	1775	26.24	742	849	1,216	1,475	1,425	1,340	1,392	1,804	2,174
Ipswich	Essex	1633	1634	33.21	4,562	2,553	3,300	4,658	6,201	6,348	8,544	11,158	12,987
Kingston	Plymouth	1620	1726	18.55	1,004	1,313	1,655	1,955	2,505	2,783	4,302	7,362	11,780
Lakeville	Plymouth	1717	1853	29.54	—	—	1,160	958	1,419	1,780	3,209	5,931	9,821
Lancaster	Worcester	1643	1653	27.65	1,460	1,862	1,932	2,478	2,461	2,963	3,958	6,334	7,380
Lanesborough	Berkshire	1753	1765	28.96	2,142	1,319	1,308	780	1,054	1,321	2,933	3,131	2,990
LAWRENCE	Essex	1655	1847	6.75	—	—	17,639	62,559	94,270	84,323	70,993	63,175	72,043
Lee	Berkshire	1760	1777	26.51	1,170	1,384	4,420	3,596	4,085	4,222	5,271	6,247	5,985
Leicester	Worcester	1713	1714	22.70	1,076	1,252	2,748	3,416	3,635	4,851	8,177	9,446	10,471
Lenox	Berkshire	1750	1775	21.48	1,169	1,315	1,711	2,942	2,691	2,884	4,253	6,523	5,077
LEOMINSTER	Worcester	1653	1740	28.81	1,189	1,790	3,522	12,392	19,744	22,226	27,929	34,508	41,303
Leverett	Franklin	1713	1774	22.90	524	857	964	744	695	688	914	1,471	1,663
Lexington	Middlesex	1640	1713	16.48	941	1,200	2,329	3,831	6,350	13,187	27,691	29,479	30,355
Leyden	Franklin	1738	1809	18.09	989	974	606	379	330	260	343	498	772
Lincoln	Middlesex	1650	1754	14.56	740	706	718	1,127	1,042	1,783	5,613	7,098	8,056

Littleton	Middlesex	1686	1698	16.46	854	955	1,063	1,179	1,277	1,651	5,109	6,970	8,184
Longmeadow	Hampden	1644	1783	9,03	744	1,171	1,376	811	2,618	5,790	10,565	16,301	15,633
LOWELL	Middlesex	1653	1826	13.38	—	—	36,827	94,969	112,759	101,389	92,107	92,418	105,167
Ludlow	Hampden	1751	1755	27.14	560	1,246	1,174	3,536	7,470	8,181	13,805	18,150	21,209
Lunenburg	Worcester	1721	1728	26.63	1,277	1,209	1,212	1,332	1,634	2,195	6,334	8,405	9,401
LYNN	Essex	1629	1635	10.47	2,291	4,515	19,083	68,513	99,148	98,123	94,478	78,471	89,050
Lynnfield	Essex	1638	1814	10.22	491	596	866	888	1,165	2,287	8,398	11,267	11,542
MALDEN	Middlesex	1640	1649	5.08	1,033	1,731	5,865	33,664	49,103	58,010	57,676	53,386	56,340
Manchester	Essex	1626	1645	7.72	965	1,201	1,698	2,522	2,466	2,472	3,932	5,424	5,228
Mansfield	Bristol	1659	1775	20.22	983	1,222	2,114	4,006	6,255	6,530	7,773	13,453	22,414
Marblehead	Essex	1629	1649	4.40	5,661	5,630	7,646	7,582	7,324	10,856	18,521	20,126	20,377
Marion	Plymouth	1679	1852	14.28	—	—	918	902	1,288	2,030	2,881	3,932	5,123
MARLBOROUGH	Middlesex	1657	1660	20.99	1,554	1,952	5,911	13,609	15,028	15,154	18,819	30,617	36,255
Marshfield	Plymouth	1632	1640	28.35	1,269	1,532	1,870	1,810	1,379	2,419	6,748	20,916	24,324
Mashpee	Barnstable	1660	1870	23.86	308	150	322	303	242	434	867	3,700	12,946
Mattapoisett	Plymouth	1750	1857	17.46	—	—	1,483	1,061	1,277	1,608	3,117	5,597	6,268
Maynard	Middlesex	1638	1871	5.24	—	—	—	3,142	7,086	6,812	7,695	9,590	10,433
Medfield	Norfolk	1651	1651	14.43	731	892	1,082	2,926	3,595	4,384	6,021	10,220	12,273
MEDFORD	Middlesex	1630	1630	8.21	1,029	1,474	4,842	18,244	39,038	63,083	64,971	58,076	55,765

Statistics on Massachusetts Towns and Cities (*continued*)

City/Town	*County*	*Year Settled*	*Year Incorporated*	*Size (sq. mi.)*	*Population*								
					1790	*1820*	*1860*	*1900*	*1920*	*1940*	*1960*	*1980*	*2000*
Medway	Norfolk	1657	1713	11.60	1,035	1,523	3,195	2,761	2,956	3,297	5,168	8,447	12,448
MELROSE	Middlesex	1629	1850	4.73	—	—	2,532	12,962	18,204	25,333	29,619	30,055	27,134
Mendon	Worcester	1660	1667	17.73	1,555	2,254	1,351	911	961	1,315	2,068	3,108	5,286
Merrimac	Essex	1638	1876	8.66	—	—	—	2,131	2,173	2,320	3,261	4,451	6,138
Methuen	Essex	1642	1725	22.41	1,297	1,371	2,566	7,512	15,189	21,880	28,114	36,701	43,789
Middleborough	Plymouth	1660	1669	69.98	4,526	4,687	4,553	6,885	8,453	9,032	11,065	16,404	19,941
Middlefield	Hampshire	1780	1783	24.13	608	755	748	410	280	201	315	385	542
Middleton	Essex	1659	1728	14.27	682	596	940	839	1,195	2,348	3,718	4,135	7,744
Milford	Worcester	1662	1780	14.79	839	1,160	9,132	11,376	13,471	15,388	15,749	23,390	26,799
Millbury	Worcester	1716	1813	15.84	—	926	3,296	4,460	5,653	6,983	9,623	11,808	12,784
Millis	Norfolk	1657	1885	12.17	—	—	—	1,053	1,485	2,278	4,374	6,908	7,902
Millville	Worcester	1662	1916	4.92	—	—	—	—	2,224	1,722	1,567	1,693	2,724
Milton	Norfolk	1636	1662	13.10	1,039	1,502	2,669	6,578	9,382	18,708	26,375	25,860	26,062
Monroe	Franklin	1800	1822	10.85	—	—	236	305	173	207	210	179	93
Monson	Hampden	1715	1775	44.84	1,331	2,126	3,164	3,402	4,826	5,597	6,712	7,315	8,359
Montague	Franklin	1715	1775	31.02	906	1,074	1,593	6,150	7,675	7,582	7,836	8,011	8,489

Monterey	Berkshire	1739	1847	26.55	—	—	758	455	282	320	480	818	934
Montgomery	Hampden	1767	1780	15.01	449	604	371	273	229	178	333	637	654
Mount Washington	Berkshire	1692	1779	22.22	261	467	321	123	73	57	34	93	130
Nahant	Essex	1630	1853	1.04	—	—	380	1,152	1,318	1,835	3,960	3,947	3,632
Nantucket	Nantucket	1641	1713	49.53	4,620	7,266	6,094	3,006	2,797	3,401	3,559	5,087	9,520
Natick	Middlesex	1718	1781	14.88	615	849	5,515	9,488	10,907	13,851	28,831	29,461	32,170
Needham	Norfolk	1680	1711	12.50	1,130	1,227	2,658	4,016	7,012	12,445	25,793	27,901	28,911
New Ashford	Berkshire	1762	1835	13.65	460	358	239	107	116	87	165	159	247
NEW BEDFORD	Bristol	1640	1787	18.99	3,313	3,947	22,300	62,442	121,217	110,341	102,477	98,478	93,768
New Braintree	Worcester	1709	1775	20.76	939	888	805	500	394	439	509	671	927
New Marlborough	Berkshire	1738	1775	47.85	1,550	1,668	1,782	1,282	1,010	956	1,083	1,160	1,494
New Salem	Franklin	1737	1775	45.04	1,543	2,146	957	807	512	357	397	688	929
Newbury	Essex	1635	1635	23.97	3,972	3,671	1,444	1,601	1,303	1,599	2,519	4,529	6,717
NEWBURYPORT	Essex	1635	1764	8.30	4,837	6,852	13,401	14,478	15,618	13,916	14,004	15,900	17,189
NEWTON	Middlesex	1639	1691	17.90	1,360	1,850	8,382	33,587	46,054	69,873	92,384	83,622	83,829
Norfolk	Norfolk	1795	1870	15.10	—	—	—	980	1,159	2,294	3,471	6,363	10,460
NORTH ADAMS	Berkshire	1737	1878	20.59	—	—	—	24,200	22,282	22,213	19,905	18,063	14,681
North Andover	Essex	1644	1855	26.63	—	—	2,343	4,243	6,265	7,524	10,908	20,129	27,202

Statistics on Massachusetts Towns and Cities (*continued*)

City/Town	*County*	*Year Settled*	*Year Incorporated*	*Size (sq. mi.)*	*Population* 1790	1820	1860	1900	1920	1940	1960	1980	2000
North Attleborough	Bristol	1669	1887	19.05	—	—	—	7,253	9,238	10,359	14,777	21,095	27,143
North Brookfield	Worcester	1664	1812	21.11	—	1,095	2,760	4,587	2,610	3,304	3,616	4,150	4,683
North Reading	Middlesex	1651	1853	13.26	—	—	1,203	1,035	1,286	2,886	8,331	11,455	13,837
NORTHAMPTON	Hampshire	1654	1656	34.63	1,628	2,854	6,788	18,643	21,951	24,794	30,058	29,286	28,978
Northborough	Worcester	1672	1775	18.47	619	1,018	1,565	2,164	1,753	2,382	6,687	10,568	14,013
Northbridge	Worcester	1704	1775	17.33	569	905	2,633	7,036	10,174	10,242	10,800	12,246	13,182
Northfield	Franklin	1673	1714	34.18	868	1,584	1,712	1,966	1,775	1,975	2,320	2,386	2,951
Norton	Bristol	1669	1711	27.91	1,428	1,600	1,848	1,826	2,374	3,107	6,818	12,690	18,036
Norwell	Plymouth	1634	1849	20.97	—	—	1,774	1,560	1,348	1,871	5,207	9,182	9,765
Norwood	Norfolk	1678	1872	10.47	—	—	—	5,840	12,627	15,383	24,898	29,711	28,587
Oak Bluffs	Dukes	1642	1907	7.14	—	—	—	1,100	1,047	1,584	1,419	1,984	3,713
Oakham	Worcester	1749	1775	20.99	772	986	959	588	477	423	524	994	1,673
Orange	Franklin	1746	1810	35.03	784	829	1,622	5,520	5,393	5,611	6,154	6,844	7,518
Orleans	Barnstable	1693	1797	13.94	—	1,343	1,678	1,123	1,012	1,451	2,342	5,306	6,341
Otis	Berkshire	1735	1773	35.77	605	981	998	476	361	364	473	963	1,365

Oxford	Worcester	1687	1693	26.71	1,000	1,562	3,034	2,677	3,820	4,623	9,282	11,680	13,352
Palmer	Hampden	1727	1775	31.43	809	1,197	4,082	7,801	9,896	9,149	10,358	11,389	12,497
Paxton	Worcester	1749	1775	14.87	558	613	725	459	489	791	2,399	3,762	4,386
PEABODY	Essex	1626	1855	16.45	—	—	6,549	11,523	19,552	21,711	32,202	45,976	48,129
Pelham	Hampshire	1738	1743	24.82	1,040	1,278	748	462	503	568	805	1,112	1,403
Pembroke	Plymouth	1650	1712	21.53	1,954	1,297	1,524	1,240	1,358	1,718	4,919	13,487	16,927
Pepperell	Middlesex	1720	1775	22.79	1,132	1,439	1,895	3,701	2,468	3,114	4,336	8,061	11,142
Peru	Berkshire	1767	1771	26.05	1,041	748	499	253	149	142	197	633	821
Petersham	Worcester	1733	1754	54.27	1,560	1,623	1,465	853	642	923	890	1,024	1,180
Phillipston	Worcester	1751	1786	23.70	740	916	764	441	354	481	695	953	1,621
PITTSFIELD	Berkshire	1752	1761	40.70	1,992	2,768	8,045	21,766	41,763	49,684	57,870	51,974	45,793
Plainfield	Hampshire	1770	1807	21.29	458	936	639	404	332	264	237	425	589
Plainville	Norfolk	1661	1905	10.98	—	—	—	—	1,365	1,302	3,810	5,857	7,683
Plymouth	Plymouth	1620	1620	97.57	2,995	4,348	6,272	9,592	13,045	13,100	14,445	35,913	51,701
Plympton	Plymouth	1662	1707	14.92	956	930	994	488	469	532	821	1,974	2,637
Princeton	Worcester	1743	1771	35.39	1,016	1,261	1,201	975	682	713	1,360	2,425	3,353
Provincetown	Barnstable	1700	1727	8.35	454	1,252	3,206	4,247	4,246	3,668	3,389	3,536	3,431
QUINCY	Norfolk	1625	1792	16.51	—	—	1,623	6,778	23,899	47,876	75,810	87,409	88,025
Randolph	Norfolk	1710	1793	10.08	—	1,546	5,760	3,993	4,756	7,634	18,900	28,218	30,963

Statistics on Massachusetts Towns and Cities (*continued*)

		Year	Year	Size	Population								
City/Town	*County*	*Settled*	*Incorporated*	*(sq. mi.)*	*1790*	*1820*	*1860*	*1900*	*1920*	*1940*	*1960*	*1980*	*2000*
Raynham	Bristol	1652	1731	20.30	1,094	1,071	1,746	1,540	1,695	2,141	4,150	9,085	11,739
Reading	Middlesex	1639	1644	9.84	1,802	2,797	2,662	4,969	7,439	10,866	19,259	22,678	23,708
Rehoboth	Bristol	1636	1645	47.25	4,710	2,740	1,932	1,840	2,065	2,736	4,953	7,570	10,172
REVERE	Suffolk	1630	1846	5.95	—	—	921	10,395	28,823	34,405	40,080	42,423	47,283
Richmond	Berkshire	1760	1765	18.95	1,255	923	914	679	561	624	890	1,659	1,604
Rochester	Plymouth	1638	1686	33.76	2,644	3,034	1,232	986	1,047	1,269	1,559	3,205	4,581
Rockland	Plymouth	1673	1874	10.02	—	—	—	5,327	7,544	8,087	13,119	15,695	17,670
Rockport	Essex	1623	1840	7.02	—	—	3,237	4,592	3,878	3,556	4,616	6,345	7,767
Rowe	Franklin	1762	1785	23.78	443	851	619	549	333	233	231	336	351
Rowley	Essex	1638	1639	19.01	1,772	1,825	1,278	1,391	1,249	1,533	2,783	3,867	5,500
Royalston	Worcester	1762	1765	41.99	1,130	1,424	1,486	958	819	795	800	955	1,254
Russell	Hampden	1782	1792	17.71	—	491	605	793	1,237	1,242	1,366	1,570	1,657
Rutland	Worcester	1716	1722	35.42	1,072	1,262	1,076	1,334	1,743	2,181	3,253	4,334	6,353
SALEM	Essex	1626	1630	7.99	7,921	12,731	22,252	35,956	42,529	41,213	39,211	38,276	40,407
Salisbury	Essex	1638	1640	15.74	1,780	2,006	3,310	1,558	1,701	2,376	3,154	5,973	7,827
Sandisfield	Berkshire	1750	1762	52.51	1,742	1,646	1,585	661	460	421	536	720	824

Sandwich	Barnstable	1630	1638	42.61	1,991	2,484	4,479	1,448	1,458	1,360	2,082	8,727	20,136
Saugus	Essex	1630	1815	10.58	—	748	2,024	5,084	10,874	14,825	20,666	24,746	26,078
Savoy	Berkshire	1777	1797	36.03	—	852	904	506	436	300	277	644	705
Scituate	Plymouth	1630	1635	16.90	2,856	3,305	2,227	2,470	2,534	4,130	11,214	17,317	17,863
Seekonk	Bristol	1636	1812	18.63	—	2,775	2,662	1,673	2,898	4,912	8,399	12,269	13,425
Sharon	Norfolk	1650	1775	23.58	1,034	1,010	1,377	2,060	2,467	3,737	10,070	13,601	17,408
Sheffield	Berkshire	1726	1733	47.82	1,899	2,476	2,621	1,804	1,435	1,709	2,138	2,743	3,335
Shelburne	Franklin	1756	1775	23.22	1,183	1,022	1,448	1,508	1,436	1,636	1,739	2,002	2,058
Sherborn	Middlesex	1652	1674	16.89	801	811	1,129	1,483	1,558	1,022	1,806	4,049	4,200
Shirley	Middlesex	1720	1775	15.81	677	922	1,468	1,680	2,260	2,608	5,202	5,124	6,373
Shrewsbury	Worcester	1722	1727	20.78	963	1,458	1,558	1,626	3,708	7,586	16,622	22,674	31,640
Shutesbury	Franklin	1735	1761	26.68	674	1,029	798	382	242	191	265	1,049	1,810
Somerset	Bristol	1677	1790	7.12	1,151	1,116	1,793	2,241	3,520	5,873	12,196	18,813	18,234
SOMERVILLE	Middlesex	1630	1842	3.93	—	—	8,025	61,643	93,091	102,177	94,697	77,372	77,478
South Hadley	Hampshire	1659	1775	17.76	759	1,047	2,277	4,526	5,527	6,856	14,956	16,399	17,196
Southampton	Hampshire	1732	1775	28.58	829	1,160	1,130	1,012	814	950	2,192	4,137	5,387
Southborough	Worcester	1660	1727	13.78	837	1,030	1,854	1,921	1,838	2,231	3,996	6,193	8,781
Southbridge	Worcester	1730	1816	20.38	—	1,066	3,575	10,025	14,245	16,825	16,523	16,665	17,214
Southwick	Hampden	1770	1775	31.15	841	1,255	1,188	1,040	1,194	1,579	5,139	7,382	8,835

Statistics on Massachusetts Towns and Cities (*continued*)

City/Town	*County*	*Year Settled*	*Year Incorporated*	*Size (sq. mi.)*	*Population 1790*	*1820*	*1860*	*1900*	*1920*	*1940*	*1960*	*1980*	*2000*
Spencer	Worcester	1721	1775	33.15	1,322	1,548	2,777	7,627	5,930	6,641	7,838	10,774	11,691
SPRINGFIELD	Hampden	1636	1641	31.70	1,574	3,914	15,199	62,059	129,614	149,554	174,463	152,319	152,082
Sterling	Worcester	1720	1781	30.52	1,428	1,710	1,881	1,420	1,305	1,713	3,193	5,440	7,257
Stockbridge	Berkshire	1734	1739	22.84	1,336	1,377	2,136	2,081	1,764	1,815	2,161	2,328	2,276
Stoneham	Middlesex	1645	1725	6.03	381	615	3,206	6,197	7,873	10,765	17,821	21,424	22,219
Stoughton	Norfolk	1713	1726	16.25	1,994	1,313	4,830	5,442	6,865	8,632	16,328	26,710	27,149
Stow	Middlesex	1681	1683	17.68	801	1,071	1,641	1,002	1,101	1,243	2,573	5,144	5,902
Sturbridge	Worcester	1729	1738	37.39	1,704	1,633	2,291	2,058	1,573	2,227	3,604	5,976	7,837
Sudbury	Middlesex	1638	1639	24.37	1,290	1,417	1,691	1,150	1,121	1,754	7,447	14,027	16,841
Sunderland	Franklin	1713	1714	14.36	462	597	839	771	1,289	1,085	1,279	2,929	3,777
Sutton	Worcester	1704	1714	32.48	2,642	2,056	2,676	3,328	2,578	2,949	3,638	5,855	8,250
Swampscott	Essex	1629	1852	3.08	—	—	1,530	4,548	8,101	10,761	13,294	13,837	14,412
Swansea	Bristol	1632	1667	22.12	1,784	1,933	1,430	1,645	2,334	4,684	9,916	15,461	15,901
TAUNTON	Bristol	1638	1639	47.29	3,804	4,520	15,376	31,036	37,137	37,395	41,132	45,001	55,976
Templeton	Worcester	1751	1762	31.49	950	1,331	2,816	3,489	4,019	4,601	5,371	6,070	6,799
Tewksbury	Middlesex	1637	1734	20.70	958	1,008	1,744	3,683	4,450	6,261	15,902	24,635	28,851

Tisbury	Dukes	1660	1671	7.19	1,142	1,223	1,631	1,149	1,275	1,966	2,169	2,972	3,755
Tolland	Hampden	1750	1810	31.93	—	692	596	275	192	129	101	235	426
Topsfield	Essex	1635	1650	12.80	780	866	1,292	1,030	900	1,150	3,351	5,709	6,141
Townsend	Middlesex	1676	1732	32.66	933	1,482	2,005	1,804	1,575	2,065	3,650	7,201	9,198
Truro	Barnstable	1700	1709	20.70	1,193	1,241	1,583	767	554	585	1,002	1,486	2,087
Tyngsborough	Middlesex	1661	1809	16.86	382	808	626	773	1,044	1,634	3,302	5,863	11,081
Tyringham	Berkshire	1735	1762	18.77	1,397	1,443	730	386	267	213	197	344	350
Upton	Worcester	1728	1735	21.65	833	1,088	1,986	1,937	1,693	2,249	3,127	3,886	5,642
Uxbridge	Worcester	1662	1727	29.29	1,308	1,551	3,133	3,599	5,384	6,417	7,789	8,374	11,156
Wakefield	Middlesex	1639	1812	7.35	—	—	3,207	9,290	13,025	16,223	24,295	24,895	24,804
Wales	Hampden	1726	1775	16.21	606	683	677	773	419	367	659	1,177	1,737
Walpole	Norfolk	1659	1724	20.56	1,005	1,366	2,037	3,572	5,446	7,443	14,068	18,859	22,824
WALTHAM	Middlesex	1634	1738	12.41	882	1,677	6,397	23,481	30,915	40,020	55,413	58,200	59,226
Ware	Hampshire	1717	1775	34.85	773	1,154	3,597	8,263	8,525	7,557	7,517	8,953	9,707
Wareham	Plymouth	1678	1739	36.68	854	952	3,186	3,432	4,415	6,364	9,461	18,457	20,335
Warren	Worcester	1664	1742	27.50	899	1,112	2,107	4,417	3,467	3,531	3,383	3,777	4,776
Warwick	Franklin	1739	1763	37.19	1,246	1,256	932	619	327	444	426	603	750
Washington	Berkshire	1760	1777	38.20	588	750	948	377	240	267	290	587	544
Watertown	Middlesex	1630	1630	4.06	1,091	1,518	3,270	9,706	21,457	35,427	39,092	34,384	32,986

Statistics on Massachusetts Towns and Cities (*continued*)

City/Town	County	Year Settled	Year Incorporated	Size (sq. mi.)	Population 1790	1820	1860	1900	1920	1940	1960	1980	2000
Wayland	Middlesex	1638	1780	15.29	801	962	1,188	2,303	1,935	3,505	10,444	12,170	13,100
Webster	Worcester	1713	1832	12.53	—	—	2,912	8,804	13,258	13,186	13,680	14,480	16,415
Wellesley	Norfolk	1660	1881	10.05	—	—	—	5,072	6,224	15,127	26,071	27,209	26,613
Wellfleet	Barnstable	1724	1775	20.47	1,117	1,472	2,322	988	826	890	1,404	2,209	2,749
Wendell	Franklin	1754	1781	31.65	519	958	704	492	346	391	292	694	986
Wenham	Essex	1635	1643	7.75	502	1,105	847	1,090	1,220	2,798	3,897	4,020	4,440
West Boylston	Worcester	1642	1808	12.69	—	886	2,509	2,314	1,624	1,822	5,526	6,204	7,481
West Bridgewater	Plymouth	1651	1822	15.48	—	1,055	1,846	1,711	2,908	3,247	5,061	6,359	6,634
West Brookfield	Worcester	1664	1848	20.67	—	—	1,548	1,448	1,281	1,387	2,053	3,026	3,804
West Newbury	Essex	1635	1819	13.90	—	1,279	2,202	1,558	1,492	1,515	1,844	2,861	4,149
West Springfield	Hampden	1660	1774	16.75	2,367	3,246	2,105	7,105	13,443	17,135	24,924	27,042	27,899
West Stockbridge	Berkshire	1766	1775	18.34	1,034	1,589	1,158	1,058	1,062	1,244	1,280	1,390	1,416
West Tisbury	Dukes	1669	1892	25.46	—	—	—	442	345	260	360	1,010	2,467
Westborough	Worcester	1675	1717	21.05	934	1,326	2,913	5,400	5,789	6,463	9,599	13,619	17,997
WESTFIELD	Hampden	1660	1669	46.85	2,204	2,668	5,055	12,310	18,604	18,793	26,302	36,465	40,072
Westford	Middlesex	1635	1729	30.25	1,229	1,409	1,624	2,624	3,170	3,830	6,261	13,434	20,754

Westhampton	Hampshire	1762	1778	27.07	683	896	608	469	305	403	583	1,137	1,468
Westminster	Worcester	1737	1770	35.64	1,176	1,634	1,840	1,327	1,343	2,126	4,022	5,139	6,907
Weston	Middlesex	1642	1713	17.17	1,010	1,041	1,243	1,834	2,282	3,590	8,261	11,169	11,469
Westport	Bristol	1670	1787	53.01	2,466	2,633	2,767	2,890	3,115	4,134	6,641	13,763	14,183
Westwood	Norfolk	1640	1897	11.15	—	—	—	1,112	1,358	3,376	10,354	13,212	14,117
Weymouth	Norfolk	1630	1635	16.70	1,469	2,407	7,742	11,324	15,057	23,868	48,177	55,061	53,988
Whately	Franklin	1672	1771	20.46	736	1,076	1,057	769	1,234	979	1,037	1,341	1,573
Whitman	Plymouth	1670	1875	6.70	—	—	—	6,155	7,147	7,759	10,485	13,534	13,882
Wilbraham	Hampden	1730	1763	22.22	1,555	1,979	2,081	1,595	2,780	3,041	7,387	12,053	13,473
Williamsburg	Hampshire	1735	1775	25.57	1,049	1,087	2,095	1,926	1,866	1,684	2,186	2,237	2,427
Williamstown	Berkshire	1749	1765	46.73	1,769	2,010	2,611	5,013	3,707	4,294	7,322	8,741	8,424
Wilmington	Middlesex	1639	1730	17.08	710	786	919	1,596	2,581	4,645	12,475	17,471	21,363
Winchendon	Worcester	1753	1764	42.53	946	1,263	2,624	5,001	5,904	6,575	6,237	7,019	9,611
Winchester	Middlesex	1640	1850	5.90	—	—	1,937	7,248	10,485	15,081	19,376	20,701	20,810
Windsor	Berkshire	1767	1771	35.13	916	1,085	839	507	403	314	384	598	875
Winthrop	Sufiolk	1635	1852	1.56	—	—	544	6,058	15,455	16,768	20,303	19,294	18,303
WOBURN	Middlesex	1640	1642	12.86	1,727	1,519	6,287	14,254	16,574	19,751	31,214	36,626	37,258
WORCESTER	Worcester	1673	1684	37.16	2,095	2,962	24,960	118,421	179,754	193,694	186,587	161,799	172,648
Worthington	Hampshire	1764	1768	32.04	1,116	1,276	1,041	675	409	471	597	932	1,270

Statistics on Massachusetts Towns and Cities (*continued*)

		Year	*Year*	*Size*	*Population*								
City/Town	*County*	*Settled*	*Incorporated*	*(sq. mi.)*	*1790*	*1820*	*1860*	*1900*	*1920*	*1940*	*1960*	*1980*	*2000*
Wrentham	Norfolk	1669	1673	22.02	1,767	2,801	3,406	2,720	2,808	4,674	6,685	7,580	10,554
Yarmouth	Barnstable	1639	1639	24.13	2,678	2,232	2,752	1,682	1,229	2,286	5,504	18,449	24,807

MASSACHUSETTS

Year	*Year*	*Size*	*Population*								
Settled	*Incorporated*	*(sq. mi.)*	*1790*	*1820*	*1860*	*1900*	*1920*	*1940*	*1960*	*1980*	*2000*
1620	1629	7,838.68	378,787	523,287	1,231,066	2,805,346	3,852,356	4,316,721	5,148,578	5,737,093	6,349,097

Museums, Historic Sites, and State Parks

Museums and Historic Sites

Adams National Historic Park
P.O. Box 531
Quincy, MA 02269
(617) 773-1177
www.nps.gov/adam

Addison Gallery of American Art
Chapel Avenue
Andover, MA 01810
(978) 749-4017
www.addisongallery.org

Arrowhead
Berkshire County Historical Society
780 Holmes Road
Pittsfield, MA 01201
(413) 442-1793
www.mobydick.org

The Berkshire Museum
39 South Street
Pittsfield, MA 01201
(413) 443-7171
www.berkshiremuseum.org

Blackstone Valley National Historical Corridor
One Depot Square
Woonsocket, RI 02895
(401) 762-0250

Boston National Historic Park
The People and Places program
15 State Street
Boston, MA 02109
(617) 242-5690
www.nps.gov/bost

Boston Tea Party Ship and Museum
Congress Street Bridge
Boston, MA 02210
(617) 338-1773
www.bostonteapartyship.com

Bostonian Society/Old State House
206 Washington Street
Boston, MA 02109
(617) 720-3292
www.bostonhistory.org

Cape Cod Museum of Natural History
P.O. Box 1710
Brewster, MA 02631
(508) 896-3867
www.ccmnh.org

Charles River Museum
154 Moody Street
Waltham, MA 02154
(781) 893-5410
http://users.rcn.com/crmi

Chesterwood
P.O. Box 48
Stockbridge, MA 01262
(413) 298-3579
www.chesterwood.org

The Children's Museum
300 Congress Street
Boston, MA 02210
(617) 426-6550
www.bostonkids.org

Children's Museum at Holyoke
444 Dwight Street
Holyoke, MA 01040
(413) 536-7048
www.childrensmuseumholyoke.org

Sterling and Francine Clark Art Institute
Smith Street
Williamstown, MA 01267
(413) 458-8109
www.clarkart.edu

The Commonwealth Museum and State Archives
220 Morrissey Boulevard
Boston, MA 02125
(617) 727-9268

The Computer Museum
300 Congress Street
Boston, MA 02210
(617) 426-2800
www.mos.org/tcm/tcm.html

Concord Museum
200 Lexington Road, Box 146
Concord, MA 01742
(978) 369-9763
www.concordmuseum.org

DeCordova Museum and Sculpture Park
51 Sandy Pond Road
Lincoln, MA 01773
(978) 259-3604
www.decordova.org

Essex Shipbuilding Museum
Waterlane Center
66 Main Street, Box 277
Essex, MA 01929
(978) 768-6441
www.essexshipbuildingmuseum.org

Fitchburg Art Museum
185 Elm Street
Fitchburg, MA 01420
(978) 345-4207
www.fitchburgartmuseum.org

Fruitlands Museum
Prospect Hill
Harvard, MA 01451
www.fruitlands.org

Fuller Museum of Art
455 Oak Street
Brockton, MA 02401
(508) 588-6000
www.fullermuseum.org

Isabella Stewart Gardner Museum
2 Palace Road
Boston, MA 02115
(617) 278-5123
www.gardnermuseum.org

Hancock Shaker Village
P.O. Box 927
Pittsfield, MA 01202
(413) 443-0188
www.hancockshakervillage.org

Harvard University Museums:
Cultural and Natural History
26 Oxford Street
Cambridge, MA 02138
(617) 496-5402
www.harvard.edu/museums

Busch-Reisinger, Fogg, and Sackler Art Museums
32 Quincy Street
Cambridge, MA 02138
(617) 495-9400
www.artmuseums.harvard.edu

Heritage Plantation
P.O. Box 566
Sandwich, MA 02563
(508) 888-3300
www.heritagemuseumsandgardens.org

Higgins Armory Museum
100 Barber Avenue
Worcester, MA 01606
(508) 853-6015
www.higgins.org

Historic Deerfield, Inc.
Box 321
Deerfield, MA 01342
(413) 774-5581
www.historic-deerfield.org

House of Seven Gables
54 Turner Street
Salem, MA 01970
(978) 744-0981
www.7gables.org

The Jackson Homestead
527 Washington Street
Newton, MA 02158
(617) 552-7238
www.ci.newton.ma.us/jackson

Kendall Whaling Museum
27 Everett Street
Sharon, MA 02067
(781) 784-5642
www.kwm.org

John F. Kennedy Library & Museum
Columbia Point
Boston, MA 02125
(617) 929-4553
www.cs.umb.edu/jfklibrary

Lexington Historical Society
Hancock-Clarke House, Buckman Tavern, Munroe Tavern
P.O. Box 514
Lexington, MA 02173
(781) 861-0928
www.lexingtonhistory.org

Marine Museum at Fall River
70 Water Street
Fall River, MA 02721
(508) 674-3533
www.marinemuseum.org

Mead Art Gallery, Amherst College
Amherst, MA 01002
(413) 542-2335
www.amherst.edu/~mead

Minuteman National Historic Park
Battle Road-Route 2A
Lexington, MA 02173
(617) 862-7753
www.nps.gov/mima

Mount Holyoke Art Museum
South Hadley, MA 01075
(413) 538-2245
www.mtholyoke.edu/offices/artmuseum

Museum of Afro-American History/
African Meeting House
46 Joy Street/Smith Court
Boston, MA 02114
(617) 742-1854
www.afroammuseum.org

Museum of American Textile History
491 Dutton Street
Lowell, MA 01854
(978) 441-0400
www.athm.org/home2.htm

Museum of Fine Arts, Boston
465 Huntington Avenue
Boston, MA 02115
(617) 369-3309
www.mfa.org

Museum of the National Center of
Afro-American Artists
300 Walnut Avenue
Boston, MA 02119
(617) 442-8514
www.ncaaa.org/museum.html

Museum of Our National Heritage
33 Marrett Road
Lexington, MA 02173
(781) 861-6559
www.monh.org

Museum of Science
Science Park
Boston, MA 02114
(617) 723-2511
www.mos.org

Nantucket Historical Association
Nantucket, MA 02554
(508) 228-1736
www.nha.org

New Bedford Whaling Museum
18 Johnny Cake Hill
New Bedford, MA 02740
(508) 997-0046
www.whalingmuseum.org

New England Aquarium
Central Wharf
Boston, MA 02110
(617) 973-5232
www.neaq.org/index.flash4.html

New England Science Center
222 Harrington Way
Worcester, MA 01604
(508) 791-9211

Old Colony Historical Society
66 Church Green
Taunton, MA 02780
(508) 822-1622
www.oldcolonyhistoricalsociety.org

Old South Meeting House
301 Washington Street
Boston, MA 02108
(617) 482-6439
www.oldsouthmeetinghouse.org

Old Sturbridge Village
One Old Sturbridge Village Road
Sturbridge, MA 01566
(508) 347-3362
www.osv.org

Orchard House/Alcott Home
399 Lexington Road Box 343
Concord, MA 01742
(978) 369-5617
www.louisamayalcott.org

Peabody Museum/Essex Institute
East India Square
Salem, MA 01970
(978) 745-1876
www.pem.org

Pilgrim Hall Museum
75 Court Street
Plymouth, MA 02360
(508) 746-1620
www.pilgrimhall.org

Plimoth Plantation
P.O. Box 1620
Plymouth, MA 02362
(508) 746-1622
www.plimoth.org

Paul Revere House
19 North Square
Boston, MA 02113
(617) 523-1676
www.paulreverehouse.org

Norman Rockwell Museum
9 Glendike Road, Box 308
Stockbridge, MA 01262
(413) 298-4100
www.nrm.org

Salem Maritime National Parks and Historic Site
174 Derby Street
Salem, MA 01970
(978) 740-1680
http://salemmaritime.areaparks.com

Saugus National Park Ironworks
244 Central Street
Saugus, MA 01906
(781) 233-0050

Schooner Ernestina Commission
State Pier, Box 2010
New Bedford, MA 02741
(508) 992-4900
www.ernestina.org

Smith College Art Museum
Elm Street at Bedford Terrace
Northampton, MA 01063
(413) 584-2700
www.smith.edu/artmuseum

Society for the Preservation of New England Antiquities
141 Cambridge Street
Boston, MA 02114
(617) 227-3956
www.spnea.org

Springfield Armory
One Armory Square
Springfield, MA 01105
(413) 734-8551
www.nps.gov/spar

Springfield Museums:
Museum of Fine Arts, G. V. Smith Museum, Connecticut Valley Historical Museum, Science Museum
220 State Street
Springfield, MA 01103
(413) 739-3871
www.quadrangle.org

Storrowton Village Museum
1305 Memorial Avenue
West Springfield, MA 01089
(413) 787-0316
www.thebige.com/storrowton.html

Tsongas Industrial History Center
Boott Cotton Mills Museum
400 Foot of John Street
Lowell, MA 01852
(978) 970-5080
www.uml.edu/tsongas/index2.htm

U.S.S. Constitution Museum
Charlestown Navy Shipyard
P.O. Box 1812
Boston, MA 02129
(617) 426-1812
www.ussconstitutionmuseum.org

Wellesley College Art Museum
Jewett Center
Wellesley, MA 02181
(781) 235-0320
www.wellesley.edu/DavisMuseum

Williams College Museum of Art
Main Street
Williamstown, MA 01267
(413) 597-2429
www.williams.edu/WCMA

Worcester Art Museum
55 Salisbury Street
Worcester, MA 01609
(508) 799-4406
www.worcesterart.org

State Parks

Division of Forests and Parks
100 Cambridge Street
Boston, MA 02202
(617) 727-3180
www.state.ma.us/dem/forparks.htm

BERKSHIRES:

Mt. Greylock State Reservation
(413) 499-4262
www.state.ma.us/dem/parks/mgry.htm

Natural Bridge State Park
Western Gateway Heritage State Park
(Hoosac Tunnel)
(413) 663-6312
www.state.ma.us/dem/parks/nbdg.htm

CONNECTICUT RIVER VALLEY:

Gardner Heritage State Park
(978) 630-1497
www.state.ma.us/dem/parks/ghsp.htm

Holyoke Heritage State Park
(413) 534-1723
www.state.ma.us/dem/parks/hhsp.htm

Skinner State Park
(413) 586-0350
www.state.ma.us/dem/parks/skin.htm

CENTRAL:

Blackstone River and Canal Heritage State Park
(508) 278-6486
www.state.ma.us/dem/parks/blst.htm

NORTHEAST:

Bradley Palmer State Park
(978) 887-5931
www.state.ma.us/dem/parks/brad.htm

Great Brook Farm State Park
(978) 369-6312
www.state.ma.us/dem/parks/gbfm.htm

Halibut Point State Park
(978) 546-2997
www.state.ma.us/dem/parks/halb.htm

Lawrence Heritage State Park
(978) 794-1655
www.state.ma.us/dem/parks/lwhp.htm

Lowell Heritage State Park
(978) 453-0592
www.state.ma.us/dem/parks/llhp.htm

Maudslay State Park
(978) 465-7223
www.state.ma.us/dem/parks/maud.htm

GREATER BOSTON:

Borderland State Park
(508) 238-6566
www.state.ma.us/dem/parks/bord.htm

Boston Harbor Islands Park
(781) 740-1605
www.nps.gov/boha

Lynn Heritage State Park
(781) 598-1974
www.state.ma.us/dem/parks/lnhp.htm

Roxbury Heritage State Park
(617) 445-3399
www.state.ma.us/dem/parks/rxhp.htm

Walden Pond State Reservation
(978) 369-3254
www.state.ma.us/dem/parks/wldn.htm

SOUTHEAST:

Dighton Rock State Park
(508) 644-5522
www.state.ma.us/dem/parks/digr.htm

Fall River Heritage State Park
(508) 675-5759
www.state.ma.us/dem/parks/frhp.htm

Myles Standish Monument State Reservation
(781) 866-2580
www.state.ma.us/dem/parks/mssm.htm

Pilgrim Memorial State Park
(508) 866-2580
www.state.ma.us/dem/parks/plgm.htm

Colleges and Universities

American International College
100 State Street
Springfield 01109
(413) 742-3142
www.aic.edu

Amherst College
100 Boltwood Avenue
Amherst 01002
(413) 542-2000
www.amherst.edu

Anna Maria College
50 Sunset Lane
Paxton 01612
(508) 849-3300
www.annamaria.edu

Assumption College
500 Salisbury Street
Worcester 01609
(888) 882-7786
www.assumption.edu

Atlantic Union College
P.O. Box 100
S. Lancaster 01561
(800) 282-2030
www.atlanticuc.edu

Babson College
231 Forest Street
Babson Park 02457
(781) 235-1200
www.babson.edu

Bay Path College
588 Longmeadow Street
Longmeadow 01106
(413) 565-1000
www.baypath.edu

Becker College
61 Seaver Street
Worcester 01609
(508) 791-9241
www.beckercollege.edu

Bentley College
175 Forest Street
Wilbraham 02452
(781) 891-2000
www.bentley.edu

Berklee College of Music
1140 Boylston Street
Boston 02215
(617) 266-1400
www.berklee.edu

Boston College
122 College Road
Chestnut Hill 02467
(617) 552-4820
www.bc.edu

Boston Conservatory
8 The Fenway
Boston 02215
(617) 536-6340
www.bostonconservatory.edu

Boston University
25 Buick Street #1
Boston 02215
(617) 353-2000
www.bu.edu

Brandeis University
415 South Street
Waltham 02454
(781) 736-2000
www.brandeis.edu

Bridgewater State College
Gates House
Bridgewater 02325
(508) 531-1237
www.bridgew.edu

Clark University
950 Main Street
Worcester 01610
(508) 793-7711
www.clarku.edu

College of the Holy Cross
1 College Street
Worcester 01610
(508) 793-2011
www.holycross.edu

Curry College
1071 Blue Hill Avenue
Milton 02186
(617) 333-0500
www.curry.edu

Eastern Nazarene College
23 East Elm Avenue
Quincy 02170
(617) 745-3000
www.enc.edu

Elms College
291 Springfield Street
Chicopee 01013
(413) 594-2761
www.elms.edu

Emerson College
120 Boylston Street
Boston 02116
(617) 824-8500
www.emerson.edu

Emmanuel College
400 The Fenway
Boston 02115
(617) 735-9715
www.emmanuel.edu

Endicott College
376 Hale Street
Beverly 01915
(978) 927-0585
www.endicott.edu

Fitchburg State College
160 Pearl Street
Fitchburg 01420
(978) 345-2151
www.fsc.edu

Framingham State College
100 State Street
Framingham 01701
(508) 620-1220
www.framingham.edu

Gordon College
255 Grapevine Road
Wenham 01984
(978) 927-2300
www.gordon.edu

Hampshire College
893 West Street
Amherst 01002
(413) 549-4600
www.hampshire.edu

Harvard University
1350 Massachusetts Avenue
Cambridge 02138
(617) 495-1000
www.harvard.edu

Lasell College
1844 Commonwealth Avenue
Newton 02466
(617) 243-2000
www.lasell.edu

Lesley University
29 Everett Street
Cambridge 02138
(617) 349-8544
www.lesley.edu

Massachusetts College of Art
621 Huntington Avenue
Boston 02115
(617) 879-7000
www.massart.edu

Massachusetts College of Liberal Arts
at North Adams
375 Church Street
North Adams 01247
(413) 662-5000
www.mcla.mass.edu

Massachusetts College of Pharmacy
Boston 02115
(617) 732-2934
www.mcp.edu

Massachusetts Institute of Technology
77 Massachusetts Avenue
Cambridge 02139
(617) 253-1000
www.mit.edu

Massachusetts Maritime Academy
101 Academy Drive
Buzzards Bay 02532
(508) 830-5000
www.mma.mass.edu

Merrimack College
315 Turnpike Street
North Andover 01845
(978) 837-5000
www.merrimack.edu

Mount Holyoke College
50 College Street
South Hadley 01075
(413) 538-2000
www.mtholyoke.edu

Mount Ida College
777 Dedham Street
Newton Centre 02459
(617) 928-4500
www.mountida.edu

New England College of Optometry
424 Beacon Street
Boston 02115
(617) 266-2030
www.ne-optometry.edu

Newbury College
129 Fisher Avenue
Brookline 02445
(617) 730-7000
www.newberry.edu

Nichols College
P.O. Box 5000
Dudley 01571
(508) 213-1560
www.nichols.edu

Northeastern University
360 Huntington Avenue
Boston 02115
(617) 373-2000
www.northeastern.edu

Pine Manor College
400 Heath Street
Chestnut Hill 02467
(617) 731-7000
www.pmc.edu

Regis College
235 Wellesley Street
Weston 02493
(781) 768-7000
www.regiscollege.edu

Salem State College
352 Lafayette Street
Salem 01970
(978) 542-6000
www.salemstate.edu

Simmons College
300 The Fenway
Boston 02115
(617) 521-2000
www.simmons.edu

Simon's Rock College
84 Alford Road
Great Barrington 01230
(413) 528-0771
www.simons-rock.edu

Smith College
7 College Lane
Northampton 01063
(413) 584-2700
www.smith.edu

Springfield College
263 Alden Street
Springfield 01109
(413) 748-3000
www.spfldcol.edu

Stonehill College
320 Washington Street
Easton 02357
(508) 565-1000
www.stonehill.edu

Suffolk University
8 Ashburton Place
Boston 02108
(617) 573-8000
www.suffolk.edu

Tufts University
Medford 02155
(617) 627-5000
www.tufts.edu

University of Massachusetts

Amherst
Amherst 01003
(413) 545-0111
www.umass.edu

Boston
1000 Morrissey Blvd
Boston 02125
(617) 287-5000
www.umb.edu

Dartmouth
285 Old Westport Road
North Dartmouth 02747
(508) 999-8000
www.umassd.edu

Lowell
One University Ave
Lowell 01854
(978) 934-4000
www.uml.edu

Medical Center at Worcester
55 Lake Avenue North
Worcester 01655
(508) 856-2000
www.umassmed.edu

Wellesley College
106 Central Street
Wellesley 02481
(781) 283-1000
www.wellesley.edu

Wentworth Institute of Technology
550 Huntington Avenue
Boston 02115
(617) 989-4590
www.wit.edu

Western New England College
1215 Wilbraham Road
Springfield 01119
(413) 782-3111
www.wnec.edu

Westfield State College
P.O. Box 1630
Westfield 01086
(413) 572-5300
www.wsc.mass.edu

Wheaton College
Norton 02766
(508) 286-8200
www.wheatonma.edu

Wheelock College
200 The Riverway
Boston 02215
(617) 879-2000
www.wheelock.edu

Williams College
Williamstown 01267
(413) 597-3131
www.williams.edu

Worcester Polytechnic Institute
100 Institute Road
Worcester 02451
(508) 831-5000
www.wpi.edu

Worcester State College
486 Chandler Street
Worcester 01602
(508) 929-8000
www.worcester.edu

Two-Year Colleges

Bay State College
122 Commonwealth Avenue
Boston 02116
(617) 236-8000
www.baystate.edu

Berkshire Community College
1350 West Street
Pittsfield 01201
(413) 499-4660
www.berkshirecc.edu

Bristol Community College
777 Elsbree Street
Fall River 02720
(508) 678-2811
www.bristol.mass.edu

Bunker Hill Community College
250 New Rutherford Avenue
Boston 02129
(617) 228-BHCC
www.bhcc.mass.edu

Cape Cod Community College
2240 Iyanough Road
W. Barnstable 02668
(508) 362-2131
www.capecod.mass.edu

Dean College
99 Main Street
Franklin 02038
(877) 879-3326
www.dean.edu

Fisher College
118 Beacon Street
Boston 02116
(617) 236-8800
www.fisher.edu

Franklin Institute of Boston
41 Berkeley Street
Boston 02116
(617) 423-4635
www.ohwy.com/ma

Greenfield Community College
1 College Drive
Greenfield 01301
(413) 775-1000
www.gcc.mass.edu

Holyoke Community College
303 Homestead Avenue
Holyoke 01040
(413) 538-7000
www.hcc.mass.edu

Laboure College
2120 Dorchester Avenue
Boston 02124
(617) 296-8300
www.laboure.edu

Marian Court College
35 Little's Point Road
Swampscott 01907
(781) 595-6768
www.mariancourt.edu

Massachusetts Bay Community
College
50 Oakland Street
Wellesley 02481
(781) 239-3000
www.mbcc.mass.edu

Massasoit Community College
1 Massasoit Blvd
Brockton 02302
(508) 588-9100
www.massasoit.mass.edu

Middlesex Community College
33 Kearney Square
Lowell 01852
(800) 818-3434
www.middlesex.mass.edu

Mt. Wachusett Community College
444 Green Street
Gardner 01440
(978) 630-9110
www.mwcc.mass.edu

North Shore Community College
1 Ferncroft Road
Danvers 01923
(978) 762-4000
www.nscc.mass.edu

Northern Essex Community College
100 Elliott Street
Haverhill 01830
(978) 556-3000
www.necc.mass.edu

Quincy College
34 Coddington Street
Quincy 02169
(800) 698-1700
www.quincycollege.com

Quinsigamond Community College
670 W. Boylston Street
Worcester 01606
(508) 853-2300
www.qcc.mass.edu

Roxbury Community College
1234 Columbus Avenue
Boston 02120
(617) 427-0060
www.rcc.mass.edu

Springfield Technical Community College
1 Armory Square
Springfield 01105
(413) 781-7822
www.stcc.mass.edu

Stockbridge School of Agriculture
University of Massachusetts
115 Stockbridge Hall
Amherst 01003
(413) 545-2222
www.umass.edu/stockbridge

Suggested Reading

General histories of Massachusetts include Richard D. Brown and Jack Tager, *Massachusetts: A Concise History* (Amherst: University of Massachusetts Press, 2000); Joseph Conforti, *Imagining New England: Explorations of Regional Identity from the Pilgrims to the Mid-Twentieth Century* (Chapel Hill: University of North Carolina Press, 2001); John T. Cumbler, *Reasonable Use: The People, the Environment, and the State, New England, 1790–1930* (New York: Oxford University Press, 2001); Albert Bushnell Hart, ed., *Commonwealth History of Massachusetts: Colony, Province, and State,* 5 vols. (New York: States History Company, 1927–1930); John D. Haskell Jr., ed., *Massachusetts: A Bibliography of Its History* (Boston: G. K. Hall, 1976); Martin Kaufman et al., *A Guide to the History of Massachusetts* (Westport, Conn.: Greenwood, 1988); Jack Tager et al., *Massachusetts Politics: Selected Historical Essays* (Westfield: Institute for Massachusetts Studies, 1998); Richard W. Wilkie and Jack Tager, eds., *Historical Atlas of Massachusetts* (Amherst: University of Massachusetts Press, 1991); Peter Temin, ed., *Engines of Enterprise: An Economic History of New England* (Cambridge: Harvard University Press, 2000).

General works on Boston include Ronald Formisano and Constance Burns, eds., *Boston, 1700–1980: the Evolution of Urban Politics* (Westport, Conn.: Greenwood, 1984); Lawrence Kennedy, *Planning the City Upon a Hill: Boston since 1630* (Amherst: University of Massachusetts Press, 1992); Thomas H. O'Connor, *Boston A to Z* (Cambridge: Harvard University Press, 2000), *The Hub: Boston Past and Present* (Boston: Northeastern University Press, 2001), and *Eminent Bostonians* (Cambridge: Harvard University Press, 2002); Douglass Shand-Tucci, *Built in Boston: City and Suburb, 1800–1950* (Amherst: University of Massachusetts Press, 1988); Jack Tager, *Boston Riots: Three Centuries of Social Violence* (Boston: Northeastern University Press, 2001); Walter Muir Whitehill and Lawrence Kennedy, *Boston: A Topographical History: Third Enlarged Edition* (Cambridge: Harvard University Press, 2000).

On the colonial period in general, the reader can turn to Charles McLean Andrews, *The Colonial Period of American History,* vol. 1 (New Haven: Yale University Press, 1934); Perry Miller, *The New England Mind: The Seventeenth Century*

(New York: Macmillan, 1939), and *The New England Mind: From Colony to Province* (Cambridge: Harvard University Press, 1953); Samuel Eliot Morison, *Builders of the Bay Colony* (1930; Boston: Houghton Mifflin, 1958); Darren Staloff, *The Making of an American Thinking Class: Intellectuals and Intelligentsia in Puritan Massachusetts* (New York: Oxford University Press, 1998).

On early English colonial settlements, see Virginia DeJohn Anderson, *New England's Generation: The Great Migration and the Formation of Society and Culture in the Seventeenth Century* (Cambridge: Cambridge University Press, 1991); David Grayson Allen, *In English Ways: The Movement of Societies and the Transferal of English Local Law and Custom to Massachusetts Bay in the Seventeenth Century* (Chapel Hill: University of North Carolina Press, 1981); Louise A. Breen, *Transgressing the Bounds: Subversive Enterprises among the Puritan Elite in Massachusetts, 1630–1692* (New York: Oxford University Press, 2001); Francis J. Bremer, *The Puritan Experiment: New England Society from Bradford to Edwards* (New York: St. Martins, 1976); David Cressy, *Coming Over: Migration and Communication between England and New England in the Seventeenth Century* (New York: Cambridge University Press, 1987); James and Patricia Deetz, *The Times of Their Lives: Life, Love, and Death in Plymouth Colony* (New York: W. H. Freeman, 2000); Richard S. Dunn, *Puritans and Yankees: The Winthrop Dynasty of New England, 1630–1717* (Princeton: Princeton University Press, 1962); Edwin Gaustad, *Roger Williams: Prophet of Liberty* (New York: Oxford University Press, 2001); Philip J. Greven Jr., *Four Generations: Population, Land, and Family in Colonial Andover, Massachusetts* (Ithaca: Cornell University Press, 1970); Stephen Innes, *Labor in a New Land: Economy and Society in Seventeenth-Century Springfield* (Princeton: Princeton University Press, 1983); David Thomas Konig, *Law and Society in Puritan Massachusetts: Essex County, 1629–1692* (Chapel Hill: University of North Carolina Press, 1979); George D. Langdon Jr., *Pilgrim Colony: A History of New Plymouth, 1620–1691* (New Haven: Yale University Press, 1966); Kenneth A. Lockridge, *A New England Town, The First Hundred Years: Dedham, Massachusetts, 1636–1736* (New York: Norton, 1970); John Frederick Martin, *Profits in the Wilderness: Entrepreneurship and the Founding of New England Towns in the Seventeenth Century* (Chapel Hill: University of North Carolina Press, 1991); James G. Moseley, *John Winthrop's World: History as a Story, the Story as History* (Madison: University of Wisconsin Press, 1992); Sumner Chilton Powell, *Puritan Village: The Formation of a New England Town* (Middletown, Conn.: Wesleyan University Press, 1963); Darrett B. Rutman, *Winthrop's Boston* (Chapel Hill: University of North Carolina Press, 1965); Kenneth Silverman, *The Life and Times of Cotton Mather* (New York: Harper and Row, 1984); Roger Thompson, *Sex in Middlesex: Popular Mores in a Massachusetts County, 1649–1699* (Amherst: University of Massachusetts Press, 1986); Selma R. Williams, *Divine Rebel: The Life of Anne Marbury Hutchinson* (New York: Holt, Rinehart and Winston, 1981).

Information about Native Americans can be found in Alfred Cave, *The Pequot*

War (Amherst: University of Massachusetts Press, 1996); Richard W. Cogley, *John Eliot's Mission to the Indians before King Philip's War* (New York: Cambridge University Press, 1999); William Cronon, *Changes in the Land: Indians, Colonists, and the Ecology of New England* (New York: Hill and Wang, 1983); James D. Drake, *King Philip's War: Civil War in New England* (Amherst: University of Massachusetts Press, 2000); Yasuhide Kawashima, *Puritan Justice and the Indian: White Man's Law in Massachusetts, 1630–1763* (Middletown, Conn.: Wesleyan University Press, 1986); Douglas Edward Leach, *Flintlock and Tomahawk: New England in King Philip's War* (New York: Macmillan, 1958); Jill Lepore, *The Name of War: King Philip's War and the Origins of American Identity* (New York: Knopf, 1998); Daniel Mandell, *Behind the Frontier: Indians in Eighteenth-Century Eastern Massachusetts* (Lincoln: University of Nebraska Press, 1996); Jean M. O'Brien, *Dispossession by Degrees: Indian Land and Identity in Natick, Massachusetts, 1650–1790* (New York: Cambridge University Press, 1997); Howard S. Russell, *Indian New England before the Mayflower* (Hanover, N.H.: University Press of New England, 1980); Neal Salisbury, *Manitou and Providence: Indians, Europeans, and the Making of New England, 1500–1643* (New York: Oxford University Press, 1982); Alden T. Vaughan, *The New England Frontier: Puritans and Indians, 1620–1675* (Boston: Little, Brown, 1965).

On witchcraft prosecutions in New England, see Paul Boyer and Stephen Nissenbaum, *Salem Possessed: The Social Origins of Witchcraft* (Cambridge: Harvard University Press, 1974); John Putnam Demos, *Entertaining Satan: Witchcraft and the Culture of Early New England* (New York: Oxford University Press, 1982); Carol F. Karlsen, *The Devil in the Shape of a Woman: Witchcraft in Colonial New England* (New York: Norton, 1987); Marion L. Starkey, *The Devil in Massachusetts: A Modern Inquiry into the Salem Witch Trials* (New York: Knopf, 1949); Richard Weisman, *Witchcraft, Magic, and Religion in Seventeenth-Century Massachusetts* (Amherst: University of Massachusetts Press, 1984).

For information about eighteenth-century Massachusetts, see Fred Anderson, *A People's Army: Massachusetts Soldiers and Society in the Seven Years' War* (Chapel Hill: University of North Carolina Press, 1984); Richard L. Bushman, *King and People in Provincial Massachusetts* (Chapel Hill: University of North Carolina Press, 1985); David W. Conroy, *In Public Houses: Drink and the Revolution of Authority in Colonial Massachusetts* (Chapel Hill: University of North Carolina Press, 1995); Lorenzo J. Greene, *The Negro in Colonial New England, 1620–1776* (New York: Columbia University Press, 1942); Christine Leigh Heyrman, *Commerce and Culture: The Maritime Communities of Colonial Massachusetts, 1690–1750* (New York: Norton, 1984); Phyllis W. Hunter, *For the Love of Goods: Massachusetts Merchants in the Atlantic World* (Ithaca: Cornell University Press, 2001); Christopher M. Jedry, *The World of John Cleaveland: Family and Community in Eighteenth-Century New England* (New York: Norton, 1979); Douglas Lamar Jones, *Village and Seaport: Migration and Society in Eighteenth-Century Massachusetts* (Hanover, N.H.:

University Press of New England, 1981); Benjamin W. Labaree, *Patriots and Partisans: The Merchants of Newburyport, 1764–1815* (New York: Norton, 1975); Gloria Main, *People of a Spacious Land: Families and Culture in Colonial New England* (Cambridge: Harvard University Press, 2002); William E. Nelson, *Dispute and Conflict Resolution in Plymouth County, Massachusetts, 1725–1825* (Chapel Hill: University of North Carolina Press, 1981); Gregory H. Nobles, *Division throughout the Whole: Politics and Society in Hampshire County, Massachusetts, 1740–1775* (New York: Cambridge University Press, 1983); William D. Piersen, *Black Yankees: The Development of an Afro-American Subculture in Eighteenth-Century New England* (Amherst: University of Massachusetts Press, 1988); Robert J. Taylor, *Western Massachusetts in the Revolution* (Providence: Brown University Press, 1954); Patricia J. Tracy, *Jonathan Edwards, Pastor: Religion and Society in Eighteenth-Century Northampton* (New York: Hill and Wang, 1980); Daniel Vickers, *Farmers and Fishermen: Two Centuries of Work in Essex County, Massachusetts, 1630–1830* (Chapel Hill: University of North Carolina Press, 1994); G. B. Warden, *Boston, 1689–1776* (Boston: Little, Brown, 1970); Michael Zuckerman, *Peaceable Kingdoms: New England Towns in the Eighteenth Century* (New York: Knopf, 1970).

Sources on the American Revolution include Bernard Bailyn, *The Ordeal of Thomas Hutchinson* (Cambridge: Harvard University Press, 1974); Richard D. Brown, *Revolutionary Politics in Massachusetts: The Boston Committee of Correspondence and the Towns, 1772–1774* (Cambridge: Harvard University Press, 1970); David Hackett Fischer, *Paul Revere's Ride* (New York: Oxford University Press, 1994); Esther Forbes, *Paul Revere and the World He Lived In* (Boston: Houghton Mifflin, 1942); William Fowler, *The Baron of Beacon Hill: A Biography of John Hancock* (Boston: Houghton Mifflin, 1980), and *Samuel Adams: Radical Puritan* (New York: Longman, 1997); Edith Gelles, *Portia: The World of Abigail Adams* (Bloomington: Indiana University Press, 1995); Robert A. Gross, *The Minutemen and Their World* (New York: Hill and Wang, 1976); Benjamin Woods Labaree, *The Boston Tea Party* (New York: Oxford University Press, 1964); William Pencak, *War, Politics, and Revolution in Provincial Massachusetts* (Boston: Northeastern University Press, 1981), and *America's Burke: The Mind of Thomas Hutchinson* (Washington, D.C.: University Press of America, 1982); Jane Triber, *A True Republican: The Life of Paul Revere* (Amherst: University of Massachusetts Press, 1998); John W. Tyler, *Smugglers and Patriots: Boston Merchants and the Advent of the American Revolution* (Boston: Northeastern University Press, 1986); Andrew S. Walmsley, *Thomas Hutchinson and the Origins of the American Revolution* (New York: New York University Press, 1999); John J. Waters Jr., *The Otis Family in Provincial and Revolutionary Massachusetts* (Chapel Hill: University of North Carolina Press, 1968); Alfred Young, *The Shoemaker and the Tea Party: Memory and the American Revolution* (Boston: Beacon Press, 1999); Hiller B. Zobel, *The Boston Massacre* (New York: Norton, 1970).

On the politics of the new nation, see James M. Banner Jr., *To the Hartford Con-*

vention: The Federalists and the Origins of Politics in Massachusetts (New York: Knopf, 1970); John L. Brooke, *The Heart of the Commonwealth: Society and Political Culture in Worcester County Massachusetts, 1713–1861* (New York: Cambridge University Press, 1989); Paul Goodman, *The Democratic-Republicans of Massachusetts* (Cambridge: Harvard University Press, 1964); Robert A. Gross, ed., *In Debt to Shays: The Bicentennial of an Agrarian Rebellion* (Charlottesville: University Press of Virginia, 1993); Van Beck Hall, *Politics without Parties: Massachusetts, 1780–1791* (Pittsburgh: University of Pittsburgh Press, 1972); Martin Kaufman, ed., *Shays' Rebellion: Selected Essays* (Westfield, Mass.: Institute for Massachusetts Studies, 1987); William E. Nelson, *Americanization of Common Law: The Impact of Legal Change on Massachusetts Society, 1760–1830* (Cambridge: Harvard University Press, 1975); Stephen E. Patterson, *Political Parties in Revolutionary Massachusetts* (Madison: University of Wisconsin Press, 1973); Leonard Richards, *The Revolution That Failed: Making Sense of Shays's Rebellion* (Philadelphia: University of Pennsylvania Press, 2002); David P. Szatmary, *Shays' Rebellion: The Making of an Agrarian Insurrection* (Amherst: University of Massachusetts Press, 1980).

For information on economic issues in late-eighteenth- and early-nineteenth-century America, see Edward Byers, *The Nation of Nantucket: Society and Politics in an Early American Commercial Center, 1680–1820* (Cambridge: Harvard University Press, 1986); Christopher Clark, *The Roots of Rural Capitalism: Western Massachusetts, 1780–1860* (Ithaca: Cornell University Press, 1990); Clarence H. Danhof, *Change in Agriculture: The Northern U.S., 1820–1870* (Cambridge: Harvard University Press, 1969); Robert Doherty, *Society and Power: Five New England Towns, 1800–1860* (Amherst: University of Massachusetts Press, 1977); Jay R. Dolan, *The Yankee Pedlars of New England* (New York: Potter, 1964); George Sweet Gibb, *The Saco-Lowell Shops: Textile Machinery Building in New England, 1813–1949* (Cambridge: Harvard University Press, 1950); Edward C. Kirkland, *Men, Cities, and Transportation: A Study in New England History, 1820–1900* (Cambridge: Harvard University Press, 1948); Samuel Eliot Morison, *The Maritime History of Massachusetts, 1783–1860* (Boston: Houghton Mifflin, 1961); Howard S. Russell, *A Long Deep Furrow: Three Centuries of Farming in New England* (Hanover, N.H.: University Press of New England, 1976).

Works on the industrial revolution include Mary Blewett, *Constant Turmoil: The Politics of Industrial Life in Nineteenth-Century New England* (Amherst: University of Massachusetts Press, 2000); John T. Cumbler, *Working-Class Community in Industrial America: Work, Leisure, and Struggle in Two Industrial Cities, 1880–1930* (Westport, Conn.: Greenwood, 1979); Robert F. Dalzell, *Enterprising Elite: The Boston Associates and the World They Made* (Cambridge: Harvard University Press, 1987); Alan Dawley, *Class and Community: The Industrial Revolution in Lynn, Massachusetts* (Cambridge: Harvard University Press, 1976); Paul Faler, *Mechanics and Manufacturers in the Early Industrial Revolution: Lynn, Massachusetts, 1780–1860* (Albany: State University Press of New York, 1981); John S. Garner,

The Model Company Town: Urban Design through Private Enterprise in Nineteenth-Century New England (Amherst: University of Massachusetts Press, 1984); Oscar Handlin and Mary Flug Handlin, *Commonwealth: A Study of the Role of Government in the American Economy: Massachusetts, 1774–1861* (New York: New York University Press, 1947); William F. Hartford, *Money, Morals, and Politics: Massachusetts in the Age of the Boston Associates* (Boston: Northeastern University Press, 2001); Gary Kulik et al., eds., *The New England Mill Village: 1790–1860* (Cambridge: MIT Press, 1982); Judith McGaw, *Most Wonderful Machine: Mechanization and Social Change in Berkshire Paper Making, 1801–1885* (Princeton: Princeton University Press, 1987); Jonathan Prude, *The Coming of the Industrial Order: Town and Factory Life in Rural Massachusetts, 1810–1860* (New York: Cambridge University Press, 1983); Winifred Rothenberg, *From Market-Place to a Market Economy: The Transformation of Rural Massachusetts, 1750–1850* (Chicago: University of Chicago Press, 1992); Carl Seaburg et al., *The Incredible Ditch: A Bicentennial History of the Middlesex Canal* (Medford, Mass.: Medford Historical Society, 1997); Carl Siracusa, *A Mechanical People: Perceptions of the Industrial Order in Massachusetts, 1815–1880* (Middletown: Wesleyan University Press, 1979); Ronald Story, *The Forging of an Aristocracy: Harvard and the Boston Upper Class, 1800–1870* (Middletown: Wesleyan University Press, 1980); Conrad Vedick Wright and Katheryn Viens, eds., *Entrepreneurs: The Boston Business Community, 1700–1850* (Boston: Massachusetts Historical Society, 1997).

On nineteenth-century Boston, see Dorothy C. Broadus, *Genteel Rhetoric: Writing High Culture in Nineteenth-Century Boston* (Columbia: University of South Carolina Press, 1999); Matthew Crocker, *The Magic of the Many: Josiah Quincy and the Rise of Mass Politics in Boston, 1800–1830* (Amherst: University of Massachusetts Press, 1999); Betty Farrell, *Elite Families: Class and Power in Nineteenth-Century Boston* (Albany: State University of New York Press, 1993); Frederic Cople Jaher, *The Urban Establishment: Upper Strata in Boston, New York, Charleston, Chicago, and Los Angeles* (Urbana: University of Illinois Press, 1982); Peter Knights, *The Plain People of Boston, 1830–1860* (New York: Oxford University Press, 1971), and *Yankee Destinies: The Lives of Nineteenth-Century Ordinary Bostonians* (Chapel Hill: University of North Carolina Press, 1991); Roger Lane, *Policing the City: Boston, 1822–1885* (New York: Atheneum, 1971); Moying Li-Marcus, *Beacon Hill: The Life and Times of a Neighborhood* (Boston: Northeastern University Press, 2002); Thomas H. O'Connor, *Civil War Boston: Home Front and Battlefield* (Boston: Northeastern University Press, 1997); Tamara P. Thornton, *Cultivating Gentlemen: The Meaning of Country Life among the Boston Elite, 1785–1860* (New Haven: Yale University Press, 1989); Sam Bass Warner Jr., *Streetcar Suburbs: The Process of Growth in Boston, 1870–1900* (Cambridge: Harvard University Press, 1962).

Sources on women in early New England include Mary Blewett, *Men, Women, and Work: Class, Gender, and Protest in the New England Shoe Industry* (Urbana:

University of Illinois Press, 1988), and *The Last Generation: Work and Life in the Textile Mills of Lowell, Massachusetts, 1910–1960* (Amherst: University of Massachusetts Press, 1990); Thomas J. Brown, *Dorothea Dix: New England Reformer* (Cambridge: Harvard University Press, 1998); Ardis Cameron, *Radicals of the Worst Sort: Laboring Women in Lawrence, Massachusetts, 1860–1912* (Urbana: University of Illinois Press, 1993); Nancy Cott, *The Bonds of Womanhood: Woman's Sphere in New England, 1780–1835* (New Haven: Yale University Press, 1970); Sarah Deutsch, *Women and the City: Gender, Space, and Power in Boston, 1870–1940* (New York: Oxford University Press, 2000); Thomas Dublin, *Women at Work: The Transformation of Work and Community in Lowell, Massachusetts, 1826–1860* (New York: Columbia University Press, 1979), and *Farm to Factory: Women's Letters, 1830–1860* (New York: Columbia University Press, 1981); Gillian Gill, *Mary Baker Eddy* (Reading, Mass.: Perseus Press, 1998); Debra Gold Hansen, *Strained Sisterhood: Gender and Class in the Boston Female Anti-Slavery Society* (Amherst: University of Massachusetts Press, 1993); Susan Juster, *Disorderly Women: Sexual Politics and Evangelicalism in Revolutionary New England* (Ithaca: Cornell University Press, 1994); Carolyn J. Lawes, *Women and Reform in a New England Community, 1815–1860* (Lexington: University Press of Kentucky, 2000); Susan L. Porter, ed., *Women of the Commonwealth: Work, Family, and Social Change in Nineteenth-Century Massachusetts* (Amherst: University of Massachusetts Press, 1996); Douglas Shand-Tucci, *The Art of Scandal: The Life and Times of Isabella Stewart Gardner* (New York: HarperCollins, 1997); Madeline Stein, *Louisa May Alcott: A Biography* (Boston: Northeastern University Press, 1999); Martha H. Verbrugge, *Able-Bodied Womanhood: Personal Health and Social Change in Nineteenth-Century Boston* (New York: Oxford University Press, 1988); Gary Williams, *Hungry Heart: The Literary Emergence of Julia Ward Howe* (Amherst: University of Massachusetts Press, 1999).

On working people and mobility in nineteenth-century Massachusetts, see Henry Bedford, *Socialism and the Workers in Massachusetts, 1886–1912* (Amherst: University of Massachusetts Press, 1966); Mark Erlich, *With These Hands* (Philadelphia: Temple University Press, 1988); Michael Frisch, *Town into City: Springfield and the Meaning of Community, 1840–1880* (Cambridge: Harvard University Press, 1972); Howard M. Gitelman, *Workingmen of Waltham: Mobility in American Urban Industrial Development, 1850–1890* (Baltimore: Johns Hopkins University Press, 1974); James Green and Hugh Donahue, *Boston's Workers* (Boston: Boston Public Library, 1980); William Hartford, *Working People of Holyoke: Class and Ethnicity in a Massachusetts Mill Town, 1850–1960* (New Brunswick: Rutgers University Press, 1990); Alexander Keyssar, *Out of Work: The First Century of Unemployment in Massachusetts* (New York: Cambridge University Press, 1986); Roy Rosenzweig, *Eight Hours for What We Will: Workers and Leisure in an Industrial City, 1870–1920* (New York: Cambridge University Press, 1983); Stephan Thernstrom, *Poverty and Progress: Social Mobility in a Nineteenth-Century City* (Cambridge: Harvard University Press, 1964), and *The Other Bostonians: Poverty and Progress in the American Metropolis, 1880–1970* (Cambridge: Harvard University Press, 1973).

The history of Massachusetts reformers is recounted in Richard H. Abbott, *Cotton and Capital: Boston Businessmen and Anti-slavery Reform, 1854–1868* (Amherst: University of Massachusetts Press, 1991); Charles Capper and Conrad E. Wright, eds., *Transient and Permanent: The Transcendentalist Movement and Its Context* (Boston: Massachusetts Historical Society, 1999); Gary Collison, *Shadrach Minkins: From Fugitive Slave to Citizen* (Cambridge: Harvard University Press, 1977); Linda Gordon, *Heroes of Their Own Lives: The Politics and History of Family Violence, Boston, 1860–1960* (New York: Viking, 1988); Brian Gratton, *Urban Elders: Family, Work, and Welfare among Boston's Aged, 1890–1950* (Philadelphia: Temple University Press, 1986); Gerald N. Grob, *The State and the Mentally Ill: A History of Worcester State Hospital in Massachusetts, 1830–1920* (Chapel Hill: University of North Carolina Press, 1966); Kathryn Grover, *The Fugitives' Gibraltar: Escaping Slaves and Abolitionism in New Bedford, Massachusetts* (Amherst: University of Massachusetts Press, 2001); Peter Holloran, *Boston's Wayward Children: Social Services for Homeless Children, 1830–1930* (Rutherford, N.J.: Fairleigh Dickinson University Press, 1989); Daniel Walker Howe, *The Unitarian Conscience: Harvard Moral Philosophy, 1805–1861* (Cambridge: Harvard University Press, 1970); Donald M. Jacobs, ed., *Courage and Conscience: Black and White Abolitionists in Boston* (Bloomington: Indiana University Press, 1993); Henry Mayer, *All on Fire: William Lloyd Garrison and the Abolition of Slavery* (New York: St. Martins, 1998); Russell Duncan, *Where Death and Glory Meet: Colonel Robert Gould Shaw and the Fifty-fourth Massachusetts Infantry* (Savannah: University of Georgia Press, 1999); Eric C. Schneider, *In the Web of Class: Delinquents and Reformers in Boston, 1810s–1930s* (New York: New York University Press, 1992); Albert J. von Frank, *The Trials of Anthony Burns: Freedom and Slavery in Emerson's Boston* (Cambridge: Harvard University Press, 1998).

On the role of immigration in New England history, see Gerald J. Brault, *The French-Canadian Heritage in New England* (Hanover, N.H.: University Press of New England, 1986); Donald B. Cole, *Immigrant City: Lawrence, Massachusetts, 1845–1921* (Chapel Hill: University of North Carolina Press, 1963); A. G. Evans, *Fanatic Heart: A Life of John Boyle O'Reilly, 1844–1890* (Boston: Northeastern University Press, 1997); Gerald H. Gamm, *Urban Exodus: Why the Jews Left Boston and the Catholics Stayed* (Cambridge: Harvard University Press, 1999); Oscar Handlin, *Boston's Immigrants*, rev. ed. (Cambridge: Harvard University Press, 1959); Marilyn Halter, *Between Race and Ethnicity: Cape Verdean American Immigrants, 1860–1965* (Urbana: Illinois University Press, 1993); Lawrence Harmon and Hillel Levine, *The Death of an American Jewish Community: A Tragedy of Good Intentions* (New York: Free Press, 1992); Paula M. Kane, *Separatism and Subculture: Boston Catholicism, 1900–1920* (Chapel Hill: University of North Carolina Press, 1994);

Brian C. Mitchell, *The Paddy Camps: The Irish of Lowell, 1821–61* (Urbana: University of Illinois Press, 1987); Thomas O'Connor, *The Boston Irish: A Political History* (Boston: Northeastern University Press, 1995), *Fitzpatrick's Boston, 1846–1866: John Bernard Fitzpatrick, Third Bishop of Boston* (Boston: Northeastern University Press, 1984), and *Boston's Catholics* (Boston: Northeastern University Press, 1998); James M. O'Toole, *Militant and Triumphant: William Henry O'Connell and the Catholic Church in Boston, 1859–1944* (Notre Dame: University of Notre Dame Press, 1992); John F. Stack Jr., *International Conflict in an American City: Boston's Irish, Italians, and Jews, 1935–1944* (Westport, Conn.: Greenwood, 1979); Paula J. Todisco, *Boston's First Neighborhood: The North End* (Boston: Boston Public Library, 1976); Reed Ueda and Conrad E. Wright, eds., *Faces of Community: Immigrant Massachusetts, 1860–2000* (Boston: Northeastern University Press, 2002); Jerry R. Williams, *And Yet They Come: Portuguese Immigration from the Azores to the United States* (New York: Center for Migration Studies, 1982).

On blacks in Massachusetts, see Adelaide M. Cromwell, *The Other Brahmins: Boston's Black Upper Class, 1750–1950* (Fayetteville: University of Arkansas Press, 1994); Ronald P. Formisano, *Boston against Busing: Race, Class, Ethnicity in the 1960s and 1970s* (Chapel Hill: University of North Carolina Press, 1991); Stephen R. Fox, *The Guardian of Boston: William Monroe Trotter* (New York: Atheneum, 1971); James Oliver Horton and Lois E. Horton, *Black Bostonians: Family Life and Community Struggle in the Antebellum North* (New York: Holmes and Meier, 1979); James Jennings and Mel King, eds., *From Access to Power: Black Politics in Boston* (Cambridge, Mass.: Schenkman Books, 1986); Mel King, *Chain of Change: Struggles for Community Development through Community Control* (Boston: South End Press, 1980); George A. Levesque, *Black Boston: African-American Life and Culture in Urban America* (New York: Garland, 1994); David Levering Lewis, *W. E. B. Du Bois: The Fight for Equality and the American Century, 1919–1963* (New York: Henry Holt and Company, 2000); J. Anthony Lukas, *Common Ground* (New York: Alfred A. Knopf, 1985); Alan Lupo, *Liberty's Chosen Home: The Politics of Violence in Boston* (1977; Boston: Beacon Press, 1988); Manning Marable, *From the Grassroots* (Boston: South End Press, 1980); Elizabeth H. Pleck, *Black Migration and Poverty: Boston, 1865–1900* (New York: Academic Press, 1979); Jane Roessner, *A Decent Place to Live: From Columbia Point to Harbor Point—A Community History* (Boston: Northeastern University Press, 2000); Mark Schneider, *Boston Confronts Jim Crow, 1890–1920* (Boston: Northeastern University Press, 1997); Steven Taylor, *Desegregation in Boston and Buffalo: The Influence of Local Leaders* (Albany: State University of New York Press, 1998).

Works on Boston sports include Bernard M. Corbett and Joe Bertagna, *The Beanpot: Fifty Years of Thrills, Spills, and Chills* (Boston: Northeastern University Press, 2002); Tom Derderian, *Boston Marathon: The History of the World's Premier Running Event* (Champaign, Ill.: Kinetics Publishers, 1994); Joe Falls, *Boston Marathon* (New York: Macmillan, 1977); Stephen Hardy, *How Boston Played:*

Sport, Recreation, and Community, 1865–1915 (Boston: Northeastern University Press, 1982); Michael T. Isenberg, *John L. Sullivan and His America* (Champaign/Urbana: University of Illinois Press, 1988); Richard A. Johnson, *A Century of Boston Sports* (Boston: Northeastern University Press, 2001); Ed Linn, *Hitter: The Life and Turmoil of Ted Williams* (New York: Harcourt Brace, 1993); Howard Liss, *The Boston Red Sox* (New York: Simon and Schuster, 1982); Glen Stout and Richard A. Johnson, *Red Sox Century: One Hundred Years of Red Sox Baseball* (Boston: Houghton Mifflin, 2000); Russell Sullivan, *Rocky Marciano: The Rock of His Times* (Champaign/Urbana: University of Illinois Press, 2003); Ty Waterman and Mel Springer, *The Year the Red Sox Won the Series* (Boston: Northeastern University Press, 2001).

On state politics, see Richard M. Abrams, *Conservatism in a Progressive Era: Massachusetts Politics, 1900–1912* (Cambridge: Harvard University Press, 1964); Dale Baum, *The Civil War Party System: The Case of Massachusetts, 1848–1876* (Chapel Hill: University of North Carolina Press, 1984); Geoffrey Blodgett, *The Gentle Reformers: Massachusetts Democrats in the Cleveland Era* (Cambridge: Harvard University Press, 1966); Ronald P. Formisano, *The Transformation of Political Culture: Massachusetts Parties, 1790s–1840s* (New York: Oxford University Press, 1983); J. Joseph Huthmacher, *Massachusetts People and Politics, 1919–1933* (Cambridge: Harvard University Press, 1959); John R. Mulkern, *The Know-Nothing Party in Massachusetts* (Boston: Northeastern University Press, 1990); Jack Tager et al., eds., *Massachusetts in the Gilded Age: Selected Essays* (Amherst: University of Massachusetts Press, 1985); Thomas J. Whalen, *Kennedy versus Lodge: The 1952 Massachusetts Senate Race* (Boston: Northeastern University Press, 2000).

On twentieth-century Boston politics, see James J. Connolly, *The Triumph of Ethnic Progressivism: Urban Political Culture in Boston, 1900–1925* (Cambridge: Harvard University Press, 1998); Gerald H. Gamm, *The Making of New Deal Democrats: Voting Behavior and Realignment in Boston, 1920–1940* (Chicago: University of Chicago Press, 1989); Herbert Gans, *The Urban Villagers: Group and Class in the Life of Italian Americans* (1962; New York: Free Press, 1982); Mark Gelfand, *Trustee for a City: Ralph Lowell of Boston* (Boston: Northeastern University Press, 1998); Doris Kearns Goodwin, *The Fitzgeralds and the Kennedys: An American Saga* (New York: Simon and Schuster, 1987); Michael Patrick MacDonald, *All Souls: A Family History from Southie* (Boston: Beacon Press, 1999); John Mollenkopf, *The Contested City* (Princeton: Princeton University Press, 1983); Thomas H. O'Connor, *Building a New Boston: Politics and Urban Renewal, 1950–1960* (Boston: Northeastern University Press, 1993); Francis Russell, *A City in Terror: The 1919 Boston Police Strike* (New York: Viking, 1975), and *Tragedy in Dedham: The Story of the Sacco-Vanzetti Case* (New York: McGraw Hill, 1971); Charles H. Trout, *Boston: The Great Depression and the New Deal* (New York: Oxford University Press, 1977); Sam Bass Warner Jr., *The Way We Really Live: Social Change in Metropolitan Boston since 1920* (Boston: Boston Public Library, 1977).

Works on economics and metropolitan growth include Henry Binford, *The First Suburbs: Residential Communities on the Boston Periphery, 1815–1860* (Chicago: University of Chicago Press, 1984); Barry Bluestone and Mary Stevenson, *The Boston Renaissance: Race, Space, and Economic Change* (New York: Russell Sage Foundation, 2000); A. A. Bright, ed., *The Economic State of New England: Report of the Committee of New England of the National Planning Association,* 2 vols. (New Haven: Yale University Press, 1954); John T. Cumbler, *Reasonable Use: The People, the Environment, and the State: New England, 1790–1930* (New York: Oxford University Press, 2001); Matthew Edel et al., *Shaky Palaces: Homeownership and Social Mobility in Boston's Suburbanization* (New York: Columbia University Press, 1984); Robert W. Eisenmenger, *The Dynamics of Growth in the New England Economy* (Middletown: Wesleyan University Press, 1967); Richard M. Freeland, *Academia's Golden Age: Universities in Massachusetts, 1945–1970* (New York: Oxford University Press, 1992); Laurence F. Gross, *The Course of Industrial Decline: The Boott Cotton Mills of Lowell, Massachusetts, 1835–1955* (Baltimore: Johns Hopkins University Press, 1993); Bennett Harrison, *Rationalization, Restructuring, and Industrial Reorganization in Older Regions: The Economic Transformation of New England since World War II* (Cambridge: MIT Press, 1982); William Hartford, *Where Is Our Responsibility? Unions and Economic Change in the New England Textile Industry, 1870–1960* (Amherst: University of Massachusetts Press, 1996); David Luberoff, *Mega-Project: A Political History of Boston's Multibillion-Dollar Artery/Tunnel Project* (Cambridge: Taubman Center for State and Local Government, Harvard University, 1996); Marc Miller, *Irony of Victory: World War II and Lowell, Massachusetts* (Urbana: University of Illinois Press, 1988); Dorothy Nelkin, *The University and Military Research: Moral Politics at MIT* (Ithaca: Cornell University Press, 1972); Glenn Rifkin, *The Ultimate Entrepreneur: The Story of Ken Olsen and Digital Equipment Corporation* (Chicago: Contemporary Books, 1988); Susan Rosegrant and David Lampe, *Route 128: Lessons from Boston's High Tech Community* (New York: Basic Books, 1992); Peter Temin, ed., *Engines of Enterprise: An Economic History of New England* (Cambridge: Harvard University Press, 2000); Karl L. Wildes, *A Century of Electrical Engineering and Computer Science at MIT, 1882–1982* (Cambridge: MIT Press, 1985).